LIFE AND TRADITION IN
WEST YORKSHIRE

LIFE & TRADITION
in
WEST YORKSHIRE

by MARIE HARTLEY
and JOAN INGILBY

with 147 photographs
8 drawings
and a map

LONDON: J. M. DENT & SONS LTD

First published 1976

Made in Great Britain
at the Aldine Press · Letchworth · Herts
for J. M. DENT & SONS LTD
Aldine House · Albemarle Street · London

This book is set in 12 on 14 point Garamond

ISBN: 0 460 04239 4

Contents

Photographs

Drawings

Foreword and Acknowledgments

THE territory under consideration, now called West Yorkshire, may briefly be described as the wool textile area of the old West Riding, for although many other industries exist in it, textiles dominate by importance and tradition. Geographically it is a complicated region, roughly encircled by the cities and towns of Leeds, Bradford, Halifax, Huddersfield and Wakefield, an area which may be divided into the lowlands to the east and the hill country of the Pennines to the west. In the past the latter shared a culture with the rural Yorkshire dales. Similarities once abounded: insularity, the farming, the love of homeland, the sporting character of pursuits, the use of by-names, the food—oatcake—and the real beauty in spite of industry still glimpsed in some valleys and on the extensive moors. One further geographical feature elucidates the pattern of settlement, the towns and hamlets clustered in five main valleys: the Colne and the Holme valleys to the south, Calderdale to the west, the Spen valley in the centre and Airedale skirting the northern boundary.

To describe in detail such a region with its many industries, thousands of firms and tens of thousands of inhabitants would result in a kind of gazetteer. Also many subjects, for example transport, cricket, trade unionism, vernacular architecture, have received full treatment elsewhere, and a wealth of information has been published by local historians, museums and the several distinguished antiquarian societies. We have endeavoured to take a cross-section of activities illustrated by individual personal experiences. It is as Defoe said 'a noble scene of industry and application', the kind of region manufacturing goods, many for export, on which the nation including those engaged in non-productive work have for long depended and still depend for their well-being, a fact too often disregarded.

We are concerned mainly here with the West Riding around the last decade of the nineteenth century and the first quarter of this. It was a time when the capitalist system prevailed, and private enterprise flourished but experienced more difficulties than heretofore, when wages were small but food and goods cheap, when hours of work were less than formerly, when measures of social security had been

introduced but not enough, when the fearful slump of the 1920s is remembered
rather than wars or the General Strike, and when the British Empire, whether we
approve or not today, was a stabilizing factor.

We have used a tape recorder so that much is related in the speakers' own words.
What has emerged is the resilience, the stamina, the sterling qualities, the wry
humour, and by and large the happiness of men and women working hard, living
in poor conditions, and with only the simplest pleasures attainable. Cynics say that
people were only happy because they knew nothing better, but happiness is
happiness in whatever circumstances or walk of life it is experienced. We have
set down our findings without bias, and make no comment except to say that the
sense of belonging to home, street, mill, chapel or church was all important and
that material prosperity alone, however desirable, is not enough.

We are indebted to a great many people of whom most mentioned in the text are
omitted here on account of space. Without the constant care and helpfulness of
Mrs M. R. Hartley whose home in Leeds became ours for many weeks over a
period of two years this book would not have been possible. In the Huddersfield
district we received generous hospitality and introductions from Mrs P. D.
Crowther of Lindley and Mr and Mrs J. D. Hartley of Fixby.

We also wish to thank the following for information and for introducing us to
their staff: Mr A. G. Crowther of W. & E. Crowther Ltd, Crimble Mill, Slaith-
waite and Mrs Crowther who encouraged us from first to last, Mr W. Asquith,
Mr R. A. Hornshaw and Miss D. Blewitt of Lister and Co. Ltd, Manningham
Mills, Bradford and Low Mills, Addingham, Mr T. P. Lambert and Mr W.
Gallimore of John Foster and Son Ltd, Black Dyke Mills, Queensbury, Mr M. W.
Shelton of Thomas Burnley and Sons Ltd, Gomersal Mills, Mr A. E. Pease of
Lock Hill Mills, Sowerby Bridge and Mrs Pease and Mrs G. R. Stansfeld, Mr
S. J. E. Huxley of Joshua Ellis and Co. Ltd, Batley Carr Mills, Mr M. Pearson of
John Crossley and Sons Ltd, Dean Clough Mills, Halifax, Mr A. G. Wilson of
Salts (Saltaire) Ltd.

Many have kindly shown us round their works, lent us unpublished material
and in some cases read the MS: Mr J. F. Alcock of the Hunslet Engine Company
Ltd, Mr J. G. Walker of James Walker and Sons Ltd, Mirfield, Mr M. D. Aykroyd
of Firth Carpets Ltd, Heckmondwike, Mr W. Wormald of Wormalds and Walker
Ltd, Dewsbury, Mr S. J. S. Walker of Joseph Sykes Bros (English Card Clothing
Ltd), Lindley, the staff of James Holdsworth Bros Ltd, Mirfield, Mr R. L. Smith of
George Hattersley and Sons Ltd, Keighley, Mr L. Barker of the C.W.S. Ltd,
Hebden Bridge, Mr H. G. Marshall of Marshalls (Halifax) Ltd, Mr P. K. Stead and
Mr E. H. Crack of Charles F. Stead and Co. Ltd, Leeds, Mr P. Schofield of

Schofields (Leeds) Ltd, Mr J. A. Horrox of Brown, Muff Ltd, Bradford, Colonel A. Monteith, Ingleby Arncliffe, Mr W. Cook, formerly of Whitehead-Miller G-J (Printers) Ltd, Leeds, Mr T. M. Little of David Little and Co. Ltd, Leeds, Mr A. Summers of Cullingworth Summers, Batley, Mr D. Asquith of Emu Wools Ltd, Keighley, Mr P. B. Haigh of John Haigh and Sons Ltd, Huddersfield, Mr P. Kirk of Kirk and Steel Ltd, Morley, Mr G. Dracup of Samuel Dracup and Sons Ltd, Bradford, Mr G. E. Phelon of David Crabtree and Son Ltd, Bradford, Mr H. S. Sykes of Harding (Leeds) Ltd, Mr P. W. Sutcliffe and Mr Aquilla Morris of the British Picker Company Ltd, Todmorden, Mr M. Popplewell of the BBA Group Ltd, Cleckheaton, Mr T. Day of Henry Day and Sons Ltd, Dewsbury, Mr R. Addis of John Fowler and Co (Leeds) Ltd, Mr C. T. Green of Thomas Green (Silsden) Ltd, Mr W. A. Winter, Bingley, Mr W. Walton and Mr J. I. Hartley of Walton Bros (Halifax) Ltd, Mr J. A. R. Maude of Boldron, Mr and Mrs F. Walkley and Mr J. Uttley of Huddersfield and Hebden Bridge, Mr F. N. Drury of Joshua Tetley and Son Ltd, Leeds.

We should like to thank in particular Mr G. W. Atkinson, Morley, Mr T. B. Fletcher and Mr J. R. Hepper, Leeds, Mr and Mrs J. C. Atack, Hebden Bridge, Mr and Mrs E. Walker, Batley, Mr and Mrs G. E. Buckley, Delph, Mr and Mrs K. F. B. Roberts and Mr F. Burley, Holmbridge, Miss C. F. Wright, formerly of Gomersal, Mrs O. M. Bedford and Miss M. G. Phillips, Gildersome, Mr B. Barnes, Saddleworth, Mr J. Ogden, Mr I. Dewhirst and Mr E. D. Dewhirst, Keighley, Mrs G. C. Roper, Pannal, Miss V. Watson, Scarcroft, Mr W. H. Murgatroyd, Bramley, Mr H. N. Sykes, Almondbury, Sir Harry Hardy, Morley, Mr S. Lee Vincent, formerly of Leeds, Mr J. Mitchell, Bradford, Mr R. Lingard, East Bergholt, Mr G. E. Bowman, Bovingdon, Mr J. Bradley, Shelf, Mrs A. Newell, Queensbury, Mr R. L. Sunderland, Halifax, Mr J. Mortimer, Mytholm, Mrs A. O. Pullan and Mrs M. I. Rigg, Rawdon, Mr F. Else and Mr F. Horsfall, Heptonstall, Mr and Mrs J. Mitchell, Pudsey, Mr H. Sykes, Slaithwaite.

We are indebted to Mr Stewart Sanderson for access to the records at the Institute of Dialect and Folk Studies at the University of Leeds. Mr C. S. Fowler of the *Halifax Courier* Ltd has shown us files in their library and Mrs Shirley Kaye persuaded readers to send in life stories, many of which we have used. Several directors, curators and keepers of museums have helped with information, suggestions for research and old photographs: Mr C. M. Mitchell of Leeds City Museums, Mr R.-A. Innes and Miss P. F. Millward of the Calderdale Museums, Miss Anne Ward of Cliffe Castle Museum, Keighley, Mr E. W. Aubrook and Mr R. A. McMillan of the Tolson Memorial Museum, Huddersfield, Mr S. W. Feather and Mr G. Hollingshead of the Bradford Industrial Museum, Mr P. C. D.

Brears, then of Clarke Hall, Wakefield, Miss A. V. Diver of Bolling Hall Museum, Mr J. Goodchild then of Cusworth Hall Museum, Doncaster, Mr P. Kelley of the Museum of Industry and Science, Armley Mills, Leeds, Mr J. Stafford of Oldham Museum. We also thank and acknowledge information from the chief and reference librarians at the Central and Public libraries at Leeds, Bradford, Halifax, Huddersfield, Batley, Keighley, Oldham, Saddleworth at Uppermill, the County Library at Taunton, the archives department of Leeds Central Library, and the Yorkshire Archaeological Society.

M. H. and J. I.

Photographic Acknowledgments

Of the 147 photographs the fifty undated ones are the authors'. We acknowledge the loan of the remainder with the numbers of the plates as follows: Mr J. C. Atack, 6; Mrs G. E. Buckley, 7; Tolson Memorial Museum, Huddersfield, 10, 40; Bagshaw Museum, Batley, 11; Miss P. Smith, 12; Mr J. G. Walker, 15; Mr A. G. Crowther, 16; Mr M. Pearson, 17; Mr S. J. S. Walker, 18, 60; Miss H. Holmes, 19; Mr R. A. Hornshaw, 20, 21, 37, 67; Mr L. Barker, 24–8; Harding (Leeds) Ltd, 29; C. H. Wood, 30, 50; T. Burnley and Sons Ltd, 32; Bradford Industrial Museum, 33, 48; Mrs E. Taylor, 34; Mr R. L. Smith, 36, 66; Mr J. Jessop, 38; Mr M. D. Aykroyd, 39· Mr G. H. Gledhill, 41, 68; Mr J. Goodchild, 42, Bath and West and Southern Counties Society, 45; Mr B. Burrows, 51; Mr A. Summers, 52; Mr T. Day, 53; Mrs A. Marlow, 54; Mr G. W. Atkinson, 55, 139; Mr C. Westerby, 56, 133; Mr P. B. Haigh, 57, 58; Mr S. J. E. Huxley, 59; Mr P. W. Sutcliffe, 63; Mr M. Popplewell, 65; Mr H. Morton, 75, 121; Shibden Hall Museum, 76, 143; Mr W. A. N. Brooke, 77, 81; Mr P. V. Charlesworth, 78; National Coal Board, 79; Mr R. Addis, 72; Mr J. F. Alcock, 73; Kirkstall Forge Engineering Ltd, 74; Central Library, Bradford, 80, 82, 112; Mrs A. Tupman, 83, 90; Central Library, Leeds, 84; Mr W. Pickles, 85; Mr C. B. Pratt, 86, 141; Miss A. K. Sutton, 87, 142; Mr J. N. Charlesworth, 91; Public Library, Heckmondwike, 92, 132; Mr Ian Dewhirst, 93; Mr W. H. Murgatroyd, 94; Mrs F. Tomasso, 95; Mr T. Farmer, 96; Mrs M. H. Gartside, 97; Mr Peter Schofield, 111; Mr T. Beaumont, 113;

Mr W. A. Potts, 114; Mr W. Cook, 115; Mrs B. Smith, 118; Mr E. and Mr S. Coates, 120; Mr M. Anderson, 122, 123; Mr C. M. Mitchell, 124–7; *The Halifax Courier* Ltd, 128, Mr J. Uttley, 129; Mr C. T. Green, 130; *The Yorkshire Post*, 131; *Bradford Telegraph and Argus*, 135; Mr G. E. Crowther, 136; Mr R. Hall, 138; Miss E. Hinchliffe, 140; Mrs A. Longstaff, 144; Science Museum, London, drawing of the Crank Mill, Morley.

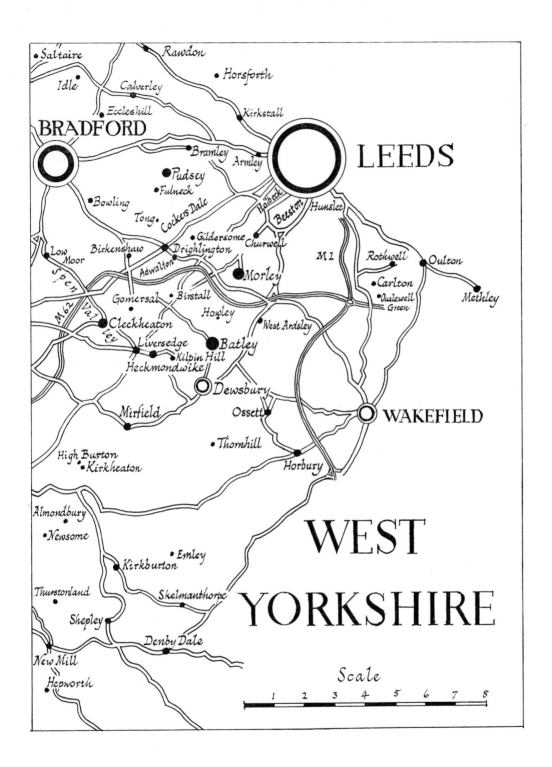

Saltaire • • Rawdon
Idle • • Horsforth
Calverley • • Kirkstall
Eccleshill •
BRADFORD
• Bramley • Armley
Pudsey • • Fulneck
Bowling • Tong • Cockers Dale
Low Moor • Birkenshaw • Drighlington
• Gildersome • Churwell
Adwalton • Morley
Spen Valley • Gomersal • Birstall
M62 • Cleckheaton • Howley
Liversedge • Kilpin Hill
Heckmondwike • Batley
• West Ardsley
Mirfield • Dewsbury
Ossett •
Thornhill •
High Burton • Kirkheaton
Horbury •
Almondbury •
• Newsome

LEEDS
Holbeck Beeston Hunslet
M 1
Rothwell • • Oulton
• Carlton • Methley
Ouzlewell Green

WAKEFIELD

WEST
YORKSHIRE

Kirkburton • Emley
Thurstonland • Skelmanthorpe
Shepley •
Denby Dale •
New Mill •
Hepworth •

Scale
1 2 3 4 5 6 7 8

A noble scene of industry and application is spread before you here . . .

Defoe

1 Recollections of the Domestic System

THE antiquity and continuity of the wool textile industry is cause for marvel. Dating back as an industry in Yorkshire and widespread in the country in the Middle Ages, it was drawn in the eighteenth century to the West Riding where, formed by zealous merchants and a multitude of clothiers based on home-work-shops, a unique structure had developed.[1] This fragmentation, this mass of small units, by and large squeezed out in the last century and up to the 1920s, but still discernible, offered opportunity and encouraged enterprise, that allied with ample natural resources, carried people and industry triumphantly through the building of mills, the installation of machinery, the reorganization of the work force, immense if fluctuating trade, in short the travail of the Industrial Revolution and beyond.

In the last decades of the eighteenth century following on inventions, the many processes of cloth manufacture—spinning, carding, weaving, finishing—were being mechanized. At the same time the clothiers then enjoying rapidly expanding trade built three-storied houses with their full-width windows lighting workrooms for weaving broadcloth. These, to be seen in the Colne valley and the Saddleworth district, are still striking relics of the domestic system in transition (*see plates 1 and 3*). In the same period old corn and fulling mills were adapted for scribbling (carding), and new purpose-built water-driven mills, known as country mills, for one or more of the processes of scribbling, dyeing, fulling (milling), and spinning began to be erected on the rivers and tributary streams (*see plates 6–7*). As machinery was introduced it is well known that it was attended by strikes and by the Luddite, Chartist and Plug Riots.

A reminder of these disturbed times was the widespread practice of watchmen firing flintlocks or blunderbusses at nine o'clock at night as for example at Lee

---

[1] William White, *History, Gazetteer, and Directory of the West Riding of Yorkshire*, 1837, vol. I, p. 512, states that about 1800 there were from Leeds to the Lancashire border nearly 6,000 master clothiers who employed besides their wives and children 30,000 to 40,000 people.

Bridge Mills, Halifax, and Acre Mills, Lindley, near Huddersfield. When a watch-man was set on at Gillroyd Mills, Morley, in 1843, after the Plug Riots, he had 'to go on duty and Fire his Gun at nine o'clock at night from 1st October to 1st April and at ten o'clock for the rest of the year'.[1] At Black Dyke Mills, Queensbury, the custom only ceased in the 1930s and at Dewsbury Mills in the 1960s.

In this turmoil 'of all the operatives connected with the trade', wrote James in 1857, 'he [the piece-maker or weaver] was on the whole the most uncomplaining and praiseworthy'.[2] Weaving was the last major process to leave the home-work-shop. The clothier's house and the weaver's cottage, the pivot on which the domestic system had revolved, for long remained the places to which the warp and weft were brought, the places from which the woven cloth was taken to the mill to be scoured and fulled, and brought back to be stretched on tenters and then taken to be sold. (These processes undertaken in the home varied according to the period, the machinery introduced and the proximity of a mill.)[3] Some clothier's houses had dye houses near by, as at High Kinders, Saddleworth, and every village too had several small workshops for cloth dressing (finishing). 'The Clothiers,' wrote Baines, in 1858, 'by their industry and frugality, find themselves able to compete with the factory owners whose great works and complicated machinery incur heavy expenses.'[4]

None the less the adjustment from hand to power looms (like that from the employment of children in the home to the factory) was temporarily painful. It was only at first, following on the invention of the flying shuttle and when machinery was small, that the piece-makers benefited.[5] In 1795 because of the French war they could earn 39*s*. 6*d*. a week, a sum which dropped to 15*s*. in 1810 and to 5*s*. in 1830, both decades of national crises. They became known as poverty-knockers (a term derived from the sound of the loom), and lived on porridge, oatcake, barley bread, milk, potatoes and some bacon. Marauding parties in the Colne valley raided warehouses; others went in singing companies to the Sheffield district to earn money; children turned to begging.

A halfway stage was the erection of loom-shops to accommodate hand-loom

[1] MS. Committee Book, 1835–61, Gill Royds Company Mill, Archives Department, Leeds City Libraries.

[2] John James, *History of the Worsted Manufacture in England*, 1857, p. 479.

[3] See W. B. Crump and G. Ghorbal, *History of the Huddersfield Woollen Industry*, 1935; A. Easther, *A Glossary of the Dialect of Almondbury and Huddersfield*, 1883; B. Barnes, *Saddleworth Heritage*, 1975.

[4] E. Baines, *Yorkshire Past and Present*, 1858, vol. IV, p. 629.

[5] See P. E. Razzell and R. W. Wainwright, *The Victorian Working Class. Selections from the Morning Chronicle, 1849*, 1973.

weavers for convenience under one roof (*see plate* 19). In some cases a row of single-storied cottages was built with a chamber for looms across the whole of a floor above them.[1] Sir Harry Hardy of Morley recollects that in the last quarter of the nineteenth century his grandfather had a shed for sixty journeymen weavers at Skelmanthorpe, near Huddersfield.

Very many mills for long simultaneously employed both hand- and power-loom weavers. The former were now called in-weavers if employed in the mill and out-weavers if still working at home. In the 1840s a shed for hand looms was incorporated in a new mill built by the Akroyds at Copley. In 1858 Wormalds and Walker had 161 hand looms of which twenty-six were worked by in-weavers and the rest by out.[2] At Armley Mills, Leeds, the looms were never connected to a power supply, and were rented by the weavers. At Gillroyd Mills when new power looms were installed in 1860 they were let for 3s. 3d. a week, with all the parts found and a tuner engaged who earned 32s. a week. At Butt End Mills, Cleckheaton, Mrs D. White (b. 1883) remembers that her father, B. H. Goldthorp, employed six old hand-loom weavers working out their days. They used to give her Pomfret cakes covered with fluff out of their pockets.

In the worsted industry power looms could be used at faster speeds than hand looms and therefore replaced them in the first half of the century. But in the woollen trade hand looms were no less slow than power. 'Until well after 1866 the thud of the treadle and the clack of the picker against the shuttle was work-music in Batley homes.'[3] In 1860 there were in Batley 1,260 hand-loom weavers earning 9s. to 10s. a week.[4] But during the Franco-Prussian War power looms were rapidly installed, and hand looms continued only here and there (*see plates* 12–14). By this time women as spinners, weavers and menders had become essential to the running of a mill.

Certain districts by tradition made certain materials. In 1841 Thomas Cook, the main founder of Wormalds and Walker, blanket-makers of Dewsbury Mills, observed: 'This neighbourhood is studded with multitudes of small makers whose property may not, nor does, average £100.'[5] An enclave of the blanket-makers lived at Kilpin Hill, near Heckmondwike (which from 1811 for a few years had a

[1] H. A. Bodey, *Industrial History in Huddersfield*, 1972, for the beginning of the firm of George Mallinson & Sons, Linthwaite in the Colne valley.

[2] F. J. Glover, 'Dewsbury Mills, a History of Wormalds and Walker Ltd', University of Leeds, Ph.D. thesis, 1959.

[3] T. C. Taylor, *One Hundred Years*, 1946.

[4] S. Jubb, *History of the Shoddy Trade*, 1860.

[5] F. J. Glover, ibid.

blanket hall). Here the eighteenth- and early nineteenth-century cottages are remembered as home-workshops with loom chambers, scouring places and tenter fields 'once dressed out in snow-white drapery' of blankets. In 1850 the blanket weavers of Kilpin Hill and neighbourhood banded together to fix piecework rates (*see plate* 11).[1]

Only ten years later the movement down into the valley to the banks of the Calder began. In 1866 John Walker of Kilpin Hill was invited to become a partner of Hague Cook & Wormald, eventually to become Wormalds and Walker. Here, too, in 1750 another Walker, James, living on a small farm at Capas Heights and starting with one loom, began to employ weavers in cottages near by. He bought and scoured wool, wove blankets, milled, tentered and raised the pieces, which each gave some twenty blankets, and took them for sale to the piece hall at Halifax. When in 1868–72 his grandsons built Holme Bank Mills on the Calder at Mirfield, other people from Kilpin Hill moved down to work for them. In 1932 the firm built a mill at Witney. Similarly the Bruce family business was moved from Heckmondwike to Clive Mills on the Calder, and four daughters getting up at 5 a.m. are remembered going there to whip blankets.[2]

Clothiers and often weavers living on a farm or a smallholding kept a horse or a donkey, a cow or cows, and a pig, clothed themselves in their own stuffs, and in the Pennine hills dug peat for fuel. Living expenses were small, reckoned in the 1830s at 5s. 2d. a week a head to clothe and feed a family out of a combination of farming and cloth manufacture.[3] Donkeys for transporting pieces, coal and any other goods were part of the system. There were said to be as many of them as people in Thurstonland near Huddersfield.[4]

The upper floors of houses, often stone-flagged, held the loom or looms and a bobbin wheel, and where houses were built into the hillside access to loom chambers was gained directly at the back, or on flat ground by a flight of outside stone steps to the 'takin-in' door (*see plate* 3). Rockfold, a three-storied building at Golcar, now pulled down, was known as "'t sheet o' pins' because the long rows of windows resembled pins as they used to be sold on sheets of paper. In such a house processes such as beaming (preparing the warp for the loom), sometimes *lecking* (scouring the cloth with urine and pig's dung to cleanse it of grease), or spinning (by this time on a hand-spinning jenny) took place in the middle chamber.

[1] Leaflet at the Bagshaw Museum, Batley.
[2] Information from Mr Harold Walker, Mr J. G. Walker, and Mr and Mrs E. Walker.
[3] Beardsell, 'An historical account of our trade from the time of becoming a Partner in 1828'. Transcript of MS. lent by Mr S. Beardsell.
[4] Mary A. Jagger, *The History of Honley*, 1914.

Often smells and when raw wool was prepared fleas were endemic. A common piece of furniture in the downstairs living quarters was a put-up bed, even two, sometimes of solid mahogany. Children often slept in the loom chamber, and in one house in the Colne valley in a hammock, reached with difficulty, slung above the loom.

The loom itself was the property of the weaver, and in 1830 costing £2 11s., it strained a man's means.[1] They were made by local joiners such as the Stansfields of Almondbury, near Huddersfield, who generally had one on the bench for winter work. Latterly they were sold to technical colleges, foreign countries, and the last, made there in 1947 by Mr W. S. Schofield, who had worked for and followed the Stansfields, cost £120. The frame, 9 feet high, was of deal and the going part (*sley* board) beech, and they were finished with a high polish like the best furniture (*see diagram on page* 23).

In 1832 James Beardsell wrote from London to ask his wife to send him some papers 'in the Money drawer in our loom'. Women, when weaving, rocked their babies by fastening the cradle band to the sley board, and they washed and baked at night while the men wove by the light of 'a farding cannel at each end of the loom'.[2] When shuttles had to be thrown, all wore hooves on their hands, and children had to wind so many bobbins before going to school.

At Halifax the piece hall, opened on 1 January 1779, the only one left intact in Yorkshire, is undoubtedly the finest monument to the wool textile industry in the eighteenth century to be seen in England, and recollections of people carrying their pieces to it are numerous. Crowds of clothiers, who having paid £28 4s. owned one of the 315 rooms, and weavers, charged 1d. for each piece brought in, converged on it on market days. Nancy Ickeringill, 'a big powerful woman, six feet tall, and with a Roman nose', who lived on a farm at Haworth, carried her pieces to Halifax, and Grace Southwell of Denholme hired herself to transport pieces across the moors and was in consequence known as 'the packhorse'.

On the other side of Halifax at Longley near Norland Moor lived William Whitaker, a hand-loom weaver, who following a packhorse track down and up steep hillsides transported his pieces to Halifax. 'One shoulder was always lower than the other', says Mrs S. E. Grayshan, his granddaughter. 'They all were. One old man was quite down on one side.' The trough to which all neighbours brought urine is still there in front of the houses where William lived. Eventually he started work at Rawson's Mill in the Ryburn valley. During the Luddite Riots truncheons

[1] E. Sigsworth, *Black Dyke Mills*, 1958, p. 147.
[2] Mrs A. Tupman (b. 1882), Heptonstall.

had been issued to the work force, and one passed on to William has been handed down in the family.

In the Holme valley Mrs A. Howard remembers her grandmother, Mary Haigh (1826–1920) known as Mary a' t' Mount', who was born at Holme Woods, one of the high little moorland farms then usually occupied by hand-loom weavers. Down in the valley were the small mills for spinning, scouring and fulling, and Mary herself took the cloth there on horseback. Working when it suited, often until midnight, the family hung up a curtain so that people should not see in. But in some households here two buckets of peat were brought in every night, and when 'those were done it were bedtime'.

Many hand-loom weavers eventually found employment in quarries, in the building of reservoirs, and in such jobs as delivering goods for shops with a horse and cart. A few, earning mere pittances, wove to the end of their days supported by younger members of the family, or they took up secondary occupations such as baking oatcake or mangling clothes. The last in a district acquired fame (*see plates* 11–12).

Mr Joe France, the retired manager of Cellars Clough Mill, Marsden (b. 1882), recollects the Colne valley in his boyhood. 'Times were hard and it bred a hard people. But in those weaving hamlets on the hillsides they never thought of locking their doors, and if anyone fell on evil days the others always helped out.' His grandfather, Joseph Sykes, known as Knuckle, built Shaw Field, never so called but always referred to as New 'Oile (Hole), still to be seen tucked into the hillside between Slaithwaite and Marsden. He was a man of some means and education who pursued work and hunting in about equal parts. His house was furnished with the solid carved oak pieces of former days, and hounds generally basked on the hearthrug in front of the fire. 'When the weavers heard the bay of the hounds it was more than they could stand. They dropped their work and set off hunting. Later as candle lights glimmered from windows people said: "So-and-so's *inning* up [catching up]."'

Besides making cloth, Joseph set up hand looms whenever they were required and kept a stock of parts—sleys, beams, shuttles. He used to go a *a-bunting*, that is he fetched warp and weft from Longroyd Bridge, five miles away, on donkeys and delivered it round to the cottages. The general trade of the valley was then linsey, a cheap cloth with a cotton warp and a woollen weft, mostly a faded blue or natural brown in colour, sold in Lancashire and to miners. (Cotton warps were introduced in 1834.) Joseph Sykes had one special sixteen-treadle loom, on which an old man who was an expert designer, and who always wore a top hat when working, wove fancy waistcoating. Pieces were sent to Manchester, usually by train, although many people walked there across the moorlands. After a successful deal Knuckle declared a free house for the day at the Dartmouth Arms, Slaithwaite; but on Sundays he wore his best broadcloth and conducted Bible readings at teatime.

When he was very small Mr France helped his grandfather in various ways. If the yarns were snarling and difficult to handle, he *bruzzed* bobbins put in a frame. 'You filled your mouth with water and made a mist by blowing air and water out at the same time.' (Another method was to dip a basket of weft in water and *wuzz* it on a stick (*see plate* 4).) 'And when they were beaming another warp for the loom in the middle chamber they used to put me underneath on a little buffet. They were going through their *raddles* that is separating and opening out the warp into so many threads to go on the beam. [The raddle, of which the top bar was detachable, was a long wooden framework with thick vertical wires through which the yarn was threaded.] The men put a *stang* [pole] through a hole in the centre of the beam, and turned it over, and at the other end the threads were running through these raddles. If a thread broke I had to shout and they stopped winding. They'd take their pieces to be scoured at Shaw Carr, an old mill no longer there. Tentergates were all over; sometimes stone, sometimes wooden posts carried them. A piece was between sixty and seventy yards long, and it was hooked on and held tight. They had to watch the weather.' Similarly the weaver looked for a fine day on which to size his warp, hanging it to dry between gate-posts or on pegs driven into walls.

Life at the end of the last century on the bleak Pennine plateau of green pastures, stone walls, and isolated weavers' houses between the Colne and Deanhead valleys is remembered by Mr J. T. Gee of Outlane. His parents, Tom and Alice Gee, and their five children lived in a cottage at Prospect Place on condition that Alice wove for the owner, George Brook, a clothier of Jacob's Well, Round Ings, less than a mile away.

Both parents could weave, but Tom was employed as a horseman for Edward Sykes, the owner of Gosport Mills at Outlane, built about 1860. Before then the Sykeses had put out their scribbling and spinning to the country mills and had taken in the pieces from the weavers all round. 'It was a busy spot.' Once Gosport Mills were built the workers left the country mills and went there. 'My grandad', says Mr Gee, 'was in at the building of it. Living in the Deanhead valley, he walked over, and became manager and designer. His children, ten of them, all worked at Gosport. He'd a big mending table, and they all took their own food and sat round having breakfast together.'

Alice wove the same cotton-warp cloth that was made in the Colne valley just over the hill. 'I went to bed many a time with the loom going and mother singing. Oh aye!' For Christmas they used to buy half a pig, curing it in the cellar. Alice had to have a 'double draw' to pay for it, that is to weave two pieces in a week and earn double the usual money which was 8s. 6d. a piece. When the shuttle had not run off clean, the bits were put in a little basket and one of Jack's jobs was to wind them steadily out on *coppins* (cops) to be used again. Three of the family beamed the warp (wound it on a beam). Usually a six-cut warp, this made six pieces, 'a fair length' which had to be *cuttled* up (folded backwards and forwards) and tentered on some light railings with nails on them. Those who had a donkey transported the piece tied on with a girth called a *wantey*. But young Gee took his in a wheelbarrow, held on tightly with a canvas belt, to Round Ings where it was taken in at the landing. George Brook weighed out the weft, that is the coppins, and wrapped them up in canvas to fit the shape of the barrow.

One of their friends used his donkey for cuttling pieces. Two people standing at each side drew the cloth across the animal's back, folding it on to a table. Then the donkey died. When the next piece was delivered, the clothier complained that it had not enough pile on it. The wooden stand substituted had failed to brush it up. 'My father said, "You'll have to buy another donkey."'

As in all these districts farming was linked with daily life. Milk was 2½d. a quart, 1d. for old milk for baking with. One of their neighbours, Sam Morton, a cattle dealer, journeyed regularly to Ireland, and Tom Gee helped out with the milking. 'It was surprising how the whole of the time was filled with doing something.' His wife, Polly Morton, was a big strong woman. They used to meet the cows which had arrived by train at Slaithwaite and had galloped off up Crimble Clough. 'Don't worry,' Polly used to say, 'they'll slow down before you get to the top of Crimble.'

'My mother worked all the year round. They were workers in those days. They were grand days though. We were happy. I can remember my first suit. It was blue. My father used to buy odd lengths at the mill [pattern lengths made for showing to customers] and mother made them up. When a lad was going to get married they used to say, "Can she bake and wesh?"'

At the age of thirteen Jack Gee started to work for his uncle at Parkwood Mill, Longwood, for 5s. a week, out of which his mother gave him 1s. for pocket money. The wage rose by 1s. a week until he was earning 12s.; 18s. to £1 was then a good wage. 'I was a big lad, and I'd always to work over [overtime]. I got all this and put half of it in the bank.' Mr and Mrs Gee were mayor and mayoress of Huddersfield in 1955–6, and Mrs Gee was mayor in her own right in 1964–5.

When William Cudworth wrote *Round About Bradford* in 1876 he had seen many disused hand looms 'awaiting their doom as firewood'. A hundred years later we found machinery and a hand loom, formerly one of six, in a small factory for making heald rugs at Pudsey, run for the first fifty years of this century by the Johnstone family. (Another of the looms is to be seen at the Moravian Museum, Fulneck.) Heald rugs have a long pile of twisted worsted dyed red, green, rust and black, and used in kitchens and farmhouses were valued for their hard-wearing qualities.

The three-storied house, probably originally occupied by a clothier, dates back at least to 1833, and is a reminder of the once populous clothing villages round about.[1] The top floor, 35 feet square, extending over the whole building, holds the machinery and the remaining looms (*see plates* 13–14). The Johnstones bought in yarn and processed it ready for weaving with the machines—a doubler, cheese winder and a hank winder—driven by a gas turbine and later by electricity, and they employed half-timers who learnt to weave in a fortnight by throwing the empty shuttle from side to side and treadling rhythmically with their feet. Older women working full time could each make three rugs, one yard by two, in a day.

[1] *Commercial Directory* 1816–17 gives '164 manufacturers who attended the Mixed and Coloured Cloth Halls at Leeds from Armley, Rawdon, Calverley, Churwell, Gildersome, Farsley, Bramley, Horsforth, Stanningley, Low Wortley, Pudsey'.

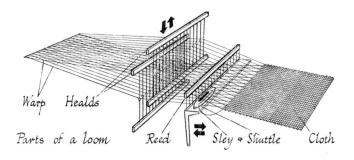

Warp   Healds

Parts of a loom   Reed   Sley & Shuttle   Cloth

2 Mills and Manufacturers

FROM the 1770s onwards mills to contain the new machinery began to be built. Opportunity to make a start was there for anyone who was capable, hard working, shrewd, far-sighted and as was said of Robert Moore, the mill-owner in *Shirley*, 'keen o' making brass and getting forrards'. Briefly mills were initially built by three means: by private individuals, by landlords who let 'room and power', and most often by groups of men who on the lines of friendly societies subscribed small sums of money to build and run company mills. Thus many gained a foothold.

Most were drawn from the ranks of the clothiers, some from landowning families, and a few from outside the county. Many borrowed from banks, which in the early nineteenth century were sometimes run by the large textile firms. Hague and Cook of Dewsbury Mills printed their own bank-notes. It was not until the 1850s to the 1870s, the climactic period of the industry, that large mills, of which foremost examples are Saltaire Mills (1853) and Manningham Mills (1873), were erected all at one time (*see plate* 21).

Nor was opportunity for the many confined to the early days. Mills constantly changed hands as the clothiers, now manufacturers, rose and fell. One man's disaster was another man's chance. An abandoned mill could be bought cheaply. Clogs to clogs in three generations (and sometime less) echoes down the years. Most eventually became family concerns with almost always a dominant member of one generation laying foundations for those who followed. Sometimes sons lost all that their fathers had built up. Manufacturers had constantly to install new machinery, change to new raw materials and new cloths, overcome the dire effects of tariffs imposed by foreign governments especially American, and the cycles of trade peculiar to the industry. 'Trade comes in the night' expresses their unpredictable nature. The awesome slumps of the early 1920s and 1930s put many out of business altogether. Wars from the eighteenth century onwards, bringing in their train army contracts for uniform cloths and blankets benefited trade, saved firms from disaster, and earned capital to surmount later recessions.

Throughout the nineteenth century mills were added to, pulled down, burnt down, rebuilt and extended. Almost without exception they were destroyed by fire at least once. In cotton mills the spinners worked in bare feet, incurring the hazard of *spells* (splinters) from wooden floors as at Spring Mill in the Ryburn Valley, so that their clogs did not strike sparks. These disasters resembled a *blitzkrieg* from whose ashes new and better mills arose. Mill fires, an unforgettable sight of crashing beams and leaping flames, had dire effects on both owners and workers, and encouraged the provision of private fire-engines and brigades, and also fireproof building techniques for which cast-iron columns and girders were advocated as early as 1801 by James Watt. In this century water sprinkling systems were introduced.

Low Mills, Addingham, the second worsted spinning mill in the country, was built on the river Wharfe in 1790 by John Lister and John Cockshott (*see plate* 20). The first of the great steam-driven mills, Park Mills at Bean Ing, Leeds, built in 1792, was the vision of the first of the great entrepreneurs, Benjamin Gott. 'It sprang from nothing, an ideal, a dream of a new age of industrialization material-ized in brick and iron, in steam and machinery.'[1] Two years later John Marshall, also in Leeds, started the first of his flax-spinning mills that culminated in the Egyptian-style Temple Mill in 1840. Bradford's first worsted mill with a 15 h.p. engine was built in 1798[2] (and only fifty years later a writer in the *Morning Chron-icle* commented that 'fortunes have been made in Bradford with a rapidity almost unequalled even in the manufacturing districts'). In the 1830s the building of woollen mills in the Dewsbury area was 'immense, enough to astonish anybody'. At Batley, short of water power, the era of mill building dated from the late 1840s to 1860.

As we have noted many little mills, each with dams, goits and water-wheels, were built in the smaller Pennine valleys: twenty-four on the river Holme and its tributaries down to Holmfirth, now only three mills left;[3] eight cotton and two silk built between the 1780s and the 1840s on Colden Water in upper Calderdale, now none; eight cotton, one corn, and one woollen in Cragg Vale, now none; ten in the Blackburn valley on the Black Brook, south of Halifax, for corn, fulling, cotton, paper, wire, woollen, and worsted,[4] now six, three woollen, one waste, one paper and one carpet; and over 100 on the waters of the Tame and its tributaries in

---

[1] W. B. Crump, 'The Leeds Woollen Industry 1780–1820', *Thoresby Society* vol. XXXII, 1929.

[2] J. James, *History of Bradford*, 1866.

[3] J. M. Hinchliffe, 'A Dissertation on the Mills of the Upper Holme Valley', Huddersfield Poly-technic School of Architecture, unpublished thesis.

[4] See Augustus Muir, *The History of Bowers Mills*, 1969.

Saddleworth. In these areas bordering on Lancashire the manufacturers who built the cotton mills had changed from the woollen to the cotton trade, and many were to revert later to wool. In 1838 there were 140 cotton mills employing 10,000 persons in the West Riding.

Many of these mills were demolished when reservoirs were made. But also for several reasons—accessibility, the more efficient steam power needing coal, and transport provided by canals and railways—industry moved into the main valleys. The complex of huge mills in the Colne valley was developed from 1860 to 1890 and the last, called Titanic, was built as its name implies in 1912. By 1884 the total number of mill-owners had risen to 1,108.

Built from stone quarried near at hand and evolving in design from the corn mills, the clothiers' homes and the loomshops, mills were first small and square and developed into the familiar long, many-storied, many-windowed edifices. Like castles and abbeys they roughly conform to a basic design. Entering through a sometimes handsome gateway, the mill yard paved with setts allowed for the arrival and despatch of goods and was so large at Bean Ing that it held tenters. At the entrance was the time office or 'penny 'oile' (see Chapter 4), and on one side of the yard either adjoining the warehouse or a separate building stood the owner's house which in time was vacated for a new house built at a discreet distance. Because weaving came late into the mills, one-storied weaving sheds usually with saw-tooth roofs fill in available ground.

Interior stone spiral staircases in the corners to save space as at St Peg Mill, Cleckheaton, Clough House Mills, Slaithwaite, or Washpits Mill, Holmfirth, were common. Machinery was in fact too closely packed together. At Spring Mill in the Ryburn valley Mr Irvin Berry remembers that when the little piecer wanted to put bobbins in at the back of the spinning frames, he lay on the floor to let the mules run over him and lay down again to get out. In weaving sheds when a new warp was required, the beam had to be lifted shoulder high into position on the loom by several overlookers.

Shallow projecting gables as at Low Mills, Addingham, and Dean Clough Mills, Halifax, accommodated privies on each floor, with a cast-iron pipe down the full height. Towers, with later water tanks for the sprinklers put on top, contained hoists, and the engine house is distinguished by tall narrow windows. Those symbols of the power house and the Industrial Revolution, chimneys, rose higher and higher, and some of their owners, Samuel Cunliffe Lister of Manningham Mills, Bradford, Thomas Taylor of Blakeridge Mills, Batley, John Edward Crowther of Bank Bottom Mills, Marsden, and Armitage Haigh of Priestroyd Ironworks, Huddersfield, on their completion or when they were being repaired, climbed to the top. Dams once needed for water for the water-wheels (and remembered as paradise for skaters in frosty winters), were still essential to provide water for the various processes. Single-storied buildings are now regarded as more functional; yet, there the mills stand in the industrial landscape, grand and huge, monuments to human endeavour and endurance, symbols of an industry 'epic in its destiny and traditions'.

Innumerable examples might be given of the humble beginnings of large important firms. Jeremiah Ambler began in 1789 as a rope-maker and founded what was to become a large important mohair and worsted spinning firm at Bradford, and C. & J. Hirst began in a cottage at Longwood in the Colne valley, and eventually had five mills and 1,400 employees. In Batley J. T. and T. Taylor, who eventually were to employ 1,600 people, become famous for their profit-sharing scheme and for Theodore Taylor, who lived to be 102, started with £300 and an eight-day clock.

A diary describes how the Beardsell family business at Holme House in the Holme valley was built up. In 1828 James Beardsell, a small clothier, took his four sons into partnership, and one of them, Isaac, the hard-working member, increased the trade in three years from the making of four pieces a week to twenty. Their success rested on Isaac's skill in designing at the time of the changeover from kerseys to fancy goods. He wrote in 1835; 'There was nothing for which I felt more ambitious than to bring out some new pattern which would take the lead', and he produced amongst others 'the grouse pattern . . . a right pattern brought out at the right time'. In 1836 they took Digley Mill on Digley Brook at the rent of £140 a year, and the Beardsells became some of the leading manufacturers in the Holme valley.[1]

Or take John Buckley (1754–1825), a yeoman clothier, who built two water-driven mills, one with his cousin about 1767, Lower and Upper Broadhead in the Castleshaw valley, near Delph (see plate 7). Two of John's five sons, Henry and Hugh, frequently journeyed abroad, one to New York and the other to Lisbon where they joined English colonies of merchants. Henry sold woollen goods and bought cotton, and Hugh sold fine quality broadcloth and remarkably beautiful printed shawls destined for Spain. In 1821 Hugh advised that canary, buff, scarlet and orange were the favourite colours, and, because there were other makers of shawls from Saddleworth, that competition was keen (see plates 8–9). In 1879

[1] Isaac Beardsell, 'An Historical Account of our Trade from the time of becoming a Partner in 1828', transcript of MS. lent to us by Mr Stephen Beardsell. For patterns of fancy goods see those designed by W. Etchells in the mid-nineteenth century in the Tolson Memorial Museum, Huddersfield.

members of the Buckley family moved to the better equipped Linfitts Mill on the river Tame.[1]

In passing it may be noted that life at Broadhead and Holme House was pleasant and dignified. A boarding school existed in the Castleshaw valley, and one of Hugh Buckley's sons took violin lessons which he disliked and used a string for his fishing-rod. Peter, one of the Beardsell brothers, enjoyed shooting woodcock, and whilst staying at Buxton visited Chatsworth House.

In that shawl-wearing century Saddleworth and the upper Colne valley from about 1820 were the main centres of manufacture. Little mills at Marsden and Slaithwaite made them. One built in Crimble Clough in 1832 dyed and finished silk shawls, and a maker, Shoddy Sam (Samuel Shaw), is remembered gathering wool caught on bilberry bushes on the moors. Elsewhere worsted yarn was spun for them. S. Cunliffe Lister invented a fringe-twisting machine, as did Joseph Craven of Thornton, near Bradford, a member of a firm that drew the trade in shawl cloths away from Paisley.[2] *The Yorkshire Textile Directory*, 1919, gives forty-four flannel and shawl manufacturers of whom sixteen makers are in the Saddleworth district. One of the last, James Bailey of Uppermills made travelling rugs and little shawls costing 2s. 6d. for the kaffirs in South Africa.

Morley provides examples of both a 'room and power' and a company mill. In the first category the Crank Mill is in any case famous as one of the earliest mills powered by steam; and it was built in 1790 for £1,250 by Lord Dartmouth and leased to John and Joseph Webster at £100 a year and later to others (*see drawing on page 34*). In the second category Gillroyd Mills are antedated by many, for instance Healey Mill built at Ossett in 1765, but its first committee book survives.[3]

The Gill Royds Mill Company, as it was then spelt, was started in December, 1834, by a group of twelve men (one of whom was the father of the Right Honourable H. H. Asquith, prime minister from 1908 to 1916). Over a period they subscribed £30 a share to build a public fulling and scribbling mill to which dyeing was soon added. To finish and equip the mill they borrowed money, mortgaged the premises to complete them, urged Hird, Dawson and Hardy of Low Moor to build the engine, and after two years' effort paid £4,413 for the building, five cottages and a dam, out of which the architect, Mark Holmes, received £75 4s. 1d. They then appointed from time to time a date for the 'Mill Feast', celebrated by a dinner, and

[1] Documents and shawls shown to us by Mr and Mrs G. E. Buckley.
[2] William Cudworth, *Round about Bradford*, 1876.
[3] John Goodchild, 'The Ossett Mill Company', *Textile History*, 1968–70, vol. I, No. I, pp. 47–61; MS. Committee Book, Gill Royds Mill Company, 1835–61, Archives department, Leeds Central Library.

pay day for all who had had goods processed. Over the years new buildings were added to include spinning in 1858 and weaving in 1860. A severe fire destroyed the mill in 1885, but it was built up again by the company. In time shareholders sold out and founded their own businesses, and one of them, John Hartley (1847–1919), first leased then bought the mill which was run by his descendants until 1966.

Meanwhile in mid-century the founders of the great mills of the high noon of the Yorkshire textile industry, almost all based on worsted and the new materials— alpaca, mohair and waste silk—emerged: John Crossley (1772–1837), who leased a mill at Dean Clough, Halifax, in 1802, and founded a carpet factory which a hundred years later was employing 5,000 workpeople; John Foster (1799–1878), the son of a farmer and colliery owner, who in 1835 started to build Black Dyke Mills at Queensbury between Halifax and Bradford, who was followed by William Foster, the dominant figure, and who in the 1870s were employing 3,500 work-people; Titus Salt (1803–76), who was foremost in discovering the use of alpaca and built the mills and a model village at Saltaire; Isaac Holden (1807–97), inventor and woolcomber, who was born in Scotland and ran combing plants in France; Edward Akroyd (1810–87) of Halifax, whose family sprang from yeomen clothiers in upper Calderdale, who pioneered model housing estates in the West Riding; and Samuel Cunliffe Lister (1815–1906), inventor, discoverer of the use of waste silk and builder of Manningham Mills. All these major figures who made vast fortunes are well known and the subjects of various studies.[1]

Others rose to the fore: the Brookes at Armitage Bridge Mills, who for 'fifteen generations and through four centuries have owned and occupied a mill on the waters of the Holme'; the Firths at Heckmondwike and Brighouse building three mills, one in the United States, established a great carpet-making firm, whose ownership changed in the early years of this century to the Aykroyds; Wormalds and Walker of Dewsbury Mills started in 1811 with five corn, fulling and scribb-ling mills on the river Calder, which became the largest blanket-making firm in the country.[2]

Some mills and their owners dominated a village, such as the Shaws who built Brookroyd Mills, Holywell Green near Halifax, employed 1,200 people, had a

[1] R. Bretton, *The Crossleys at Dean Clough*, 1950; R. Balgarnie, *Sir Titus Salt*, 1877; E. M. Sigsworth, 'Sir Isaac Holden Bart: The First Comber in Europe' in *Textile and Economic History*, ed. N. B. Harte and K. G. Ponting, 1973; R. Bretton, 'Colonel Edward Akroyd', *Transactions of the Halifax Antiquarian Society*, 1948, pp. 61–100; Samuel Cunliffe-Lister, *Lord Masham's Inventions*, 1905; E. M. Sigsworth, *Black Dyke Mills*, 1958.

[2] W. B. Crump and G. Gorbal, *History of the Huddersfield Woollen Industry*, pp. 47, 117–20; *150th Anniversary, Flush Mills, Heckmondwike, near Leeds*, 1972; F. J. Glover, 'Dewsbury Mills, a history of Messrs Wormalds and Walker Ltd', University of Leeds, PhD. thesis, 1959.

private railway, and as a family firm finished in 1952.[1] At Gomersal in 1752 the Burnleys were yeomen clothiers living at Pollard Hall, and 100 years later Thomas Burnley bought the Cloth Hall Mill at Gomersal, now called Gomersal Mills, and ran it until 1913. These mills, now part of a combine, are notable for the scale of their operations and modern system for worsted spinning, combing and dyeing. In the Colne valley, besides other families, such as Hirst, Hoyle, Beaumont and Mallinson, the Crowthers, branching out from Lees Mill at Golcar, backed the building of large mills from Milnsbridge to Marsden. Bank Bottom and others run by John Edward Crowther (1862–1931) were said in his lifetime to be the largest privately owned mills in the world.

Amongst all these Cunliffe Lister was raised to the peerage, and others, amongst whom Sir Isaac Holden, who rising from poverty has the most unusual career, were given baronetcies and knighthoods. Some became members of parliament, founded banks, promoted railways, and started profit-sharing schemes. In varying degrees especially in the mid-century building era they contributed vast sums to erect churches, chapels, schools, almshouses, mechanics' institutes, model housing estates, and especially chapels for many were Nonconformists. Some built mansions, now turned into public buildings. A few—Fosters, Crossleys, Brookes, Crowthers and others—founded dynasties that still continue. In the later years of the century and in this others made fortunes and hurried away from their native places.

Many manufacturers faced adversity. They lived beyond their means, or were unlucky, or were defeated by new tariffs, and in an effort to extricate themselves from difficulty were involved in fraud, or mortgaged houses, or borrowed from relations and staff—a brother, a widowed mother, the foreman, the firer. Families quarrelled and members split off. Some colourful figures are fixed like flies in amber in local annals for their exploits such as backing plays on the London stage with dire financial results. Firms went bankrupt; men committed suicide, and even died of broken hearts. Except in fiction these agonies involving pride, home and family have been insufficiently stressed in studies of the textile trade.

Albeit strict disciplinarians and frequently powerful personalities, manufacturers were totally engrossed in the mill and often father-figures in their own world, especially before the advent of National Insurance and the Welfare State. The death of a large mill-owner shook a whole district. Usually salaries were modest and thrift was ingrained; earnings from trading were the hoped-for source of wealth. When in 1889 William Hanson, who had begun work as a little piecer at ten years old, formed his large firm of cotton spinners and doublers at Halifax into

[1] R. M. Shaw, 'The Shaws of Stainland', *Transactions of the Halifax Antiquarian Society*, 1965.

a limited company, his salary as managing director was £400 a year paid quarterly plus £100 for travelling expenses, the cost of the usual first-class ticket between Bradford and Manchester and an allowance for a journey to Germany. In 1907 the sons of the owner at one woollen mill had an extra 5s. a week allotted them on their thirtieth birthdays. At one important mill at luncheons for board meetings a director knelt down on his knees in order to measure the sherry in each glass so that all had exactly equal quantities. At Mallinson's old Eli, son of the founder, is remembered chiding a clerk for spilling and wasting a drop of ink.

Sons served an apprenticeship by going through the mill, working mill hours, thus establishing personal contact with their staff who addressed them as 'Mr John', 'Mr Harry' and so on. At Washpits Mill, Holmfirth, Mr Stephen Beardsell's grandfather went to work in 1865, his father in 1899, and he himself in 1926, when they were all three there together. In 1905 Mr Philip Kirk of the Crank Mill was 'fetched from school' when he was fifteen and has worked at the mill ever since. His father gave him nothing and he went to the 'tech.' at night, both usual practices. At the age of nineteen Mr Harold Walker of Holme Bank Mills lived in Aachen to work as a textile machinery overlooker and to learn German. One of the Shaw family spent two years in Shanghai, and another took a course in chemistry and dyeing at Bayer's in Elberfeld in Germany. As a young man Mr M. W. Shelton of Gomersal Mills spent some of his early years in mills in northern France, and his father, J. W. Shelton, used to travel on business from the Hook of Holland to Moscow and back via Vienna and Saxony with a few gold sovereigns in his pocket. As time went on sons were sent to public schools and university, and some eschewing trade turned into country gentlemen.

Women, who under the domestic system had played important roles, now only held office in wartime or became heads of firms in emergencies. For example Mrs P. D. Crowther following the death of her husband took on the chairmanship of Bank Bottom Mills in 1953, and Mrs E. M. Horsley, a director of her family firm, William Hanson, at Halifax, became secretary after the death of the holder of that office in 1952, and in 1964 the first woman president of a Chamber of Commerce in England.

Amidst all the 'hurry of work' there existed the hundreds of small firms: the top-makers at Bradford buying wool and having it combed on commission, the rag-sorting and shoddy-making establishments at Dewsbury and Batley, the makers of rugs of all kinds, the mending workshops, the fustian manufacturers of Hebden Bridge.

The rag and shoddy trade dates back to the invaluable discovery about 1813 that old rags could be ground up by machines to be re-cycled for use in the manufacture of cloth. Rags from all over the world were first auctioned at Dewsbury in 1845 by Henry Cullingworth; innumerable rag-sorting places run by members of families existed in every street in Batley and Dewsbury, and manufacturers of shoddy and mungo,[1] such as Henry Day and Sons, who started in 1844, were established. Here again thrift was the rule. Hephzibah Bruce, a rag merchant of Batley, remembered for having three husbands and three sons, sank her profits as was the custom in houses and shops.

Another firm started as a result of Jewish persecution in Europe. 'My grandfather, Samuel Strassburg, was a cloth manufacturer in the town of Pabianicz near Lodz in the Imperial Russian province of Poland.' In 1903 a son was sent to England to find a refuge, and by chance he learnt that Russian rags, called 'wants', were in demand at Dewsbury. He left for Russia, brought back two train loads, and the families changing their name to Stross settled as rag and cloth merchants in the West Riding.[2]

Cloth made of shoddy with cotton warps, besides clothing the poor, enjoyed a worldwide sale. Round the turn of the century Melton, a thick cloth, then priced at 6d. to 1s. a yard was sent in quantity to China, as were thousands of yards of cheap black coffin cloth, used in that country instead of coffins. Before the First World War low quality material could be sold at $2\frac{3}{4}d.$ a yard. But in a lifetime both the mills and the small rag sorters and mungo manufacturers have diminished in numbers as rags, bought up elsewhere, have become less available, and since synthetic materials have been introduced and heavy cloths, once a speciality, are no longer required in centrally heated buildings. Sixty years ago there were fifty-five manufacturing firms in Morley, in 1975 ten, and in Batley thirty-nine are reduced to five.[3] A feature of rags at the present day is their cleanliness and newness owing to the general use of washing machines and the habits of a throw-away society.

Another example of small units was to be found at Hebden Bridge where about 1840 the manufacture of fustian was established, followed, after the invention of the sewing machine, by the making-up of garments. (William Barker at Mayroyd Mill, was the first to use a power sewing machine.) It was general practice for the

[1] Shoddy and mungo are respectively ground up woollen and worsted rags. The unfortunate connotation of the word shoddy disguises the fact that if made from good quality wool it can be more valuable than less good pure new wool. See H. Burrows, *A History of the Rag Trade*, 1956, and *A Story of Woollen Rag Sales, 1860–1960. Centenary of Robert Thornton and Sons*, Savile Bridge, Dewsbury.

[2] MS. Notes on the Stross family of Dewsbury.

[3] Report, *Batley at Work, The Rise and Fall of a Textile Town*, 1974.

HOUSES AND INDUSTRY

1. Golcar in the Colne valley showing some of the many late eighteenth-century clothiers' houses. In 1753 of the 166 clothiers in the valley, 111 lived in and around here. An example of an early trading estate, it is now a conservation area. The house in the centre, one of the many home-workshops, contains the Colne Valley Museum.

2. Hebden Bridge, upper Calderdale, showing the nineteenth-century development. Most of the terraces of houses were built in the 1890s. Many of them are in tiers with one house entered from the front and another above it entered from the back. On the hilltops are seen some of the old original settlements.

EARLY INDUSTRY

3. High Kinders, Greenfield, Saddleworth, dated 1642, a fine example of a clothier's house. It takes its name from the family who built it, and it has been extended several times. Hand-loom weaving continued here until the 1880s. Note the two 'takin' in' doors at the top of the flight of steps, one blocked up.

4. Wuzzing holes at Manor Farm, Thurstonland, near Huddersfield. A stick was put in the hole, and wet wool in a skep (basket) or a metal container was hung on the stick, which was swirled round and round, thus shaking out the water.

5. Tenter posts erected about 1840, a very late date, for Wall Clough Mill on Wall Hill, Saddleworth. They would have wooden bars with hooks on to which the cloth was fastened and stretched along the top and bottom.

EARLY MILLS

6. *Low Lumb Mill, built in 1805, and High Lumb Mill, built in 1815, on Colden Water, upper Calderdale. The latter had a little gasometer. Paved paths led through the woods to them from Heptonstall (date unknown).*

7. *High and Low Broadhead, water-powered fulling mills in the Castleshaw valley, near Delph, built in the late eighteenth century. From here the Buckley family exported superfine broadcloth and fine shawls (c. 1875).*

8 & 9. *Two of a group of fine mostly woollen shawls, still preserved, made at Broadhead. They date from 1820 to 1850. The one with no fringe is white printed with a border of grey scrolling motifs and green, blue and red lozenges. The second with a long twisted fringe is elaborately printed in red, blue, orange, green, rose pink, dark and light browns and yellow.*

HAND-LOOM WEAVING
10. Mr Ishmael Whittell, hand-loom plush weaver, at Messrs Sykes and Tunnicliffe, Northfields Mill, Almondbury (1919).
11. Mr Joseph Pinder (d. 1910), the last of the Kilpin Hill blanket weavers (date unknown).

12. Timothy Feather (1825–1910), of Buckley Green, Stanbury, near Keighley, seen sitting in his 'house'. He was the last hand-loom weaver in that neighbourhood. Note the bobbin winder, and oatcake hung on a flake.

13. Mr G. H. Johnstone demonstrates weft winding from the hank to the bobbin at a small factory making heald rugs up to about 1953 in Pudsey.

14. The looms were arranged round the walls near the windows, and the weavers sat propped against the walls on two-legged buffets. Two beams were used—a pile beam seen at the top of the loom and a warp beam at the bottom.

MILL-OWNERS
15. *John Eli Walker (1848–1943) of Holme Bank Mills, Mirfield (c. 1925).*

16. *John Crowther (1817–1865), son of John Crowther (b. 1783) clothier and of Lees Mill, Golcar, Colne Valley, the founder of the Crowther dynasty.*

17. *Martha Crossley (1775–1854), wife of and driving force behind John Crossley, founder in 1802 of Crossleys Carpets at Dean Clough Mills, Halifax. Rising daily at 4 a.m., she controlled 160 hand-loom weavers, was responsible for selling the products of four looms making brace*

18. *Charlotte Sykes (1790–1852) who built Acre Mills, Lindley, near Huddersfield.*

webs and body belts, and with assistance, made and stitched every carpet they sold retail.

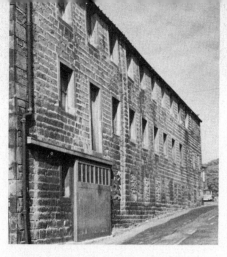

EVOLUTION OF A FIRM

19. Loomshop for sixty hand looms in Chapel Lane, Addingham, built by John Cockshott in about 1780 for weaving calico. There were five Cockshotts, calico manufacturers, in Addingham in 1822. The building was later used for the making of clog irons.

20. Low Mills, Addingham, built in 1787 by John Cockshott and John Cunliffe, the second worsted mill to be built in England. The water-wheel was at the side of the building next to the river Wharfe, and two rows of cottages, in one of which a school was held, are seen behind. The projections on the front of the two main buildings contained closets (c. 1921).

21. Ground plan of Manningham Mills, Bradford, built by Samuel Cunliffe Lister, grandson of John Cunliffe, in 1873. The architects were Andrews and Pepper of Bradford and the works then covered eleven acres of flooring and required about 3,000 h.p. to drive the machinery. The lodges spaced at intervals along the frontage gave access to the various departments. Note the rows of back-to-back houses.

MANNINGHAM MILLS · BRADFORD · YORKS. Messrs Lister & Co. Silk Spinners Manufacturers.

MILL YARD AND DAM

22. The mill yard at John Foster and Son, Black Dyke Mills, Queensbury. The office block is glimpsed on the left and the semi-round projection contains Shed Mill staircase and a lift. The chimney was built prior to 1868.

23. Gibson or Lord Holme Mill, Hardcastle Crags, upper Calderdale, a water-powered cotton mill on Hebden Water built by Abraham Gibson about 1800. It ceased work about 1900.

makers-up to buy grey cloth (undyed and uncut) from the weavers, and send it to dyers such as Moss's for dyeing and cutting. (Like velvet, the pile had to be cut to make corduroy, *see plate* 26.) Some such as Sutcliffes and Redmans developed into large concerns. But even forty years ago many little firms flourished. A man cutting out garments and his wife machining could start a business. Everyone helped everyone else. Minimal distinction between employer and employed, who in any case were often related, encouraged a close-knit egalitarian society.

One of the firms, formerly at Nutclough Mill and now at the Hebden Works, was started in 1870 by about thirty men who, suffering hardship from lack of work and inspired by the co-operative movement then developing over the border in Lancashire, each subscribed 3*d.* a week to form a co-operative workshop. They rented a room, bought corduroy to cut, sent goods to local dyers, introduced the making-up of garments and founded the Hebden Bridge Fustian Manufacturing Society which in 1873, with the aid of a loan from the Wholesale Co-operative Society, bought a little mill at Nutclough. This flourished and was enlarged to the extent that by 1914 £15,600 had been paid out in bonus on wages, and in 1918 when 765 fustian looms were in operation, the concern was sold to the Wholesale Co-operative Society for £42,000. Nutclough closed down in 1968, but the same business continues at the Hebden Works.[1]

The various types of fustian—moleskin (plain, locally called mole), and corduroy (ribbed, known as cord)—together with denims, drills and woollen kersey were used up to the mid-1950s for industrial and institutional clothing interesting for its specific design. For instance pit sinkers in Durham, Yorkshire and Kent were supplied with suits made of white kersey which had knee and shoulder patches of moleskin. Mental hospitals were provided with cord trousers and derby tweed jackets and waistcoats, and for the less amenable patients moleskin garments, padded and quilted at the front and fastening down the back. The heavier weights of corduroy were once used for breeches and leggings for gamekeepers and country gentlemen, and are still made into climbing breeches. Thousands of yards of constitutional cloth, a broad ribbed corduroy whose pile had been cut, brushed and singed under gas burners so that gold adhered to it, were sent to South Africa for gold panning. This cloth is still in demand.[2]

What materials have we seen in the mills in the 1970s? Velvet and fur fabrics

---

[1] Joseph Greenwood, *The Story of the Formation of the Hebden Bridge Fustian Manufacturing Society Ltd*, 1888; *Report of the Coming of Age Celebrations of the H.B.F.M.S.*, 23rd and 26th September, 1891; *Rules of the H.B.F.M.S.*, 1908; 'The Fustian makers of Hebden Bridge', *The Wheatsheaf*, May 1919; all lent to us by Mr L. Barker.

[2] Information from Mr J. C. Atack, formerly of Cheethams.

such as imitation mink requiring special finishing processes at Manningham Mills, Bradford, fine worsted made in short runs for men's exclusive suits, much of it exported to Japan, at Newsome Mills, near Huddersfield, colourful finely-woven blazer cloths for Oxford colleges at Uppermoor Mill, Pudsey, mohair cloths at Black Dyke Mills, Queensbury (the largest factory for that material in the world), ladies' luxury coating and fine cloths made from cashmere, camelhair, mohair, angora at Batley Carr Mills, Dewsbury, and Hopton Mills, Mirfield, tweeds for the multiple tailors at the mills in the Colne valley, a cashmere blanket at Wormalds and Walker, a pattern of the carpet woven for the *Queen Elizabeth II* at Clifton Mills, Brighouse, hosiery yarn and knitting wools at Emu Wools, Keighley, striped denims and purple corduroy for the fashion trade at the Hebden Works, velours and union cloths at the Crank Mill, Morley, tartans to be made up into house coats in Denmark and thick felt cloth to protect the petrol tanks of aeroplanes at Washpits Mill, Holmfirth. 'You live out of versatility.'

We have seen chimneys being felled, mills standing idle or used for new purposes, and men of many nationalities attending the machines. The monopoly is over; other nations make cloth too. But inherited knowledge and skills still count. Textile historians trace the beginning of decline to the 1920s. In 1958 there were in the United Kingdom 1,087 firms with 170,626 employees, and in 1974 533 firms with 82,906, of whom 62,300 are in Yorkshire. Many family businesses have been caught up in the maw of large public companies. Others continue, harried by taxation, and all still suffer the booms and recessions of trade.

3 Half-timers

MAGNET-like the textile industry drew people to the West Riding from the far corners of the British Isles and from foreign countries. The influx of the Irish had started before the years of potato famine, and colonies grew in most towns. We have met the descendants of many emigrants: craftsmen overtaken by mass production, the grandson of a candle-maker at Hinderwell near Whitby, and sons and especially daughters of miners and steel workers from South Yorkshire where employment for women was scarce. A family pioneered and others followed, at first lodging with relatives. Others, attracted to the better pay, came from Derbyshire, East Anglia, Somerset to be maids, coachmen or gardeners to the manufacturers.

In the period with which we are concerned the days of child labour and inordinately long hours had passed. Factory and Education Acts had slowly given education precedence over work. None the less although gradually modified, half-time working for children lasted from 1844, when some schooling was made compulsory, until 1922. Several early mills had their own schools as at Low Mills, Addingham, and Armley Mills, Leeds. In Halifax in 1917 there were 1,057 half-timers,[1] and the last who began in this way retired from Dean Clough Mills on 4th July 1974, after fifty-six years' work.

But as late as the 1920s the bow-legged, the K-legged, the hunch-backed were not uncommon. It was said that a seventh child was marked for life. In other words large families suffered from neglect and malnutrition resulting in rickets and anaemia. Young people carried too heavy pieces in finishing departments and women worked too near the birth of a child. It is true that children deformed from birth could find light work in a mill more readily than elsewhere. Children, having nimble fingers and a soft touch and paid tiny wages, usefully performed operations in the spinning departments. Almost everyone in a mill formerly began as a little piecener or piecer, or a little doffer. The first joined broken threads between finger and thumb, and the second took off the full bobbins from mules or spinning

[1] Notes by H. W. Harwood seen at Halifax Courier Library.

frames. (Mules used for woollen spinning and frames for worsted are different: *see plates 33 and 35*.) A big and little piecer worked under a spinner, who, for instance, earned 41*s*. out of which he paid 12*s*. to them.[1] A team to mind mules in the Colne valley was a spinner, a minder, and two pieceners, a spinner and piecener in one mule gate and a minder and piecener in the other.

School log-books record the link between school and work. For instance, 8 February 1864, 'Admitted today many new children, nineteen half-timers from Drummond's Mill', and 17 September 1866, 'Six mill girls left the school to go full time'.[2] At Staincliffe, near Batley, on 14 December 1886, the master commented that he was 'greatly disappointed with the work of half-timers. They seem to forget facts almost as soon as they are taught. Either weariness or idleness seems their great characteristic'.[3]

The system frustrated teachers who had mixed classes of full- and half-time scholars. The latter suffered, although George Cooper, a half-timer in the 1880s at the age of ten, wrote that older people were helpful and sympathetic, that he worked a thirty-three hours week for 1*s*. 6½*d*. which he proudly took home, and that most never advanced beyond the fourth or fifth standards, but in reading, composition, spelling, and geography they compared favourably with the average scholar in the 1930s. An example beyond compare of a half-timer rising above circumstances is Joseph Wright (1855–1930), who started work as a doffer at Saltaire Mills at the age of seven, and eventually handed down to posterity that feat of scholarship the *English Dialect Dictionary*.

Former half-timers, whom we have met, dependent on their age, began work at from ten to thirteen. (At thirteen you became a young person with whom women were classed.) Mrs A. Tupman (b. 1882), then of Heptonstall, says that her father, William Townsend, started work at eight as a doffer, here pronounced 'dorfer', at Low Lumb Mill, on Colden Water (*see plate 6*). Up to then he had worn a dress and a pinny and was breeched to go. He earned 1*s*. 6*d*. a week rising to 2*s*. 6*d*. and when he was thirteen or fourteen made up for lack of schooling by attending classes at the mechanics' institute. He became a weaver, then a loom tackler (repairer), married and brought up a family of five boys and a girl, and, a keen bandsman and a conductor, he lived to be ninety-one.

Mrs Tupman herself began work as a half-timer when she was ten at 'Tommy Sutcliffe's' in Hebden Bridge. One week, leaving Heptonstall at 5.30 a.m. and

[1] E. Baines, *Yorkshire Past and Present*, 1858, vol. IV, p. 629.
[2] Log-books of St Paul's Church of England School, Manningham, seen by permission of Mrs B. Hudson and the governors.
[3] L. Kemp, *Staincliffe, near Dewsbury, Church of England School Centenary Handbook, 1869–1969*.

walking down the steep track known as the Buttress, she started work at 6 a.m
going to school in the afternoon, and the other week vice versa going to work at
1.30 p.m. until 6 p.m. and on Saturdays working until one o'clock. She learnt to
machine for eight weeks without pay, was then given 1d. a week pocket money
and earned 2s. 6d. rising to 5s. a week when she was thirteen. After that it was
usual to go on piecework and earn what you could, at the most £1 a week. After
marriage she left and did not return.

Only a week younger than Mrs Tupman, Mrs A. Walton of Heptonstall (b. 2
January 1883), because of intervening legislation could not go to work until she
was eleven. She too was a machinist. The girls sat on either side of a long table,
which had gas lights down the centre (for comparison *see plate* 24). They 'worked
through', that is, made complete garments such as 'riders' (riding breeches), cord
leggings for 3d., a boy's vest (waistcoat), jacket and trousers for 9d. Piecework
prices were reckoned down to eighths of a penny. Mrs Walton's sister, Miss E.
Akroyd, continued at work for sixty years.

Mrs A. Ashworth, whose early life follows a similar pattern, lived as a child at
Lily Hall near Heptonstall. The three-storied house was divided into four dwellings including a farmhouse on the ground floor, and her family occupied the
middle part at the back—a kitchen and two bedrooms. She was one of seventeen
children, only five of whom survived. She began half-time work at the age of
eleven, and earned 2s. 6d. a week given to her by the woman who taught her to
machine. When she married, she remembers, 'You could put 10s. on t'top o'
t'sideboard and buy a week's food'. Another industrial clothing worker, Mr H.
Barrett (b. 1885) of Heptonstall, began as a half-timer and eventually worked at
Nutclough Mill for forty-five years. He said, 'There's not a man in Hebden Bridge
as has been a band-knife cutter as long as what I have. . . . If I had mi time over
again I'd go to t'Nutclough. Never a wrong word.'

Take Mrs M. A. Collins' story. She was always called a 'Feast child' because
she was born on the Whit Sunday before Adwalton Feast in 1878. Her father, a
mine manager, was killed at work in America at the same time as his brother died
in a pit accident at Bruntcliffe Pit, Morley. The telegrams bringing the news
crossed on the water. The mother took her five children to live with her father at
Drighlington and returned to the mill to weave, whilst another sister looked after
the home; a third, a dressmaker, made their clothes and the other grandfather, a
shoemaker, their boots. 'We were poor enough, but we managed.' A clever child,
she won a scholarship to the grammar school, but her mother could not afford to
let her go.

Instead, at the age of ten she went as a half-timer to Bower's Mill, where one of her aunts taught her to cap spin. Her mother retired from weaving at forty, and she took her loom at Bulrush Mill, Batley, where her sister and other members of the family worked. This meant leaving home at 5 a.m. and crossing Adwalton Moor. A party of them were once coming home in a snowstorm, and Ned, the only man, cried, 'Follow mi stick and mi coat'. Leading them in single file, he fell into a hole in the moor, Sally Dick's pond, and 'one after another we all fell in after him. We always laughed about it afterwards'. 'The owners of Bulrush were very kind, real Christians. On a wet morning they'd say, "Now lasses get into t'tentering place, and get warm before beginning work". At Christmas we'd put up mistletoe, and one of the girls had to kiss the boss. My first year it was me. Aye they were right good bosses. I wouldn't care if it was coming all ovver again.'

Another half-timer, Mr Alfred Brown, began as a doffer aged twelve at Saltaire Mills. His mother had asked if he could go and he had the required labour certificate from the education office stating the number of his school attendances. Going to the Gatehouse, he was sent to a room 'where the overlooker told you to take your coat off and you were in'. He earned 9s. 9d. a week with a rise of 3d. weekly until he started full time at 18s. 9d. 'If you could get in at Salt's, you'd accomplished something. There was always competition between Salt's and Lister's.' It was in fact generally conceded that Salt's, Lister's and Foster's were the most prestigious places to work at. In any case to get into a good mill you had to put your name down. 'Weavers were waiting to come in.'

Or consider Mr H. Johnson who came from Haworth over seventy years ago 'on a flitting'. As a half-timer, aged eleven, he began as a doffer earning 2s. a week. There were 144 spindles on a spinning frame and a set of five or six doffers with a gaffer sharing them out. A doffer started at one end of the room by taking off and replacing bobbins as the frames stopped one after another all the way down. The one who was last most times in a week had to put on knee pads and with a big piece of oily cotton rub down the alleyway. If you became a jobber lad putting on the bands to run the spindles, you earned 6d. extra. In some mills a form was provided for the doffers and when the overlooker whistled they ran, and the last was given a swipe with the alleydasher (a cleaning implement, a piece of leather attached to a picking stick which when waved created a draught which swept up fluff). In well-kept mills you could eat off the floors which were 'polished like ballrooms'.

When Mr Robert Dennis of Churwell began as a little piecer apprenticed to a spinner (but not a half-timer), one of the mules was steam driven one way and pushed by hand the other. 'Some of the old spinners directing operations sat in an armchair in the mule gate, and paid us what they thought we were worth. The more they could earn by telling us what to do the more they could pay us.' Mr Dennis doffed and put on bobbins. 'It was marvellous how you could fasten about fifty bobbins in the crook of your arm, and go right down the mule hitting about 500 spindles every time like lightning.'

The family of Mr H. Ambler at Queensbury illustrates the tradition of families following on in the same mill generation after generation. This was expected, and in any case if they occupied a mill house or cottage it was obligatory. Mr Ambler (b. 1898) worked half-time for a year in the spinning department, known as t' slave 'oile at Black Dyke Mills, moved on to learn the trade of mechanic, and has been in the mill for sixty-four years. Seven out of eight of his brothers and sisters worked there totalling 304 years in all in the mill. Until they grew up and had learnt their trade, the oldest in the family drew the wages for all.

We met several retired workers from Lock Hill Mills, Sowerby Bridge in Calderdale, formerly W. and R. K. Lee engaged in cotton spinning and doubling (*see plate* 34). Two friends, Mrs N. Broadbent and Mrs M. Shaw, worked as a pair at reeling, that is taking off and tieing up finished hanks, a top job. 'You had to work very swiftly at the same speed. May was quick at starting then slowed up; I was the other way round. They were the happiest hours of my life. We were always laughing.'

Mrs Vera Gaukrodger met her husband who was the boiler firer at Lock Hill. She worked for a year half-time as a setter putting bobbins on, 190 at one side and four sides to set. In her third year she qualified as a doffer. There were fifty-seven machines in one large room, with twenty-five doffers of whom four and a setter each had a 'share', making five shares in all. 'It was marvellous when I got to top doffing, and was given a ticket to say how many machines had to be doffed.' At sixteen, following her sister, she became a fully fledged ring doubler and 'that was really something'. Each doubler patrolled a pair of frames to join any broken threads with a 'dog' knot. (Many practised making these at home.) A doubler was never without a knife or a stone for sharpening, although many stone window-sills in mills were in use as whetstones. The knife, used for cutting off the ends of the knots neatly, wore hooves on the hand. 'I earned about 37s a week, a lot of money. I'd take it home to my mother and I'd say, "How much spending money am I going to have?" and she'd reply, "Half a crown". I used to save half of it every week.'

However undesirable the half-time system was, no one has grumbled. It was taken for granted. Others were going and you went too. For young men there were apprenticeships and night classes, whether at mechanics' institutes or 'techs.', leading to the first rungs of the ladder that led to promotion. For young women a ladder barely existed, only a better wage earned by efficiency on piece-work. Further education had often to be denied them. In 1935 the training rate for a welfare officer was 18s. A spinster, and there were many after the First World War, worked not by any means always unhappily, at the same job for fifty or sixty years. 'I had two lives, my mill life and my home life.' On the other hand marriage, usually but not always, ended a woman's career in the mill.

Many life stories illustrate success from small beginnings. It was possible by ability, hard work and good luck for men to rise to be directors. Others became heads of departments. In 1915 Mr F. Alderson began half-time work in the mill as an errand boy earning 7s. 2d. one week and 4s. 10d. the next. Two years later he moved to Manningham Mills, and by the 1930s was in charge of the finishing department. Times were so bad for about five years that to avoid sacking anyone he kept an alphabetical list of names and shared out the short-time work.

When he was twelve Mr J. Greenough went to Gomersal Mills half-time as a bobbin lad, earning 3s. a week and became cashier. His father had worked in the warehouse there for three months short of seventy years, and in his day the wages were paid in gold. Mr Greenough used to make up the wages, wrapped in pound notes placed on a rack, so that they could be paid out to about 1,000 workpeople in some twenty minutes.

Or take Mr W. Horton's career at Bank Bottom Mills, Marsden. In the bad times of the early 1920s he had gone for a job as a flour boy at the local co-operative stores, but there was a queue of boys waiting there already. He did not dare go home without work, so he went as a piecener to Crimble Mills, Slaithwaite. Moving to Bank Bottom in 1921, he proceeded from piecener, to spinner, to warper, to weaver, to finish percher, to greasy percher, to foreman mender with fifty menders and five men under him.[1] 'I liked to see everything correct and proper and the customer satisfied.'

Consider Mr W. Spink who worked at Gomersal Mills from 1911 when he went as a half-timer for twelve months, to 1965 when he was given a gold watch on retirement. He progressed from a little doffer earning 5s. 3d. one week and 2s. 9d. the next to a jobber lad (oiling round and so on), to mule spinner, to a stint in the territorial army, to card jobber, to night overlooker, to day overlooker, to manager in the carding and wool scouring. An overlooker's wage when he married was about £3 16s. a week, but a manager was salaried. In the carding he had about ninety people under him, half working day and half night. He had charge of both shifts and was often called out 'if owt had gone wrong'. Sometimes they dis-

[1] A warper prepares the warp for a loom. A finish percher examines the cloth for faults after it has been washed and scoured. A greasy percher examines it straight from the loom.

mantled the huge carding machines weighing ten tons, and moved them to another room.

The women tell a different story. Weaving was sought after for the better pay, and in spite of the noise and having to stand for hours on end, it was rewarding and companionable (as for that matter was other work in the mill). Formerly one weaver looked after one loom, and did not welcome anyone else using it. She kept it clean, sometimes coming early and providing her own brushes and even emery paper. In some work if dust penetrated the material 'buttoned'. Sometimes looms were set on fire by a spark falling on fluff. Standing in a *gate* (the passageway between the looms) the weaver could talk to her gate mate by lip-reading and shouting. 'You get very close to your mate' and an equable temper helped. In those days fines were levied for bad work, but if anything was missed, the weaver nearly cried. The best ones were given the best work, weaving the most valuable pieces. When she had finished she 'felled out'.

Weavers wore aprons and mill skirts, long and voluminous, and made of harden that washed as white as snow, and if the work were dirty a belly patch, a piece of leather about two feet square, was worn where the belly pressed against the loom (*see plates* 54 *and* 56). Aprons and skirts were utilized to carry full bobbins from the piecers in the spinning department to the looms. For twenty or thirty bobbins the apron served, but for a full doffing of 450 bobbins, six inches long full of weft, they were worked round and packed tightly into a skirt held up high with hands crossed towards the neck, and carried perhaps up four flights of steps. On Monday mornings John Hartley of Gillroyd Mills used to stand at the top of the mill yard, and if any weavers came in dirty bobbin skirts he sent them home.

'The nicest people I ever met in the mill', says Mr R. Dennis, 'were the old weavers. They'd do anything for you. They'd rush out and deliver a baby, and they'd come back and they'd weave. These were the real people. The ladies in the mill. There was a camaraderie about it that's missing today.'

Miss L. Speddings (b. 1889), whose family came from Sheffield, worked at Listers, Manningham Mills, for fifty-seven years, for the last twelve part-time. After starting in the combing, and washing and teazing raw silk, she went into the Beamsley Shed, spending three weeks being taught to weave. Her family and the mill paid the weaver, and she herself received a small sum. She often used to go home and cry, but her teacher said, '"She'll never leave. She's too interested." And I never did. When I came out I could weave anything. I taught a lot to weave. You had to work hard to get any wage.'

Miss A. E. Britton, beginning as a half-timer at Manningham Mills at the age of fifteen earning 2s. 7d. one week and 3s. 5d. the next, continued at work for forty-

eight years. She first put labels on silk reels, then on skeins for embroidery, and at
the age of seventeen to earn more money went on to weaving and eventually wove
the crimson velvet for the Coronation robes. Listers also made the thick white fur
fabric, on to which tails were sewn, for the ermine capes. Another weaver had
woven thousands of yard of moquette for the Canadian Pacific Railway, and a
third had worked at Manningham for fifty-five years, forty-five of them in the seam
finishing, and 'enjoyed every minute of it'.

Mrs Annie Marlow's story differs slightly. Her father, a farmer at Drighlington,
died on a Wednesday in March 1915, and on the following Monday when she was
thirteen, armed with her labour certificate, she started work first as a piecer earning
5s. rising by 1s. a week to 12s. She then went to Keighley and Moorhouse at
Bruntcliffe Mill and was taught to weave standing by the weaver for three or four
weeks. 'When you got on and the tuner gave you a loom and you started earning,
you gave the weaver your first week's wage. Talk about the good old days. I don't
want them back.'

Similarly in 1910 Miss Agnes Morton, whose family originally came from
Birkenhead, was taught to weave at Manningham Mills when she was sixteen. She
progressed from a single plush loom, earning on average 17s. a week, to a velvet
loom, to a double shuttle loom when the wage increased to 19s. Her sister died
leaving five children and a baby. Her husband was out of work, so her mother, a
widow, took the baby. There was then no chance of marriage, 'whoever had
married me would have had three to keep'. 'What if you were sick?' we asked,
'Sick? You couldn't be sick. You had to work it off. You got 12s. a week and
nothing for the first three days.'

Miss Olive Booth of Batley went to work for her grandfather who employed
about thirty girls pegging rugs which were sold in colliery districts. After three or
four weeks she could not see, and her mother put 'a teea leeave poultice on mi
eyes. They talk about folk today as if they were made of china'. So at thirteen she
learnt to weave in three days on an old fashioned slow loom. 'I've never worked so
hard in my life.' She continued as a weaver for fifty years. 'I wore a shawl a long
time. Mi mother said I'd worn it to ribbins because I thowt I were picturesque wi'
a shawl thrown over mi shoulder. But they weren't as warm as coats. . . . Wages
were small, but we'd some fun. The worse conditions were the more fun we had.
You may not believe that, but it's true. I tell you when I read Osbert Sitwell, I
were sorry for t'Sitwells, they'd a sorry time.'

Other jobs for women were whipping blankets and fringeing rugs and shawls
(see plate 49). In the shawl-making districts of the upper Colne valley and Saddleworth fringeing shawls was undertaken either in the mill or in the home. Men used

to carry away over their shoulders an 'end of twisting' which made fifteen shawls for their wives to fringe at night, or many boys had barrows in which to take them after school from the mill to the house. Money earned by fringeing or tazzling was invariably saved, and two well-built cottages at Slack Cote near Delph, nicknamed Twisters' Rest, were paid for in this way.[1]

Mending and burling because it was quiet clean work was much sought after. Burling, a simple task picking out knots and lumps in a piece with a burling iron, was in early days undertaken by married women to pay the rent. Mending on the other hand is skilled work, especially in worsteds, requiring training, so that menders always regarded themselves as superior. Their job, tiring for the eyes, is to repair faults—a pick or an end out—in the pieces of cloth which had been examined and marked (*see plate* 48). It used to be said that if it took a week to weave badly it would take a month to repair it. W. B. Crump records that the mending room at Bean Ing 'was the most impressive spectacle in industrial Leeds'.

We met Miss Mary Lee at Batley Carr Mills who has been a mender for fifty-nine years, and as head of the department has trained two lots of girls. When she 'got a board the forewoman had a stick and gave you a rap if you weren't doing well'. Mrs L. Addy (b. 1880) says, 'They were very particular then who they took in as menders'. Her father was horseman for Hudson Sykes and Bousfield, Springfield Mills, Morley. When she was thirteen he took her down to the mill and 'they wanted to know if we knew anybody what was a mender, and of course we did. That's how you got in. Whilst learning, we had to go for a month for nothing, then for another month for 5s. a week'. The price paid per piece varied according to its quality, and earnings came to about £1 a week. Mrs Addy worked at the mill, except for intervals (her husband died and her father was ill), all her life. 'Oh, we'd some happy times. You see we could talk when we were mending.'

[1] Mrs M. A. Gartside, Delph, Mr E. Schofield, Diggle, and Mr J. Whitehead, Delph.

4 In the Mills

THE majority o the workers lived within walking distance of the mill, or near any other job for that matter, in rows of houses built for them at 't'back o' t'mill', houses mostly now pulled down, although some of them were 'little palaces'. At the heads of the Pennine valleys where people passed through woods or over rough ground, it was customary going to work on early winter mornings to carry lighted candles in jam jars, so that, like Swaledale in the lead-mining days, a little string of lights might be seen moving along the hillsides. At Marsden in the Colne valley many came by train from Lancashire and Saddleworth, and called at the Railway Inn for a rum and coffee, formerly a popular drink costing 2*d*. or 3*d*.

It was the father's task to waken the family by shouting their names. Or some people rapped on their neighbour's adjoining wall. Or knockers-up toured set streets wakening occupants of specific houses and charging 2*d*. or 3*d*. a week. Elderly Mrs Griffiths at Manningham rattled the spikes of an old umbrella tied to a long clothes prop on bedroom windows, and called out the name of the person, the state of the weather and the time of day. Or another had a long bamboo cane with three wires with corks on the ends and took his dog for protection. A third in Leeds shouted 'Right-O' when heard and was paid 6*d*. a week.

In general workers were summoned to and let out of work originally by horns, then bells, and when steam engines were installed by buzzers or whistles, sometimes called 'Whews'. Bell turrets may be seen for instance at Batley Carr Mills and Brookroyd Mills, Holywell Green. In *A Spring-time Saunter* Whiteley Turner records that he heard one of the last of the factory bells ringing in 1913. Within recollection the different notes of the buzzers made a familiar cacophony of sound.

Women wore clogs, fringed woollen shawls and black stockings. Shawls were not an innovation, but had been standard wear for all women. Dress or Sunday shawls, made of silk or cashmere, were complementary to those worn during the week. For going to work in they were large for winter and small for summer, and were fastened with a safety-pin under the chin or thrown over the shoulder (*see plates* 56, 78, 81, 83). 'You didn't need gloves in a shawl.' Woven in checks or in plain colours, red was popular at Queensbury, and black in a honeycomb design was worn at Heptonstall 100 years ago. Sold at drapers and co-operative stores, they were advertised at a yearly clearance sale at Heckmondwike in 1897 at 2s. 11d. to 8s. 9d. each.

Those coming from a distance took their packets of food, called *jock* in Calderdale and the Colne valley and *snap* in the Leeds district, tied in a red and white spotted or flowered handkerchief often carried under the arm. Sometimes the handkerchief held a basin with a saucer on top and another basin on top of that containing the pudding. Others used baskets, not popular with younger people, or stuffed newspaper packages into their pockets. In many places tin or enamelled billy cans, of which the lid served as a cup, were taken filled with tea, and at night, well scoured, they were hung on nails outside houses to sweeten them. Or a small oval tin canister with two compartments held tea and sugar or a mixture of the two for mashing tea at the mill. Mrs Tupman remembers, 'My mother put up breakfast and dinner (bread for breakfast and teacake sandwiches for dinner) the night before all arranged round a table for the different members of the family, and my father made us a hot drink before we set out.' She carried her jock in a red flannelette bag. When all her family were working, Mrs Marlow buttered twenty-six slices of bread every morning and was often stuck fast as to what to put in. Dripping, especially 'mucky' fat, was a general favourite.

Although some firms started dining-rooms much earlier, in general canteens followed on statutory requirements in the Second World War. (A dining-room was provided by the Akroyds at Copley in 1840 and by the Hadwens at Kebroyd Mills in the Ryburn valley in the late 1880s.) Mostly food was eaten at the loom gate, or on the floor leaning against the spinning mules, or sitting on a wool-sorter's board. 'Our canteen was where we worked.' Places variously called 'snap 'oiles', 'scalding 'oiles', or the 'kettle house' contained a jacketed tank of hot water heated by steam from the engine and with a steam oven on top or near by, and often a large stone sink, usually choked with tea leaves. The billy cans could be hung in the tank to heat them, or otherwise tea was scalded in pint pots (mugs). Many retired mill workers continue the pint pot habit. Tea they think tastes better that way and also they have become accustomed to and like it half cold. Eggs for breakfast were boiled under running hot water taps. Fish and chip shops supplied mill orders (a ha'porth of each thirty times) perhaps fetched by the bobbin ligger, or a tasty fry might be bought for 3d. Meat and potato pies were favourites, and heated in the oven were sometimes marked to indicate whose they were. It is related at one mill that a greedy man often claimed the best pie regardless of the ownership. One of his mates asked his wife to bake 'a right nice mouse pie', and placed it in a prominent position in the oven. The man took it, ate it, and when he was told, 'it cured him'.

In many cases, perhaps every other day, children took their parents a hot meal in their dinner hour. When she was eleven or twelve Mrs L. Addy of Morley, who lived a good mile from where her father worked, had winter and summer to come home from school at m̓dday when she was given something to eat to put her on, carry her father's meal in a basket over her arm to the mill, eat her own dinner, and return to school for half past one. Sometimes snow lay deep on the ground. 'We did run i' them days. Children are too pampered today.'

The penny 'oile already mentioned preceded the time office, and took its name from the fine imposed on late-comers. Is the first record of this custom in *Shirley*? 'Mr Moore made him pay his penny down ere he entered.' 'You were pennied' is the remembered expression. The office was often occupied by a dour character, perhaps an old soldier, who fifty or more years ago not only 'pennied' but shut the gates five minutes after 6 a.m., so that late-comers were left standing outside until after breakfast time thus losing part of their wages. At Gomersal Mills, the penny 'oile is remembered presided over by George Crabtree, a little man who wore a checker brat down to his feet, and at Black Dyke Mills by Dan Cullen who wore a uniform and finished about 1920. Here the gates were shut and late-comers had to enter at the door of the penny 'oile and go out by another door which Cullen could bolt and unbolt from inside. He then wrote your name on a slate, sent it to the office and the money was taken off your wage. When it was realized that the employers were losing good labour penny 'oiles were dispensed with, and in any case the breakfast half hour disappeared with a shorter working week.

At the end of the day the mill *looses*, and if it is not working during holidays or strikes, or if on short time, it is standing and the staff are playing or *laiking*. 'I haven't played many Saturdays.' There were 5,000 people at Manningham Mills and when the mill loosed, 'You couldn't walk against the crowd. Folk on holiday came to look.' A football team which trained at night was once walking home in their white clothes over Crosland Moor, and a woman who saw them shouted, 'Hey, by gum, t'cemetery's looised'.

At Gillroyd Mills one Saturday in August, 1859, the engine was stopped 'to allow the workers an afternoon for a trip to Halifax'. In the 1860s in the Colne valley jollifications in the New Year were always arranged either on mill premises or at the inns, and usually consisted of tea for the women and a 'substantial' supper for the men, followed by singing and a ball. One such event took place in the tentering room. The coffee had been too well laced with rum, and the dancers lurching against the tenter hooks tore their clothes disastrously. In more modern times outings first by train, then by charabanc, later coach, to Blackpool, More-cambe, Scarborough were arranged, either subscribed to or paid for by the owners to celebrate a special occasion. For instance the firm of Hirst and Mallinson in the Colne valley sent all their operatives on a monster excursion to the British Empire Exhibition at Wembley. Rooms in the mills were decorated for Christmas or for Coronations or for visits of royalty. Clubs or raffles were run to help save for holidays or Christmas fare. Life in the mill is said to have been more friendly than now. You worked and still do not at such and such a mill but for Rhodes, Jarmains, Sykes, Roberts, Priestmans, Martins or Murgatroyds.

Many of the tasks already referred to have been either modified or made obso-lete. Weavers, now often men, look after three or four looms, or up to sixteen when automatic. Spinners do their own doffing, and they and doublers use a machine to tie knots and wear a plastic ring containing a razor blade to cut the ends. Nor are there many engine tenters and firers left, or those such as Strap Alf at Bank Bottom Mills, who attended to the belting connecting the machines with the shafting and the engine.

Two now obsolete jobs were those of velvet and cord cutting. (Velvet is a cut warp and corduroy a cut weft pile fabric; for the latter *see plate* 26.) In 1894 at Low Mills, Addingham, then and now run by Lister's, there were fifty-five hand-cutters of velvet, a number which four years later had dwindled to one owing to the introduction of the double velvet loom incorporating a mechanical cutting knife in the loom's action. The last cutter, Robert Hustwick, lived to be over ninety and remembered the care taken with the cutting of silk velvet for Queen Victoria. When the velvet left the looms it was stiffened on the back with boiled sago, stretched on a frame, and with special scissors the cutter sliced the row or race with a deft sure motion.

Another job that has gone was that of the *seeak* 'oile man. Briefly seeak was a by-product of scouring. A thick soapy liquid was run off from the scouring machines into tanks, cracked with acid, and the fatty scum run on to ash beds, dug up like thick porridge, and wrapped in sacking parcels about 18 inches square. Pressed steam was blown through the parcels which were squeezed to produce crude oil which was barrelled up for sale, and the cake residue was sold for manure often to hop fields. A dirty job, it blackened and *stalkened* (stiffened) trousers enough for them to stand up on their own. 'Wearing them was like having a treacle tin round your legs.' At Washpits Mill, Holmfirth, Sam Fattycake was in charge of the seeak 'oile, and we have met Mr Tom Godfrey (b. 1879) who was the seeak 'oile man for twenty-six of his fifty years at Crimble Mill, Slaithwaite. He remembers a dog, and others remember a hen and even the seeak 'oile man himself, falling into the tank with fearful results.

The process of dyeing, totally modernized and scientifically conducted, is also remembered as a dirty, wet, smelly job, cold and draughty in winter and hot in summer. The dyepans, now stainless steel, were square wooden boxes with a mushroom in the centre out of which dye was forced and sprayed out, and the dyer stirred the loose wool with a stang, a process called stanging (*see plate* 41). Dyers could be swung off their feet with the weights being lifted. When new stangs were bought they were tested and the heavy ones left to the last. Powdered dye was mixed with hot water in buckets, and after about half an hour of boiling material in the dyepan, a sample was taken. If it was too pale extra dye was added, called *cobbling*, a process if necessary repeated five or six times. Or if too dark the wool might be stripped with a stripping agent. Mr Hilton Sykes, a dyer's labourer for fifty-two years at Slaithwaite Dyeworks, was 'on black for a start and that's shocking stuff. After a week's holiday in August I'd just about got my hands clean.' He wore overalls, a plain navy blue smock and dyers' clogs which had uppers.

Even the wool buyer, that most important member of the staff on whom the prosperity of a mill may depend, has no longer to rely solely on his own judgment by the handle and appearance of the wool to decide the percentage of top, noil, grease and sand. Instead quality control specialists take a sample and report. A well-known verse runs:

> The men who go to the London sales
> And see the fleeces packed in bales . . .
> They make a slight miscalculation,
> Then seek another situation.[1]

In Yorkshire the Bradford Wool Exchange was until the 1960s an important mart for the wool-users of the world.[2]

At Thongsbridge in the Holme valley the firm of Wood and Burtt kept on their books some 800 farmers in the Pennine dales. Their buyer visited markets such as Leyburn and Richmond, and handling 400,000 lb. of wool a year, bought on a handshake. This kind of sales organization ceased with the Second World War.

On the other hand the job of designer, again crucial to the success of a firm, has in essence hardly changed. In well-lit quiet rooms men sit matching bunches of yarn, or show you with pride pattern books, out of which if a few are winners, even one, they will be pleased. Designers at carpet firms, engaged on large-scale stylized paintings, rely on inspiration from stone, lichen, flower heads, a Chinese

[1] Otto Mombert, *Rhymes of the Wool Market* (undated).
[2] Marie Hartley and Joan Ingilby, *The Wonders of Yorkshire*, p. 76.

vase. At Crossley's Mr T. Marchetti once produced a design which proved a best-seller derived from a piece of used blotting paper. At Firth's a popular pattern came from a micro-photo of a bar of steel. Here, none of the forty people under a well-remembered head designer were allowed to leave until he had tapped his desk twice with a pencil. In the 1920s carpets were made for as little as 2s. 11d. a yard, 3s. 4d. laid from the shop.

Nor has the job of wool sorter changed. Formerly some of the best paid of men, they used to go to work in top hats and only worked in daylight so that in mid-winter the hours were from 9 a.m. to 3 p.m. In the upper floors of mills men still work at grease-encrusted boards in front of a north light with a stand for the bales on their left and a series of skeps on their right (*see plate* 30).

In 1920 when he was sixteen Mr W. S. Barnes began an apprenticeship of five years at a Bradford works as a sorter at 12s. 6d. a week. At first he picked up bits of wool from the floor and scraped and swept it twice a day, for it was always said that 'wool was dearer than sugar'. In some places they even had a man scratching slivers off the workers' clothes as they went out of the door. As he progressed he stood by a sorter looking at the skeps and their contents. 'You think you'll never pick it up, but suddenly you've got it.' After a year, perhaps two, the apprentice is promoted to a stand. Each man adjusts to the correct height by raising himself up on extra boards. A visitor once remarked, 'What a fine set of men you've got!' The boss shouted, 'Hey lads', and when they jumped down, they were all different heights.

The sorter might deal with Australian cross-bred and Merino or English wool, but if the type were changed he singed the skeps with a roll of lighted paper. To sort he uses both touch and eyesight. Low quality is harsh and vice versa. 'Your eyes are looking for the serrations in the fibre. Light is shining on the wool, and a shadow is cast between the serrations. The finer qualities have them very near together so they are all shadow and look dull. You tear the wool off.'

When a skep is full of one quality, the sorter takes it to a square trap in the floor where the taker-off checks that it is in order. Occasionally he might bear a grudge and return it for no reason, or even in the past be open to bribery such as a bottle of beer in the skep. The wool is then tipped down into the packing floor below, put into wool sheets slung up from the roof, then skewered by using a *jerry*, a double pronged lever and in former days a *soldier*, a V-shaped tool of which one end stuck in the floor and the V supported the pack. Then it was sent, in this case, to the combers.

Lastly, two important posts in a mill—the overlookers and the managers. Much depended on the former. (It was they in the early days who had the power to ill-treat children and who wielded the alleydasher.) In charge of sections of machinery, they were important enough to be listed under their occupation in directories. Fifty years ago they ran outings and arranged cricket matches. In weaving departments they are called overlookers in Bradford, tuners in the Huddersfield and heavy woollen districts and tacklers in the region bordering on Lancashire. Tuners at Morley wore navy blue smocks, and at Heptonstall tacklers some eighty years ago white cord trousers and white cord vests, which were laid on the floor to be scrubbed clean. 'They don't know what work is today.' At Hebden Bridge Cheethams made tacklers' trousers of bluette and blue drill, also sleeved vests, with fronts of bluette and sleeves of black twilled cotton; individual tacklers sometimes requested up to a dozen pockets for their spanners.

A man in charge of women could and did give easy work to favourites, or be so popular that if he moved to another mill the women followed him. A Catholic overlooker might have all Catholics under him. Good tuners with vile tempers had to be tolerated, 'If he tunes thy loom, thou'll have nowt to do wi' his temper'. Or they conducted Christmas sings in the dinner hour.

At Gomersal Mills Mr Hartley Brook starting as an overlooker under his father, the mill manager, was told, 'Now think on your job's to see that the machinery is cleaned, greased, and that the premises you occupy are in perfect condition—no bread left about, no rats, no mice. We want none o' that. If you can't get them as works for you to do it, I shall force you to do it.'

Mr J. H. Gill of Haworth (b. 1894), who started as a half-timer at a spinning mill at the age of twelve, served a five-year apprenticeship, being paid 5s. or 6s. a week, at Hattersleys, the loom-makers at Keighley, and then worked for fifty years for a large part of the time as a weaving overlooker at Merralls, Ebor Mills, Haworth. When he began there, all were narrow looms, 55 to 60 inches wide, and a warp with four cuts (to make four pieces) was an advance. In his lifetime looms were increased in size, and warps instead of having to be changed every week or ten days were lengthened to eight or ten cuts lasting a month; and improvements such as the dobby, which controlled the movement of the heald shafts, and four boxes for shuttles at each end of the loom allowed for the weaving of different colours in the weft. Thus fancy patterns, such as tartans, could be woven as well as plain whites for piece-dyeing. He looked after twenty to twenty-four plain looms and made sure for example that cloths were of the right weight by changing the number of picks to the inch by fitting a different wheel with more, or less, teeth. Here the overlooker wore corduroy trousers and a short white smock (clean on every week), with a pocket for a red handkerchief, whilst the weaving manager in charge of the loom shed wore a longer smock.

Mr and Mrs R. J. Atwell, both born in 1892, both worked at Manningham Mills, she as a velvet weaver, he as a foreman overlooker. As Mrs Atwell said, 'It was there that I met mi fate'. In 1914 after apprenticeship he became an overlooker with a share of twenty-one looms earning 30s. to 32s. a week, and after the war took charge of a shed with 150 weavers, men and women, and thirteen other overlookers and velvet cutters. He was responsible for allotting the work, deciding which quality should go into which loom, and interviewing prospective staff. If her mother had been good, it was likely that a daughter would take after her. Women with fine delicate hands were chosen. Sweaty hands damaged light coloured velvets, and a little bag of French chalk in which to dip the fingers used to be kept at the side of the loom. He decided bonus payments (4s. a month for good work), or was told of a 'trap', a serious mistake, so that all the ends had to be taken up and even a hole might be made in the piece. To remedy this disaster other weavers often rallied round. The fine for bad work was 2d. Everything had to be perfect. '"Go fetch Bob" they would say. I knew every name. It was one happy family.'

Lastly the mill manager. It is remembered at one mill that a Scotsman who overworked the weavers had been appointed manager. One day the owner returned from lunch to find the yard full of five or six hundred of them, all threatening to throw the man in the dam. Knowing that he could not swim, there was no option but to sack him. At Gomersal Mills Mr Hartley Brook told us that he wanted to be a farmer, but his father argued him out of it, and he eventually took over as manager. 'I was brought up to make sure that when you go home, you've earned your day's wage. I've loved working at Burnley's; it's been a pleasure. I've been seeing improvements for the benefit of the workpeople, not for the boss all the time. Nobody knows what hard work's been put into this mill.'

The last sentiment echoes down the years. Changes have been immense, in hours and conditions of work, in wages, and in the machinery, so that less skill is required resulting some would say in less interest. On the other hand there is more professionalism and less loyalty. What has struck us in those to whom we have talked is pride—pride in the mill they worked in, pride in the family who owned it, pride in their own work, and pride in themselves and the way they won through.

5 Textile Machinery

THE great diversity of large and small family businesses in textile manufacture is echoed in the making of textile machinery. In the last century the many machine-makers catered for the needs of their particular districts, and were aided by the supply of iron from Low Moor and other iron works, by castings from local forges such as the old established Kirkstall Forge, and by a host of individual craftsmen who made special parts. Some were originally blacksmiths, some clock-makers, and some were linked with Lancashire, the birthplace of invention. All were engaged in improving and perfecting already established principles of construction often behind locked doors.

At the series of great exhibitions started in 1851 (for instance the London Exhibition of 1862 and that at Roubaix in France in 1911), firms won prizes bringing their inventions to the fore. Up to the Second World War machines and parts, and the men to set them up, were sent all over the world, in particular to India and Russia, but since then competition from Europe has made inroads into the former monopoly of a pioneering nation.

As we have seen early motive power was supplied by water-wheels, but of the very few *in situ* in textile mills in our area, for example that at Lumb Mill, Wain-stalls, near Halifax, none are in working order.[1] There were formerly great wheels at Rishworth Mill in the Ryburn valley ($57\frac{1}{2}$ feet in diameter and 12 feet broad), at Diggle New Mill, Saddleworth (64 feet 8 inches in diameter and 7 feet wide), and at Mytholm Mill, upper Calderdale (52 feet in diameter and 9 feet 6 inches wide). Sixty years ago the latter used to be heard 'dreaming' as with water trickling in from the buckets it was just turning over. It has been passed down that young people working in the mills rejoiced when after heavy rain water backed up the tail goit so that the wheel was stopped and work ceased.

Horse gins, another form of early motive power, worked rotary carding machines and slubbing billies, especially from 1780 to 1790 round Rawdon and

[1] G. Binns, 'Water Wheels in the Upper Calder Valley', *Halifax Antiquarian Society*, 1972; W. Pickles, 'Water Mills around Leeds', the *Dalesman*, vol. 24, 1962, pp. 435–40.

Yeadon.[1] Water-wheels continued in use after the invention of steam engines, for although unreliable, money had been put into them and they cost less to run. Many early steam engines were utilized to throw the water back on to the wheel. However, coal already used for heating dyepans and in the finishing processes was at hand, sometimes so near that it could be barrowed from day-hole to mill boiler. The age of the steam engine began.

Early engines with a crank motion were installed at the Crank Mill, Morley in 1790, Low Bridge, Damsdale and Hope Mills, Keighley,[2] the first St Peg Mill, Cleckheaton, built about 1803, and no doubt at others (*see drawing on page* 34). The engine at the Crank, replaced in 1872, antedated by three years that at Bean Ing, Leeds, a 30 to 40 h.p. Boulton and Watt rotative engine. By 1850 the changeover from water to steam power was almost complete.[3]

In 1822, besides sixteen machine-makers, there were three firms making steam engines in Leeds, of whom Fenton, Murray and Co. were the early locomotive engineers.[4] The ironworks at Low Moor, Bowling and Shelf, all made engines, and other makers started up elsewhere. At Sowerby Bridge Timothy Bates, founded in 1786, was followed by Pollitt and Wigzell, responsible for many engines in Calderdale. Mr Pollitt is remembered visiting mills every three or four years, and if his engine was well kept giving the engine tenter £1. This firm was taken over about 1933 by Cole, Marchent and Morley, founded in 1848 and still flourishing at Bradford, who made their last engine about 1926, and are the last of the long line of steam engine makers in the West Riding.

At Ready Carr, Marsden, a foundry developed from the blacksmith's shop of Enoch and James Taylor, the two brothers famous as makers of the cropping frames attacked by the Luddites, and this continued first as Taylor and Hirst, and then as Robert Taylor and Sons (Robert, 1787–1868, was their nephew) making steam engines and Lancashire boilers.[5] About 300 men and boys were employed. Mr Joe France's father worked there marking out end plates, fire boxes, water gauges and so on, and he travelled all over England, to Scotland and even France seating boilers. These monster cylinders, 30 feet long by 8 or 9 feet in diameter, were taken up the steep road to Marsden station pulled with ropes by every available man, and by twenty or thirty horses hired from local farmers. Steam traction engines next came into use for transporting and manœuvring them into

[1] P. Slater, *The Ancient Parish of Guiseley*, 1880.
[2] I. Dewhirst, *A History of Keighley*, 1974.
[3] W. B. Crump and G. Ghorbal, *History of the Huddersfield Woollen Industry*, p. 74–80.
[4] E. Baines, *History, Directory and Gazetteer of the County of York*, 1822, vol. 1, *West Riding*, p. 125.
[5] L. B. Whitehead, *Bygone Marsden*, 1942.

position in the boiler houses in mill yards—a task fraught with danger and difficulty.

As the need for more power arose, old engines were scrapped and often two or more put in to drive different parts of the mill. The engine man or tenter, keeping his charge clean and polished 'like furniture', was the king pin of the mill, and his boiler firer, who often lived in the mill yard to be at hand for stoking in the early morning, was trained to take over if the engine man was ill. Steam power from the boilers heated the premises and kept the tenter house going. Mills in the West Riding worked on Good Fridays because of the economics of maintaining the boiler fires. Every room was connected to the engine either by noisy gear wheels and shafts or by ropes and pulleys and had a danger bell which rang in the engine house. Boiler explosions, owing to faulty construction or the incompetence or even drunkenness of the engine tenter, caused deaths and were frequent enough to concern eminent engineers. On 9 June 1869 an explosion at a bobbin turners at Bingley killed thirteen people. On the other hand at Bowers Mill, in the Blackburn valley, Ben Jackson slowed down his engine to indicate mealtimes; at Gomersal Mills the engine is said to have worked the mill clock, and at Elmfield Mill, Bramley, when the engine started a fountain began to play in the owner's grounds.

Mr Arnold Townsend (b. 1883) graduated from plumber's and fitter's apprentice to millwright, to assistant engineer, and at twenty-four to engineer in charge of the five engines at Dean Clough Mills, Halifax. One was a 1,200 h.p. horizontal compound made by Pollitt and Wigzell, and another provided power for the grinding of flour to make paste to mix with colours for putting patterns on carpets. The twenty-seven boilers reduced over the years to eight consumed between 70 to 90 tons of coal a day. Arnold Townsend recollects as an apprentice crawling up narrow pipes to seal joints and inside a boiler to help lift out the bars, and working a whole week with little sleep to repair two faulty engines. Stoking was then all by hand (hopper feeds came in some sixty years ago), and the firer shovelling coal and raking off the ashes and clinkers with a huge rake streamed with perspiration.

Engines were replaced by gas engines, steam turbines, and eventually by individual electric motors on each machine, a process accelerated from the early 1930s to the 1950s. W. and E. Crowther, Crimble Mill, Slaithwaite, installed a Brush-Ljungström turbine in 1917 to replace two steam engines and were one of the first to go all-electric. A few engines, however, remain *in situ*, some silent, some working with their hovering tenter wearing a cap and holding an oily rag in the lofty precincts of the engine house.[1] One, which makes electricity at Dearnside

[1] According to a list prepared by the Industrial Section of the Bradford Archaeology Group there were eighteen engines in working order in mills in the West Riding in 1972.

Mills, Denby Dale, was built from parts by W. H. Kenyon, the present owner's grandfather, and James Lumb, engineer of Elland, in 1900. This vertical cross compound engine and its flywheel, a magnificent sight, feeds itself with oil, and seldom breaks down except when Mr Eric Kenyon goes away 'so that he takes care never to tell it'.

All engines were christened at ceremonies appropriate to the living creatures which they appeared to be, usually with the name or names of the owner's wife. 'John and Mary' at the Haggases at Oakworth included those of both husband and wife, whilst for obvious reasons some were called 'Gladstone' as at Black Rock Mills, Linthwaite, or 'Thomas Hughes' and 'Unity' as at Nutclough Mills.

The numerous extant early inventories of machinery are not matched by existing examples of the machinery itself.[1] One of these, the carding engine or card as it was formerly called, has developed in the woollen industry from a pair of small hand cards, used for teasing wool ready for spinning, to the largest machine in the mill, up to 75 feet long and with as many as eighty rotating rollers, a marvel of invention and engineering. The principle and use are still the same, that is wire teeth inserted in a foundation, once leather, now wire teeth on sheets or fillets on different bases, clothing the rollers. (Machines for carding cotton are small.) The construction of a carding machine requires three main contributors: the engineers who make the machines; the card-makers, now card clothing firms; and the card nailers, now the card mounters, who affix and renew the clothing on the rollers.

An old established firm still in the same family, John Haigh and Sons, Priestroyd Ironworks, Huddersfield, now amalgamated with Chadwicks of Cleckheaton, has since it was founded in 1835 supplied the mills in the West Riding and those in industrial towns all over the world with woollen and worsted carding machines, once costing a few hundred, now tens of thousands of pounds. Skilled craftsmen, serving apprenticeships, make the cylinders, formerly of well-seasoned mahogany, still occasionally used, then iron, now steel and aluminium. On these the card clothing is fixed not in the workshop lest it be damaged, but after installation of the machine in the mill (see plates 57–8).

Card-makers, plying their ancient and essential trade, were concentrated round Halifax, Huddersfield, Brighouse and Heckmondwike, where there were 116 in 1822. As an example, John Sykes, apprenticed to a card-maker at Elland, started a business in 1809 at Dearn House, Lindley, near Huddersfield, tanning leather, probably drawing wire, and using two machines, one called the Bendigo to cut and

---

[1] Early machines may be seen in Yorkshire at Cliffe Castle, Keighley, Bankfield Museum, Halifax, Tolson Memorial Museum, Huddersfield, Saddleworth Museum, Uppermill, Bradford Industrial Museum, Moorside Mills, Bradford, and Museum of Industry and Science, Armley Mills, Leeds.

bend the teeth and another to prick holes in the leather. Then in the card-maker's workshop or in 'setting schools', or often sitting on the doorsteps of their cottages, women and children were engaged in inserting teeth into leather straps, repeating nominies to count by and to encourage each other 'one o' me rody, two o' me rody' or naming people round the village. The tedious ill-paid work, comparable with the hand-knitting industry in organization and monotony, ceased altogether about 1870 as new machines were invented.[1]

In 1833 Charlotte Sykes, the widow of John and mother of six sons and five daughters, built Acre Mills, Lindley, and with her sons continued the business which, passed on from generation to generation, and expanding significantly from 1889 to 1912, became the largest manufacturer of card clothing for cotton in the world (see plate 18). In 1897 the firm joined three other old established companies (all be it noted in proximity to the source of iron at Low Moor), Samuel Law of Cleckheaton, John Whiteley and Sons of Halifax, and Wilson and Ingham of Mirfield, to form the now international English Card Clothing Company. These and other firms, such as James Holdsworth at Mirfield, employ skilled card-setters who each attend to a set of eleven or twelve machines making card clothing (see plates 60–2).

For his part the card nailer provided the tacks only and nailed on the leather based clothing. Metal cylinders had little wooden pegs let in for the nails, and card clothing, once made in fillets, and sheets 72, 66, 60 inches long by 6½ inches wide, is now mostly in fillets. Usually self-employed, the nailer ordered tacks by the half ton, once walked miles carrying heavy tools on his back, and charged so much a sheet or so much a cylinder.

Mr Lupton Bamforth of Marsden, a third generation of card nailers and thus employed for over fifty years, recollects: 'When you nailed a cylinder fifty inches in diameter with thirty sheets, with 240 tacks in a sheet, you get round to 7,000 tacks, 6 lb. in a cylinder, and all put in at once by hand half an inch to three quarters of an inch apart. You'd stretch the sheets with card pliers and with your foot operate a treadle to get your tension.' Now all is different. The card mounter wraps the clothing in fillets, 1½ to 2 inches wide, now often on a cotton, linen or cushion-rubber foundation instead of leather, round the cylinder in one length guided by a tension machine operated by another man.

To equip a mill the manufacturer had no need to go far afield. Take for instance Underbank Mill, which installed the machinery about 1920, in the Holme valley; the

[1] S. J. S. Walker, The History of Joseph Sykes Brothers, 1939; H. Ling Roth, 'Hand Card Making', Bankfield Museum Notes, No. XI; Malcolm Speirs, A History of the Card Setting Machine Tenters' Society, 1972.

spinning mules came from William Whiteley and Sons of Lockwood in the Colne valley, the scouring machines from France and Lodge of Honley, the looms from Hutchinson and Hollingworth, Dobcross Loom Works, Saddleworth, and the finishing plant from Sellers and Co., Folly Hall, Huddersfield, all not more than from four to ten miles away.

Keighley, perhaps from its proximity to Lancashire, early established itself as a centre for textile engineering.[1] Small family firms began as makers of parts—rollers, flyers and spindles—for early spinning frames called throstles. William Smith, who started in this way as early as 1795 in two cottages, founded a family firm which developed into Prince-Smith & Son, later Prince-Smith and Stells as others were taken over. In 1912 they employed 12,000 men and produced machinery for all the processes of worsted manufacture, exporting to many countries. In 1960 they were said to be the largest works in the world solely engaged in the production of wool combing and worsted spinning plant. The firm was itself taken over by the great Lancashire firm of Platt International in 1970.

George Hattersley and Sons of Keighley, together with Dobcross, Northrop, Platt and others such as George Hodgson of Frizinghall, Bradford, Lee and Crabtree and David Sowden of Shipley, and Briggs of Gomersal, supplied the West Riding and the world with looms. Dobcross looms, made by Hutchinson and Hollingworth at Diggle, Saddleworth, from 1861 to 1970, rivalled Hattersleys, and Hodgsons won many gold medals at international exhibitions. Also a few large manufacturers—Listers, Fosters, Crossleys, Firths and Merralls of Haworth —formerly had their own engineering shops in which looms were made. For years Joseph Reixach, a Spaniard and the son of the inventor of the velvet loom, the patent for which had been bought by Cunliffe Lister, worked for Listers. About 1918 the firm employed some eighty mechanics making annually thirty to forty single and double shuttle looms in a secret department which was closed down in the late 1950s.

Richard Hattersley (1761–1829) had come from Eccleshall, near Sheffield, in 1789 to Keighley where he started as a whitesmith, and it was his son, George (1789–1869) who in 1834 began to make looms for the worsted trade. In 1856 the firm invented the first revolving box loom which allowed colour to be used in the weft and which supplanted many of those made locally. Further patents followed, for instance the dobby in 1867, and looms were ordered by the hundred. Fitters and tuners lived and settled abroad, especially in Germany. In the early part of this century one man spent years in France starting tapestry looms for the weaving of tapestries for the walls of French châteaux (*see plate* 36).

[1] John Hodgson, *Textile Manufacture, and other Industries, in Keighley*, 1879.

After the First World War new methods allowed for much finer construction, and a new Standard model loom was introduced and exported to France, and also to Italy, Japan, China, Australia and South Africa. For delivery near at hand or in Lancashire the firm once kept thirty-two horses and sent looms ready erected. It was said in loom-making that two good years were followed by five bad. Looms sold very cheaply—in 1905 at £7 10s., a price which rose to £75 in 1914, six years later to £310, in the slump of the early 1920s £150, and in 1951 £450. Hattersley's invented a domestic foot-pedal type loom first developed for the Balkans, and later sent these and still do to the islands of Lewis, Harris and Skye for the manufacture of hand-woven Harris tweed. They took over Hodgson, Sowden, and Hutchinson and Hollingworth in amalgamations only too frequent amongst the makers of textile machines.[1]

There are in fact only three loom-makers of the fifteen existing in about 1911 left in the West Riding: Hattersleys, David Crabtree & Son, Laisterdyke, Bradford, and Wilson and Longbottom at Barnsley, the two last making carpet looms required to supply carpets to an affluent society. Crabtrees, founded in 1853, then Lee and Crabtree, provided plain looms for the mills in the Heavy Woollen District for 100 years. In 1926 they perfected and made their first Gripper Axminster loom of which they are the sole makers (see plate 39). This huge machine, of which some twenty-six are made in a year, takes four months to construct, cost in 1975 approximately £80,000, and is supplied all over the world.[2]

The many parts needed for a loom—Jacquards, sleys, reeds, healds, temples, shuttles, bobbins and pickers, of which the last three are slowly disappearing —illustrate the number and diversity of ancillary firms and craftsmen needed. Consider the Jacquard, a French invention for making figured materials, and a fascinating mechanism whereby a design is converted into perforations on cards, which by means of a harness working the healds produces the design (see plate 39). At the present day three firms, one in Manchester, and J. T. Hardaker and Samuel Dracup in Bradford, make them, of which Hardakers work in close association with Crabtrees.

Dracups was founded in 1825 by Samuel, son of Nathaniel Dracup, a shuttle-maker of Great Horton, Bradford, and is still in the same family. Formerly Jacquards were all wood (birch), but they are now mostly metal and steel. The harness is varnished linen thread or Terylene and the cards thick cardboard or plastic. Craftsmen still straighten the needles (which connect the threads with the

---

[1] Information from Colonel F. L. Smith, Mr R. L. Smith of Hattersleys and Mr T. E. Horsfall, retired Technical Manager.

[2] Information from Mr G. E. Phelon, Managing Director, David Crabtree & Son.

healds) by hand as has been the practice for 150 years. Jacquards, of which some forty types are made, may be used for designs in the finest silk, for carpets, or, one of the smallest, for weaving the name of a firm or its trademark down the selvedges of the cloth. They cost from £350 to £10,000. At Dracups we were shown a portrait of Queen Elizabeth II, a Coronation tapestry, and other remarkably fine work woven on Jacquard looms.

As for the shuttle-makers, there were thirty-four in 1849 in the West Riding, a few combined with bobbin turning and picker-making. Now there are three or four and a few in Lancashire. Shuttles ranged in size from 22 inches for blanket looms to 12 inches for silk. In the past they were made of boxwood or perhaps apple, and an apprentice knocked in the metal bushes on the ends, shaped with clogger's knives, and sand-papered the inside. There were shuttle boddiers and shuttle finishers; and a man might make a shuttle throughout, whereas now he tends one lathe and one machine fashioning one stage in the manufacture.

At Oakworth, near Keighley, shuttles have been made since the beginning of the last century in the usual three-storied building with the former living quarters on the ground floor. Built by Thomas Burwin, whose name is inscribed over a door, it formerly had a water-wheel and a beam engine, and is now run by a distant connection of the Burwins, Mr C. Fearnside. Shuttles, usually sold in pairs, one for weaving and one to be filled ready for use, are made to order. Just before the First World War they sold at 6d. or 1s. and now, made of persimmon or cornel wood imported from America, or plastics, or manufactured woods, they each sell for several pounds.

Similarly bobbin-makers, once scattered about the country especially in the Lake District, and often utilizing the water-wheels of old corn mills for power, have contracted in numbers from thousands employed in the trade to a few hundreds. Like shuttle-making bobbin-making reached a peak of demand about 1870 and flourished until the end of the Second World War. A cluster of buildings at Cote Hill, Halifax—a works, a small dam, a mill house, a chimney, and once cottages for workers, now demolished—developed from the bobbin-making begun there in 1798. Mary Bancroft, the maker in 1829, sold slubbing bobbins, mill nuts, and bobbin *broaches* (spindles). The steam engine has gone, but with complicated machines made by Fell's, the wood-working machinery firm of Kendal, and actuated by hydraulic and pneumatic power, Roberts and Hirst make large ring spinning bobbins of which the flange is sycamore and the barrel Danish beech (*see plate* 64).

So, too, sleys, reeds, healds, temples and pickers for looms require specialist knowledge for their construction. The making of pickers, the buffer which projects the shuttle every time it crosses the warp, centred round Todmorden on the Yorkshire-Lancashire border, where there were ten or twelve small firms engaged in this work. Originally they were made of wood, then leather, now water buffalo hide, and more recently plastics. All sizes and varieties for different looms are made by the British Picker Co., an amalgamation of several firms, at Todmorden (*see plate* 63).

At Leeds three firms, pioneers in the field of textile machinery, require mention: Taylor Wordsworth, amalgamated with Prince-Smith of Keighley, were the first makers of the Noble comb. Fairbairn, Lawson, Combe and Barbour made and exported the whole range of machinery for processing flax, jute and similar fibres, machine tools and other products, and now as Fairbairn Lawson exports many engineering products.

The third, Hardings, is one of the few firms of any size in the world making pins for all types of combing machines, teeth for carding and rag grinding machines and castings for Noble combs (*see plate* 29). Thomas Harding, who was born in Cambridgeshire, the son of a wool merchant, learnt the craft of making combing pins for the flax trade in Lille in France, and in 1859 founded a firm in Leeds, then the centre of that trade. Five years later he built the present works in Globe Road, with a chimney, based in design on the Lamberti Tower at Verona in northern Italy, to make a flue for the steam engine and to create a draught for an extraction plant essential to carry away the fine steel dust caused by the grinding of the steel pins. When three firms joined together and the works were enlarged in 1899 the Giotto Tower, based on the design of the famous one in Florence, took over the function of the Verona Tower. The dust, conveyed away in a complex system of underground flues, is sold to make fireworks.

Lastly, the machines used in the finishing processes, the tentering, cropping (now called cutting) machines, the latter known locally as Jerries, and the teazle raising gig, of which the last two were the cause of the Luddite Riots. The first two, although crude machines, were developed early, and they were made by William Whiteley and Sons of Lockwood, already mentioned, an important firm which no longer exists. The teazle gig consists of a revolving drum or cylinder covered with rods or spindles filled with teazle heads whose tough hooked bracts raise the nap of cloth, and is also made in the Colne valley at the present day by James Bailey, textile engineers of Slaithwaite.

Up to about 1915 teazles (*Dipsacus fullonum*) were grown in Yorkshire round Selby and Sherburn-in-Elmet where the heavy rich soil suited their cultivation, also formerly in Kent, Wiltshire, Essex and Gloucestershire. Once they were exported from Yorkshire, but instead they are imported from France and Spain to augment the small quantity still grown east of Taunton in Somerset, the only teazle growing district left in England.[1]

Taking seventeen months to grow, harvested by hand, and carefully dried on poles and in shelters (*see plates* 43–4), they then keep indefinitely. In the winter they were formerly sorted and arranged in bunches of twenty-five, called *fans* in Somerset, and bunches of ten, called *glens* (gleanings) in Yorkshire. Thirty glens were then put on a *stav* (a hazel stick 3 feet to 4 feet long, split half-way down) and sealed at the top with a willow ring (*see plate* 45). 'In the barn the stavs in rosettes looked like waxworks.' The Somerset stavs (once shipped from Bristol) were reared upright in railway box vans for despatch to Yorkshire. A grower might have had ninety packs, 1,800,000 teazles for sale. In Yorkshire 13,500 counted as a pack. Formerly dealers were both growers and merchants, such as James Bortoft of South Milford who had warehouses in Leeds. Now two remain—Edmund Taylor of Huddersfield and Sloman and Smith of Leeds who, sending pack sheets for teazles, buy in and grade them for sale. In the 1920s the price slumped to £4 a pack, rose to £18 after the Second World War, and is now nearer to £50.

In the past most mills had teazle gigs, whereas today they are only used for some knitwear, some blankets, and for cloths with a drawn finish such as quality worsted, velours and mohair, cashmere, camelhair and billiard cloths. Few firms employ a full-time teazle man, and most engage a journeyman for half a day a week or for longer as required. Skill and experience judge the strength of the teazles to be used and how long to leave the cloth, which is damped, in the gig, perhaps half an hour to two days. To keep their effect even, four or five rods out of the twenty-four on a drum are changed at one time, and the rods are also turned over (*see plates* 46–7). 350,000 teazles may be employed in one gig in a year. Wire machines have been invented, but nothing man-made quite replaces the teazles which reach to the base of the cloth and part the fibres.

Baines wrote in 1858: 'The increased speed with which everything connected

Arthur Young found 'tassels' grown as a profitable crop at Stillingfleet, near Selby, in 1771, and *White's Directory*, 1837, states that many teazle growers from Somersetshire and various parts of Yorkshire attended several inns in Leeds. See also 'A Yorkshire Plant: The Teazle', *Leeds Mercury Supplement Notes and Queries*, 1889–90; J. Billingsley, *General View of the agriculture of the County of Somerset*, 1797, pp. 110–12; *Journal of the Bath and West and Southern Counties Society*, 6th series, vol. XII, 1937–9, pp. 34–40. Also information from Mr C. George of Edmund Taylor, Huddersfield, Mr D. J. Maddick and Mr F. Brunt of Somerset, 1973. Also Mr R. A. McMillan at the Tolson Memorial Museum, Huddersfield, has kindly shown us details of teazle growing in Yorkshire given to him in the same year by Mr William Bradley of South Milford, then aged ninety.

with the [textile] trade is transacted is startling to men who remember the old times and ways.' How much more startled they would have been today by the sophisticated machines resulting from scientific research, precision engineering, and the invention of man-made fibres, all going faster and faster, taking larger packages, and lessening both the numbers of operations and labour force.

The small Bendigo machine formerly used for making teeth for card clothing.

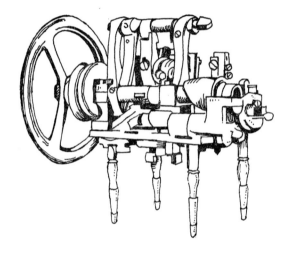

6 Paved with Gold

THE abundant natural resources of the West Riding are nowhere more in evidence than in the mineral wealth of sandstone and coal found above the millstone grit. During the last century excellent stone was at hand everywhere for the great surge of the building of houses, mills, warehouses, town halls, offices, art galleries, for pavements and for roads, not only in the West Riding but in London and elsewhere. Masterpieces in stone such as the centre of the city of Bradford (now largely rebuilt) rose on every hand.

Quarrying was formerly undertaken by farmers getting stone on their own fields, then by small men leasing a thousand or more square yards from the owners of the freehold for shallow *delphs* (quarries). Later some of these employed delvers and became stone merchants. *Huggers*, men wearing leather saddles on their backs, carrying huge slabs up ladders with broad rungs and liable to accidents, were replaced by gins and hand-cranes, which in turn were superseded by steam cranes and in the 1920s by electricity. Picks and wedges to cut stone then gave way to the plug and feather method using pneumatic drills.

In the second half of the last century new quarry owners—Armitages, Aspinalls, Briggs, Brookes, Farrars, Freemans, Marshalls, Vints and others—turned the industry into big business. Huge deep quarries were excavated, derricks pierced many skylines, and thousands of men were employed as barers, delvers, hewers, fettlers and banker masons. Although since about 1914 the numbers of quarries, many filled in, have greatly diminished, one-man quarries run in the old style remain at Spring Hall, Greetland, and Blake Hill End, in the Shibden valley (*see plate* 69), and a number of large concerns flourish.

In general two types of stone were hewn, ashlar, a sandstone with no visible grain, won in beds up to 10 feet thick, used for buildings, and the famous Elland Edge Flagrock, a stone that splits, usually called freestone, which runs along the hilltops from Huddersfield to Leeds, used for wall stones, paving, kerbstones, landings (large slabs), setts for roads, platform coping and roofing slates. Hard

York stone became and is famous especially when used for fine smooth-faced flagstones, that is paving stones.

Stone from Bramley Fall and other quarries was used for building Leeds Town Hall, that from Crosland Hill above the Colne valley for the buildings in Huddersfield, fine quality ashlar from Ringby Quarry for Halifax Town Hall, and from Bolton Woods, Bradford, stone was supplied for Manningham Mills. Colour was important and had to be matched. 'They knew a great deal about stone in London.' Stone was despatched by rail, by canal and by boat to London, America, Germany, Australia and many other countries.

At the beginning of this century on the hilltops of the Ribbleden valley near Holmfirth, a district pitted with small abandoned quarries, the Gee family lived at the Rising Sun public house combining quarrying with inn-keeping in the traditional manner. Mr Joe Gee, who was born in 1909, remembers helping in one way and another as a child, milking the cows before going to school, and that his father and grandfather before him had Longley Edge Quarry on Scholes Moor as well as Hillhouse Edge on Cartworth Moor which he and his brother worked until their retirement in 1967. From the soft rough grit at Longley Edge ridge stones for roofs and troughs for watering horses on roadsides were hewn. The troughs were hollowed out with a pick and the sides scrappled smooth and square from great blocks of stone, the largest 8 feet long, 3 feet 6 inches wide and 2 feet 9 inches deep. Similarly at other quarries huge dyepans and brewing vats were formerly hacked out by hand.

Hillhouse Edge was 'as nice a quarry as you could wish to have' and the stone 'good to work'. They employed about sixteen men including banker hands, and were equipped with steam cranes, a blacksmith's shop, two saws, a polishing machine and two horses and waggons. Men were strong in those days. A man could carry a stone slab weighing 7 cwt on his back in the old style. In the 1920s stone was delivered in the district at 2s. 6d. a super yard, whereas in 1975 it may well cost £7 or £8. At Longley Edge trade diminished about 1910, but at Hillhouse Edge it continues vigorously.

Landings, 4 to 6 inches thick, were large stone slabs used for steps, the ceilings of cellars, for pavements (when a square or a round hole might be cut in them down which coal was shot) and were despatched to London packed in straw in railway trucks. They were in constant demand for the base of memorials on graves in Christian, Jewish and municipal cemeteries. Up to about 1939 William Knight and Co., masonry contractors and stone merchants of London, used to have a standing order to deliver sixteen landings every Monday morning to the Islington and St Pancras cemeteries at Finchley. Those only 6 feet 6 inches by 2 feet 6 inches

NUTCLOUGH MILL, HEBDEN BRIDGE
24. *Sewing Room with machinists (c. 1890).*

25. *Hand-finishers and Machine Room (c. 1890).*

26. *The Cutting Room (c. 1890).*

27. *Portable Exhibition Stand. Mr Sam Moore, traveller (c. 1910).*

28. *Cutting fustian. The cloth was stretched on a frame and the cutter sliced down the race with a rapier-like knife. This is now performed by a machine (date unknown).*

WOOL AND WOOL COMBING

29. *The comb setting department at Hardings, Tower Works, Leeds. There are 50,000 pins in the large rings for Noble combs. Here the operatives are setting the pins, a highly skilled job, by placing a small steel tube over the pin and straightening if necessary. It takes three weeks to complete one ring (1950).*

30. *Wool-sorters at Manningham Mills, Bradford. They wear full-length blue and white checker brats fastened with a back button and a tape half way down, and formerly leggings, like over-trousers, also of checked cotton to button on to the trousers (early 1950s).*

31. *A Lister comb used for long hair wool, in this case mohair, at Black Dyke Mills, Queensbury.*

32. *Noble combs combing tops at Thomas Burnleys, Gomersal Mills (1950s).*

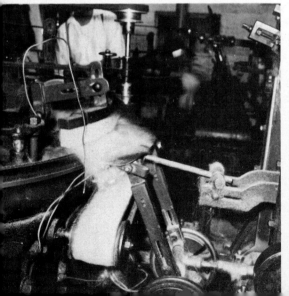

SPINNERS

33. A doffer (the boy) and a piecener (the girl) at a flyer spinning frame for worsted yarn at William Fisons, Greenholme Mills, Burley-in-Wharfedale. The piecener has stopped the flyer with her left thumb and is about to piecen with her right hand (c. 1907).

34. Cotton spinners at Lock Hill Mills, Sowerby Bridge, in the Stop Motion or Cheese Winding Room, which is decorated for the Coronation of King George VI (1937).

35. Self-acting mules for spinning woollen yarn at Gillroyd Mills, Morley. The machines move backwards and forwards on the rails drawing out and twisting the condensed slivers (from the carding machines), seen on the spools on the right, on to the bobbins in front of the women (1930s).

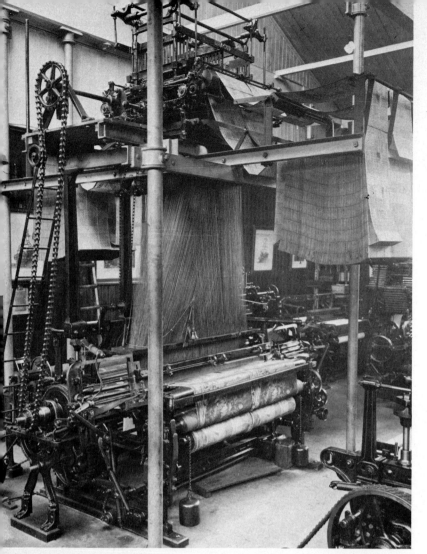

LOOMS

36. Tapestry loom built in *1908* by George Hattersley and Sons, Keighley. It was shown in operation at the Franco-British Exhibition in Paris in that year, and was awarded the Grand Prix. The tapestry being woven is of 'Bolton Abbey in the Olden Time' by Landseer owned by the Duke of Devonshire. For the production of this panel two Jacquard machines, made by S. Dracup and Co., Bradford, were used.

37. Weaving silk at Manningham Mills, Bradford (*1918*).

PATTERN AND CARPET LOOMS

38. The many pattern looms at Taylor and Littlewoods, Newsome Mills, near Huddersfield, makers of fine worsted. Only two are in use now. The dressing frame in the foreground was for dressing the warp with size (1892).

39. Mr Reggie Bird weaving carpet on a 27-inch Gripper Axminster loom made by David Crabtree and Son, Bradford, at Firth Carpets, Clifton Mills, Brighouse. The Jacquard cards above control the design and the yarns of the pile may be seen coming from the numerous bobbins on the creel (1948).

FULLING, DYEING AND TENTERING

40. *Fulling stocks installed at Armitage Bridge Mills on the river Holme, near Huddersfield, in 1813. The two sets of wooden stamps were lifted a certain distance, and when they fell they milled the cloth which was in a rounded trough below the sloping iron supports (1936).*

41. *Mr W. T. Birks at Slaithwaite Dyeworks. He is stirring loose wool in the dye-pan with a stang. Note the mushroom in the centre out of which the dye was forced and sprayed (1940s).*

42. *Blankets drying on tenters in the tenter fields at Wormalds and Walker, Dewsbury Mills, Thornhill. Tenters continued in use for blankets much later than for cloth, and these held five miles of blankets. The men on the right show the height (1920s).*

TEAZLES

43. (Above) Teazles growing in Somerset for use in Yorkshire mills. Mrs D. J. Maddick harvesting teazles at Fivehead, near Taunton.

44. (Above right) Mr D. J. Maddick has slotted the bundles on to a pole, and carries a lug of teazles to the gallows (more correctly two uprights and a crossbar) for drying.

45. (Left) The old method of packing teazles for sale. A Somerset grower with a completed stav containing twenty fan-shaped bundles each with twenty-five teazles, in all 500. Forty stavs made up a pack (date unknown).

46. (Below) Mr Norman Dawson, who has been a journeyman teazle man for fifty years, uses a setting iron to fill a rod with teazles for a raising gig at Henry Wheatleys, Hopton Mills, Mirfield.

47. (Below right) Mr Arthur Binns, overlooker, who has been at Hopton Mills for forty years, with one of the six raising gigs there.

MENDING AND FINISHING

48. (Left) E. Lofthouse mending at William Fisons, Greenholme Mills, Burley-in-Wharfedale (c. 1907).

49. (Above) Mrs J. Frain fringeing travel rugs at Joshua Ellis's, Batley Carr Mills. She twists the fringes by rubbing them up her arm, and uses whiting to assist.

50. (Below) Finish perching at George Akeds, Vicar Lane, Bradford (early 1950s).

RAGS

51. Rag sorting at J. R. Burrows, Carlinghow Mills, Batley. The operatives mostly work at riddles, and an innovation was the conveyor belt on the right (early 1930s).

52. A rag sale at Henry Cullingworth and Sons, South Street, Dewsbury. This was the last sale of a firm of rag merchants which began in 1845. The auctioneer is Mr A. Summers. Cullingworth Summers continue to conduct rag sales at Batley (1974).

53. Rag grinding machine made by George Thornes and Sons, Batley, now made by Knowles Wilson and Sons, Heckmondwike. The merchant using this machine dyes its products —shoddy and mungo—to match simple patterns (date unknown).

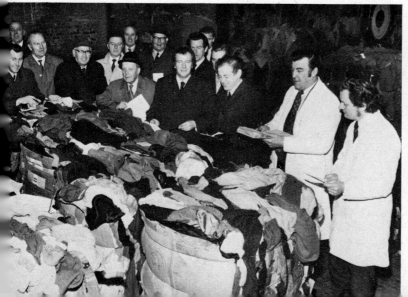

INDUSTRIAL CLOTHING

54. Weavers at Keighley and Moorhouses, Bruntcliffe Mill, Morley, wearing voluminous mill skirts made of harden, and the bibs which were separate. Mill skirts held up to 500 bobbins of weft (1916).

55. Workers at Albert Mills, Morley (c. 1902).

56. Work people at Bank Bottom Mills, Marsden, leaving the mill at Saturday dinner time. Some carry their mill skirts to be washed in readiness for Monday morning (1880s).

CARDING MACHINES

57. *Casting cylinders for carding machines in the iron foundry at John Haigh and Sons, Priestroyd Ironworks, Huddersfield (1935).*

58. *The erecting shop at John Haighs. Note the size and length of the machine more than 70 feet long. The set includes the scribbler, carder and tape condenser (1935).*

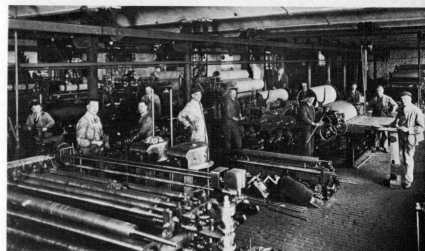

59. *Carding machine minders or feeders wearing black Italian pinafores, at Joshua Ellis and Co., Batley Carr Mills. They looked after four sets putting raw material into hoppers by hand at one end and doffing the bobbins of slubbings at the other (c. 1926).*

CARD CLOTHING

60. *Wet drawing card wire at Joseph Sykes Bros, Acre Mills, Lindley, Huddersfield, the largest firm of fine wire drawers in the United Kingdom and a member of the English Card Clothing Company. These machines made on the premises were in use from 1906 to 1960/65 (c. 1950).*

61. *A card setting machine tenter, Mr John Gledhill, at James Holdsworths, South Brook Mills, Mirfield. He runs twelve filleting machines that each put in 300 teeth a minute. The fillets 'clothe' the cylinders of the carding machine.*

62. *Mrs Irene Magee sets any missing teeth at South Brook Mills.*

ANCILLARY TRADES

63. The making department at the British Picker Company, Sandholme Mills, Todmorden. Pickers of water buffalo hide are made by folding, pressing and boring, and every one is made by weight (late 1940s).

64. Mr G. S. Hirst of Roberts and Hirst, Cote Hill, Halifax, bobbin turners, makes ring spinning bobbins.

65. Mr Cecil Fearnside, shuttle and loom accessories manufacturer, Park Works, Oakworth, near Keighley (1970).

MILL TRANSPORT

66. *Despatch of a loom from George Hattersleys, Keighley. This particular loom and its attendants may have been going to join a pageant. The firm had at one time thirty-two horses (date unknown).*

67. *Bogies, Ford lorries, steam waggons, and large lorries at Manningham Mills, Bradford (1920s).*

68. *Early lorry belonging to Tom Liversedge and Sons, Canal Bank Dyeworks, Huddersfield (1909).*

STONE

69. *Blake Hill End Quarry and Hollin Grove Farm in the Shibden valley, near Halifax, run by the Pulmans combining quarrying and farming in the old style. Note the judd walls to the left of the farmhouse.*

70. *The so-called Walls of Jericho near Egypt, north of Thornton, near Bradford. They were built as retaining walls for quarry debris.*

71. *Mr Ronnie Porter, banker mason, using a slating hammer to dress a stone roofing slate on a slate banker at the quarries and works of S. Marshall and Sons, Southowram, near Halifax.*

ENGINEERS

72. John Fowler operating his improved 4-furrow balance plough and using a Kitson and Hewitson chain-driven engine (1861).

73. Dom Carlos I built for the Benguela Railway, Angola, Portuguese West Africa, and staff at the Hunslet Engine Works, Leeds. It was built, tested, dismantled and packed for shipment in twenty-one days—thought to be a record in engine building (1905).

74. One of the two helve hammers at the Kirkstall Forge, Leeds. The complex was built in 1686, but the water-wheel shown dates from 1740. With each revolution of the wheel, the hammer struck four blows. It ceased to be worked about 1919.

and 4 inches thick were called ledgers, and the landings up to 9 feet by 6 feet 6 inches and 6 inches thick were used for the more elaborate monuments. Both were replaced by concrete in the 1930s.

Between Huddersfield and Halifax quarries surrounded the town of Elland, which gave its name to the stone used in particular from about 1800 onwards for the pavements of the expanding cities and towns. Up to the First World War a special tendering practice prevailed to prevent delays caused by late deliveries. A price was fixed for thousands of square yards of flags and kerbstones, but if a certain quantity, 200 to 300 square yards, was undelivered within twenty-four to forty-eight hours of the order being placed, the local authority concerned had the right to buy from a merchant and charge the firm tendering the difference in price.

At Lightcliffe, near Halifax, Joseph Brooke and Sons, a family firm founded in 1842, worked some twelve quarries, and pioneered the production of a crushed stone aggregate, patented in 1898 and marketed as 'Non-Slip stone', used for railway platforms, the pavements of London boroughs, and of towns from one end of England to the other. They also had quarries in Guernsey, Wales and Scandinavia. From the latter granite for dock works and monuments was shipped to Aberdeen and from there sent by rail to Halifax. The works, described in 1930 as the largest for roadway and building materials in the world, were closed down in the 1960s.[1]

Similarly at Southowram, near Halifax, the whole neighbourhood has been given over to quarrying, and is now the headquarters of Marshalls, a firm founded here by Solomon Marshall in 1891. A group of companies, one making rock drilling equipment for roadstone quarries and water boring tools, they employ 700 men. Marshalls took over Brookes and still supply York stone flags to paving contractors to the corporation of London, in recent years used for the new London Bridge, the Guildhall extension, the Houses of Parliament, and many other works. It used to be said that London's streets were paved with gold and at today's prices the saying has a more prosaic meaning. In 1937 Marshalls began to manufacture a prefabricated stone, Marshalite, very widely used for building, paving, and for garden layouts, and they are the largest manufacturers of hydraulically pressed concrete in the world.

It is a sobering thought that the best stone has been taken, and that in spite of easier methods of removing the overburden, sometimes 50 feet to 100 feet thick, quarries are almost finished. It is common practice and worth while to take up

[1] S. A. Leleux, *Brookes' Industrial Railways*, 1972.

kerbstones and re-dress, re-joint and re-use them. In the 1880s Welsh blue and
Cumberland green slates began to replace the traditional stone slates as the roofing
material for the rows and rows of houses in the cities and towns of the West Riding.
Houses may thus be dated by their roofs.

Stone slates were formerly riven or split from the lifts of stone, left to dry for a
few weeks, and then split off by the slate striker. Next they were to trim off on a
slate banker with a slate hammer (*see plate* 71), and have the scale shelled off with
an adze, a job often undertaken by Irishmen. Dick Marsden, who died in 1948,
worked at Marshalls as a slate striker from the age of eight for sixty-seven years.
Now suitable stone for riven slates is not there, even if they could be afforded.
Their scarcity and value may be judged by their once being sold by the 100 of six
score, then by the score, and now, if available at all, at so much apiece.

Behind Thornton, near Bradford, the extent of quarrying is commemorated by
the judd walls, the so-called Walls of Jericho, built as in other places for example
in the Shibden valley to retain quarry waste and so form a level field (*see plates*
69–70). A hundred years ago these enclaves of quarrymen were practically illiterate,
and dependent for education on Sunday schools held in remote chapels. Often they
relied on one of their number with a gift for figures to reckon up their piecework
earnings. In severe winters they and their families endured great hardship, and
enlightened employers found their men work or opened soup kitchens. From
Thornton huge slabs of stone, varying in size and up to 6 feet 6 inches long and 1
foot 4 inches thick, for making steam engine beds, were transported by waggon and
horses to Bradford station. Many of these were supplied from Yorkshire quarries
to Lancashire mills.

At Haworth as many as eight quarries were once worked on the moors. The
Jaggers, who moved from Ringby to Bankfield Quarry, Haworth, about 1928,
employed at one time 100 men getting stone for new buildings in Halifax and elsewhere. Rough tough horses pulled the narrow block waggons with heavy wheels.
Mr W. Jagger remembers the skill of one little man putting on the slipper brake,
fastening the wheels with a chain, and driving his three horses pulling a waggon
load weighing 10 tons down Haworth's steep Main Street.

Sandstone setts, the customary and once familiar paving material for streets,
have been gradually replaced by tarmac. In a price-list for 1901 they ranged in size
and quality from 6 inches at 48s. a rood to 'Best Yorkshire Nell Setts' 10 inches by
7 inches by 8 inches at 80s. Until the early part of this century setts were measured
for sale in roods of 14 square yards, stacked in eight rows, each 5 feet 3 inches in
length and 3 feet high.

Haworth Main Street, a splendid example of stone paving, was relaid in the

1930s. The Jaggers supplied 6-inch setts of stone 'as good and hard as you could find'. Setts were not laid on the bed, but edgeways to prevent weathering, and were bedded in tar and ashes from mill boilers. Ashes were once used for mixing with lime for plaster, and alone to improve early roads, and 6*d*. a load was paid to anyone who carted them away.

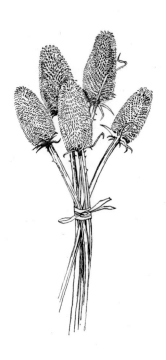

7 Miners Look Back

LIKE stone, coal was everywhere at hand for the expanding industries and influenced their siting and development. Mines and mills formerly occupied the same territory. Coal outcrops near the Elland Road football ground at Leeds, and within a three-miles radius of Dewsbury there were once forty-two working collieries. These were small and shallow such as the seven or eight at Batley, where it is said you could shout down the shaft to the men at the bottom. The historic Middleton Colliery and Waterloo Main were in or near to Leeds, and Gomersal Colliery in the very centre of our area only closed down in 1973. As pits were worked out mining moved from this, the western exposed coal-field, to the concealed field of the south-east.

None the less remembered scenes are of rows of colliers squatting on their haunches at popular meeting-places in the villages, walls against which they leant appearing as if polished with black lead, and black-faced men with black-rimmed eyes clattering home in clogs. In those early days owing to lack of experience in safety measures and regulations, terrible disasters occurred involving great loss of life, such as those at Morley Main Colliery in 1872 and Combs Colliery, Thornhill, in 1893. 'My grandfather and two of his brothers were killed in the Morley explosion. They took the bodies in coal carts to the Royal Hotel.' The strikes and lockouts, too, which punctuate the history of mining, affected not only the lives of the miners themselves but those dependent on coal for work and warmth.

Between Rothwell and Wakefield, only four or five miles south of Leeds, coal-mining began in earnest in the early part of the last century, and mining families grew out of old established communities of people with varied occupations. Batty in his *History of Rothwell* records the diminishing longevity of the inhabitants as mining developed. None the less a way of life emerged in which boys automatically followed their fathers' employment. Here, worked by fewer than twenty men, were many family pits in which strangers had no part. If a man left, his place was taken by a younger brother, a son or nephew. Lads gained their 'pit eyesight' starting with haulage in the pit bottom, and then joined their relations at the coal face.

The colliery officials and miners with whom we have talked, dedicated men, who spent their lives in coal-mining, worked both under private ownership and since 1947 under nationalization. Mr Syd Thompson of Rothwell started his mining career in north-west Durham against the wishes of his parents who did not want him to go underground, 'I ran away from school with a pal one Friday in January, 1921, when I was fourteen, and we were set on as pony drivers at 11s. a week. It seemed like a fortune. On the Monday morning at 9 a.m. along with other men and lads we just walked into the hillside down a day-hole or drift mine. I can smell the tang of the air yet, of timber, ponies, men, coal and powder reek, burning candles and the smoke from the naked lights of the oil *midgies*. It was a new world. You were moved to safety lamp seams later, a sinister tang all its own. There was great comradeship—to belong meant something—and the discipline was very strict.'

Influenced by his schoolmaster and like so many more lads throughout the mining industry at that period, he combined earning a living with attendance at night school, undertaking every type of job in the pit including 'sweating it out on your side with a hand pick in very low coal in the dim light of a safety lamp'. At technical college he first passed as a shot-firer and a deputy. 'During 1933 when I was fore-overman in charge of the shift and of mechanizing part of the pit, I had to be the first man down on the cage every morning at 3 a.m. with 350 men and lads to check and deploy. It was gruelling, with office work at night. I hardly saw my wife and kids. But there was a great spirit among us. We spent some happy times.' Finally he obtained the first- and second-class certificates of competency under the Coal Mines Acts of 1911 and 1920 which qualified him for the exacting job of under-manager or manager. Some men obtained degrees in mining engineering. This was the pattern in the 1920s and up to 1940. Today it can still obtain, but the selection is more keen, partly because of the diminished labour force, and partly because of the comprehensive facilities for education in mining now provided.

In 1940 when war had broken out Syd Thompson came from Durham to the Old Silkstone Collieries, Yorkshire, and after a short time was appointed manager of their Silkstone mine. He found the coal and wages in Yorkshire better, but the men's and the officials' attitudes very different. 'You had to live with the fellows and get to know them, and they had to get to know you before you could work together.'

Four years later he moved to Rothwell Collieries owned by J. and J. Charlesworth, a complex of eight mine shafts, employing 1,400 men, and listed as a necessitous undertaking. Here the famous Silkstone and Beeston seams were exhausted; the pit was threatened with closure, and the less attractive and thinner seams were being worked mainly for the war effort. The trade unionists, at first demanding this, that and the other, proved very difficult, until made aware of the true position and that their jobs were at stake. Within a short period production improved steadily each month, vying ultimately with those of its neighbours. After nationalization in 1947 and following the timely opening of the Skelton Grange Power Station which used the class of coal mined, the pit has been completely modernized and it still flourishes.

Mr Thompson, as the representative of the National Association of Colliery Managers, visited and assisted at several single and multiple fatalities, fires and one or two explosions, all of which mercifully lessen in numbers as safety regulations are constantly enforced and lessons learnt. Extraordinary chaos results in the roadways from an explosion. His work, too, has involved him in the closure of mines in West Yorkshire, each one a sad and chilling experience. Here, for 100 years or more a pit has employed hundreds of local men, whose work cannot easily be replaced by other forms of employment. After the removal of useful material, supplies and machinery and the clearing of the site, the shafts are filled in until no trace of the pit remains.[1]

Formerly in West Yorkshire if a man was killed, everyone came out and sacrificed their earnings. Only those who carried the dead man were paid. If a man was badly injured, it was customary too, although there existed a Miners' Sickness and Aid Fund, to take a collection for him. 'An injured miner was never well off.' Miners had snap tins the shape of a loaf, in two parts which slotted together, carried by a crank lever on the belt, and in the workings hung up on girders away from any mice or rats which came into the mine with the ponies' fodder. (In the 1924–38 period there were 2,480 horses and ponies in the 116 mines in West Yorkshire.) Glass bottles for water were replaced for safety by tin then enamel, and now by Dudley bottles which hold four to six pints all of which are welcome in the deep hot pits. Hard hats and safety helmets made their appearance before the Second World War.

Mr Maurice Westmoreland (1896–1975) was a member of one of the few old families at Rothwell engaged in mining since about 1800, and was a collier (that is a man working at the coal face) for nearly forty years until his hand was trapped in a roof fall. He started when he was thirteen at the pit bottom at Belle Isle (a pit which tapped the Beeston seam at 220 yards), pushing tubs into a cage and knock-

---

[1] Mines that have gone in the area in the last thirty years are Allerton Main, Whitwood, West Riding, Snydale, Middleton, Shaw Cross, Thornhill, Roundwood, Waterloo Main, St Johns, East Ardsley, Water Haigh, Primrose Hill and Gomersal.

ing the empty ones out for 10*d.* a day for eight and a half hours for five days and six and a half on Saturdays. His mother gave him 6*d.* a week pocket money.

Next he drove ponies, of which there were over seventy in the pit, for 1*s.* 1*d.* a day, and then as was customary joined his father in a team of three at the coal face. 'You couldn't have a better way of seeing to a fellow's welfare.' At first he filled the then small tubs, holding about 6 cwt, and in about six months was earning equal wages with his father, about £1 a day. He changed from his boots into clogs at the pit head, and worked in *bannakers* (long shorts), knelt on rubber pads, and leant his shoulder on a low buffet. Knees were calloused and cut, and Beat knee (fluid on the knee) was a common complaint. They were paid by the ton and won the best coal by *baring* (undercutting a large seam) and using chocks to hold it up. When these were removed enough coal fell down to fill five or six tubs. In this way round (large) coal, sold at a good price, was obtained without explosives.

A collier was paid for the amount of coal he got, and each tub full was distinguished by a *motty,* a numbered metal disc. When he started a miner was given a number. 'Mine was eighteen. I've never forgotten it. A motty is a symbol to a miner.' *Mottying,* cutting someone else's off and substituting their own, an occasional happening, was regarded as a heinous offence and the man was blacklisted. The master's weighman and the check-weighman, representing the miners, sat in the same office and weighed the tubs, 10 to 15 cwt. 2 to 4 lb. picks were supplied, and they used 10 lb. hammers for knocking timbers and wedges in for the supports, and two shovels, a round muck shovel and a square filling shovel. Picks were sharpened each day by the pick sharpener, and although they were numbered, some men buried their tools so that they were certain to keep their own.

When he moved to Methley Pit, Maurice rose at 4 a.m., walked a mile and three-quarters, caught a bus at 5 a.m., changed to a second, and riding to the face in tubs, was at work by 6 a.m. In some mines without riding facilities the men had to walk two to three miles and in these cases were allowed walking time. Nevertheless in a seven-hour shift this meant only five at the face to make a living. When Maurice's hand was damaged, all too common a happening, his compensation was then £4 a week dole and £4 from the pit.

'You couldn't save much to be married, but we'd plenty of coal, and the rent was 3*s.* 4*d.* a week. We went many a time to Leeds to shop or look round or to the theatre, and on Saturdays to a Rugby match. We'd three shows that day, the Empire for 6*d.*, the Royal for 9*d.* and 9*d.* for the Rugby match. We'd to walk home many a time [five miles].' Maurice was, as so many miners are, blessed with green fingers and took immense pride in his garden and greenhouse (*see plate* 147).

By the time Mr George Garfit of Rothwell left school about 1920, boys could not go into the pit until they were fourteen, so he worked for a twelve-month at an engineering works in Leeds. Like the other lads, he too began tramming tubs in the pit bottom, which was then lit by tallow candles—in his case at Beeston Pit—and after a year learning from his brother, he became a fitter. In those days providing their own tools, he and his brother maintained the pumps and condensing engines. Later when diesel engines replaced ponies and coal shearers and conveyor belts were introduced as many as fifty maintenance men were necessary, and the colliers had only to reset supports and shovel coal from the face corners.

'You never could get shut of coal dust. My mother always had to put the fireside boiler on for Dad's bath. It was hard work for mothers before pit baths came.' When first married he earned two guineas a week. His wife was always relieved when he arrived home. For holidays they travelled all over England on a motor-bicycle and sidecar, and in retirement both share the hobby of making model railway engines.

Mr Jack Priest of Ossett also at the age of fourteen at 6 a.m. on 9 April 1929 followed his father who was a deputy down the pit at Gomersal. 'When me and mi Dad were oppening t' pit out [it had been closed and was re-opened], ther'd be big grown-up men kneeling down in front of him begging for a job at 6s. a day to get a bit better for their families. . . . An official were more like a sergeant major. If he said " Jump", they'd to jump. The hand-getting colliers were proud of their skill, and worked on contract at so much a yard or ton [it was for this that a deputy formerly carried a stick, a yardstick]. When you went to your work, if you wanted bantams, poultry, pigeons, flowers or cabbage plants somebody somewhere kept 'em, and they'd be there i' t' lamp room next day. You'd ask "How much do you want for 'em?" and the answer might be a couple o' bob or nowt.'

'Mi father, me and mi brother went home and had us dinner before we got weshed. Up to us leaving school we had to stand at table for us meals. If us belly went agen t'table or if we reached for us bun before us bread, knife used to come down at back of us hands. When we started working we got a chair. We used to get us dinner about a quarter to three; then mi Dad had a nap, and I used to go to t'set pot with a *piggin* [lading can] and take two piggins of watter and fill an enamel bowl in a stone sink at side, and take two cold ens back. You used ter take yer shirt off and wesh behind yer ears and arms and chest. Yer were black breet, then mi mother used to come and wesh yer back. She used to buy harden sugar bags and boil 'em for towels and dry your back. Ooooooh! There were always notches all down yer back like. Then you'd take yer pants off and your stockings and roll yer football breeches up and put a leg in t'bowl. If you went to t'pit wi' mucky legs, you used to get some hammer. A lot of 'em, men up to thirty year old, i' them days used to be in their pit muck till nine o'clock at neet, laiking football or piggy or cricket. In t' pit rows they used to be sat on t' doorsteps i' summer time, telling t' tale i' their shirt sleeves. It's gone is that. Culture's all gone. I don't talk broad as I used to do.' Jack Priest also has his hobbies, keeping canaries and collecting pit lamps and other bygones.

The oldest of the remarkable ninety-year-olds we have met is Mr John Chapman Fox, aged ninety-seven, a surface worker in the mines for most of his life, a keen cyclist, a great fisherman, and gifted with a memory for dates and statistics. He remembers the rioting at Featherstone in 1903 when soldiers were brought in, and that it was a hot day on 30 April 1896, when sixty-three men were killed in the Micklefield Colliery disaster, and that drunkenness and fighting on Saturday nights were commonplace.

John Chapman Fox was one of a family of two girls and five boys, all over 6 feet tall, of whom all the boys went into the pits. He himself suffered from slight claustrophobia which explains his mixed career, for earnings on surface work were half the pay of those underground. In 1887 his father, a miner, who had been left money, set up as a rope and twine spinner, and here at the age of ten John began work. However, following an eleven-week-long strike at the colliery which supplied the coal for the steam engine, the enterprise failed. By 1902 when he married he had had three jobs, of which one involved walking to Hunslet four miles there and four miles back each day for five years.

Then through his parents who knew the manager at Rose Pit, Rothwell, he was given the job of stoking the nine boilers for the winding, haulage and pumping engines. Two men worked the day shift and one the night. In the first two years, often having to work a shift and a half, he lost two stones in weight and earned only 27s. a week plus overtime. After nine years he moved to more congenial work, looking after the engine which ran the machines of the repair shop for the pit. But he displeased the bosses by canvassing for a Labour candidate and was sent back to his old job, which he shortly left.

John, then thirty-six, went as a collier to Methley Junction Pit. But this meant cycling four miles, walking two more to the coal face, six miles in all before starting the day's shift. It was too much. After three days back at home his old boss offered him work at Beeston Pit where he was employed at different jobs on the surface for thirty years until the pit closed down, after which he alternated between the dole and good jobs for a few years until his retirement.

At the present day mining presents a totally different picture from the above accounts. Such is modernization within the last forty years that the miner is now a trained skilled operative using expensive and sophisticated machinery. There are no longer either colliers or trammers, and miners are not readily recognized on their way to and from work. New mining villages have replaced old stable communities. Many men have drifted or been sent to Yorkshire from other fields where pits have closed. This is now a cosmopolitan mining area.

8 Steam and Speed

THE two converging strands of opportunity and tradition meet in the development of the numerous industries other than textiles. Opportunity for work for the many and for advancement for the gifted few attracted people to cities and towns, where stimulated by the proximity of coal, the age of steam advanced. At Leeds the basis of work changed from the manufacture of cloth to engineering which drew to it a large work force of men and the clothing industry which employed a large work force of women.

Tradition is epitomized by the Kirkstall Forge, which follows the bloomeries worked on the site from about 1600. Its recent history concerns the Butler family, who at first with the Beecrofts, rented a forge and a farm near by in 1779, and manufactured goods—shovels, spades, hammers, axes and domestic ironmongery such as patten rings—and by the middle of the next century following on the invention and installation of new forging hammers made cranes, bridges, steam boilers, railway waggon wheels and axles, of which axles for motor transport became in time a prime product.

Kirkstall Forge, like Armley Mills both on the river Aire, retains industrial relics on interesting and historic sites. Two helve hammers and a collection of trade pieces are preserved (*see plate* 74). The latter were made by applicants for work, who, given iron, were asked to make an article as proof of their proficiency. In 1974 a descendant of one family who started at the forge in the 1770s still worked there.[1]

Within a few miles of Bradford other ironworks of importance to West Riding development were started at Birkenshaw in 1762, Bowling in 1788, Low Moor in 1789, Shelf in 1794 and Bierley in 1810, all of which eventually ceased. Low Moor Iron Works mined their own ironstone and coal, for which they had at one time seventy pits, and about 1870 employed 3,700 men. They built stationary steam

[1] R. A. Mott, 'Kirkstall Forge and Monkish Iron-making', Misc. vol. 15, Thoresby Society, vol LIII, p. 154, 1973; R. Butler, *The History of Kirkstall Forge*, 1954; *The History of Kirkstall Forge through seven centuries 1200–1954*, reprinted 1954. Also information from Mr J. Northrop.

engines, made plates and forgings for iron ships, armaments, supplied parts for Brunel's steamship *The Great Eastern*, suffered a serious explosion in 1914, and closed down in 1928.

On the opposite side of Leeds from Kirkstall, Hunslet Road and Jack Lane became the seat of many of the great engineering plants in West Yorkshire, plants that burgeoned into full stature in the last century, and like the iron foundries many faded away in this. Just as Matthew Murray (1765–1826) gravitated to Leeds from the North-East because of the opportunities presented there, so talented men joined him at the Round Foundry in Holbeck, and leaving, founded other works in adjoining Hunslet, such as the Airedale Foundry, which under the Kitsons became the largest of the locomotive works there.

John Fowler, who was born in Wiltshire, by his inventive genius laid the foundation of the vast works next to the Airedale Foundry in Hunslet Road. Here were made draining and ploughing equipment, steam traction engines, road rollers, locomotives, pit-head gear and winding machines, electric generators, and tanks in time of war. In its heyday 2,000 men were employed. The works in Leeds closed down in 1973. They may be said in a sense to have been supplanted in Yorkshire in so far as agricultural machinery is concerned by David Browns, a firm making gears in 1860, now employing some 4,000 people at Meltham, near Huddersfield and elsewhere, to build farm tractors exported all over the world.

Three firms in Jack Lane, Hunslet, that have gone are J. and H. McLaren, builders of steam waggons, Manning Wardle at the Boyne Engine Works, and Hudswell Clarke at the Railway Foundry. Three still in being, only the last in Jack Lane, but all connected with steam are Thomas Green whose chairman in the 1930s, Robert Blackburn, founded the Blackburn Aeroplane company, and Greenwood and Batley who made the first bandsaw for John Barran, the founder of the first of the wholesale clothing firms in Leeds, and the Hunslet Engine Company which has acquired much of the land of the Airedale, the Boyne and the Railway Foundries.[1]

The Hunslet Engine Company, started in 1864 by J. T. Leather with seven men, was the last of the great locomotive engineering firms to be founded in Leeds, and managed by three generations of Campbells and three of Alcocks, it is the one

[1] For further reading see: *Matthew Murray*, ed. E. Kilburn Scott, 1928; E. Kitson Clark, *Kitsons of Leeds 1837–1937*, 1938; R. N. Redman, *The Railway Foundry, Leeds, 1839–1969*, 1972; L. T. C. Rolt, *A Hunslet Hundred*, 1964; D. R. Bomford, 'John Fowler Memorial Lecture', Institution of British Agricultural Engineers, 1956; *Steaming*, Journal of the National Traction Engine Club, vol. 9, No. I; Alf Pepper, *Retrospect of over Fifty Years with John Fowler and Co. (Leeds) Ltd*, 1946. Records of John Fowler and Company are at the Museum of English Rural Life, University of Reading.

survivor. It owes its success to Mr Edgar Alcock, who came as works manager in 1912, and had the foresight to plan the change from steam to diesel. In 1927 his son, Mr John F. Alcock, then entering the works, was granted £5,000 to build a diesel locomotive, and assembling together a small team, he succeeded. He also began the practice of making a world tour twice a year, not only to obtain orders at once but to prepare the ground for many placed years later.

In those days up to the Second World War the head offices of the railways of the world were in London, with India as the chief customer and Germany the chief rival. As with textile machinery and mills, when engines were ordered, men went out with them, whilst others, often rising to be general managers, ran the railways themselves. For a variety of reasons, of which one is the early age of marriage, families nowadays have little wish to live abroad for a long period. Men also rose up from the shop floor as did Mr Edgar Alcock himself. Success is exemplified for example in the career of Mr W. Morrell. He started at the works at the age of fourteen in 1914, and by learning every job and attending trade school at the mechanics' institute at night, as was not unusual, he became at the age of twenty-three senior draughtsman with special responsibility for gear design—progress that would not be easy today when university trained men expect to enter at a high level. The company, which has for long encouraged apprentices, now takes in about twenty-five a year, including one or two girls.

In the drawing office when a steam locomotive was being designed a team of draughtsmen under a general supervisor took charge of the different sections—the boiler, the motion, the frame. Engines, modified for different gauges of rails, heights of tunnels and power required, were mostly individual in design, and built to exact specifications down to the paintwork, which for example might have 'to stand and look well in a hot climate after a long voyage'. When eventually one was finished, a particular whistle was blown and all available men, perhaps 200 of them, with long ropes hauled it into the yard for testing. The whole work force, having contributed to it, gained satisfaction from its completion.

In the 1920s when the first diesel was being built, hand work with simple tools was the rule. Then there were a dozen men capable of filing up a big diameter as perfectly as if it had been ground, and in the smithy others bent angle-irons, now almost a lost art. Today's skills are machine ones, and as old craftsmen retire, old skills, no longer required, are forgotten—a development echoed in many spheres.

Also in Hunslet three different firms illustrate success by supplying needs and they also demonstrate the interlinked nature of progress. Procter Brothers, wire-works, is the oldest firm in Leeds founded in Jack Lane in 1740. Noted for making the Little Nipper Mouse Trap, invented by a Herbert Atkinson, but now only a

small part of their business, they manufacture for example wire-guards for all types
of machinery. The second, Fawcetts, founded by two brothers Thomas Constantine
and John Dawson Fawcett, came from Hull and invented brick-making machinery,
now made in a factory in Hunslet Road and exported all over the world.

The third, T. F. and J. H. Braime, was also founded by two brothers, Thomas
Fletcher Braime (1864–1955) and James Henry Braime (1868–1930), both gifted
with remarkable inventive talents, whose success sprang from the invention of the
oil-can. T. F. Braime, who had been apprenticed to J. and H. McLaren, never
forgot the terrifying journey lasting half an hour driving a steam traction engine
across a wooden trestle bridge high above the Rhône.

In the 1880s they began production of the oil-can, again in Hunslet Road, in a
two-storied building rented at 7s. 6d. a week with the ground floor let off to a
tanner for 5s. Eventually short of capital they advertised in the *Yorkshire Post* for a
loan. It was answered by a clergyman who offered them his life savings, £500 (later
repaid many times over). Thomas Fletcher then designed and built large power
presses whilst James Henry invented dies and processes for the manufacture of
large metal pressings. In the First World War when their inventive talents were
turned to munitions they employed 1,250 men and women. The firm, run by their
descendants, still makes and exports oil-cans, but its main products are deep-
drawn pressings for many different industries, manufactured in workshops on the
same site as the original building but now occupying six acres.

Again the adaptation of the bandsaw, to cut several layers of cloth at once, by
Greenwood and Batley points to the same co-operation of different firms. The
invention of the sewing machine in America and the use of the bandsaw set off the
clothing concerns in Leeds, of which Hepworths, Montagu Burtons and Prices are
examples and of which Prices represents their phenomenal growth.

Henry Price, the son of a Methodist minister, left school when he was twelve,
and started work in a readymade clothing shop at 2s. 6d. a week. At nineteen he
became manager of the Grand Clothing Hall in Keighley, whilst his wife sold men's
collars, ties and socks displayed in the window of their cottage. In 1907 he opened
a tailor's shop in Silsden near Keighley. The shop prospered, another was opened
in Keighley and a third in Leeds, where an old building was taken as a clothing
factory, During the Christmas week a heavy snowstorm caused the roof to cave in,
a disaster that almost finished the whole project.

By 1930 Prices had opened thirty-five branches and the name Fifty-Shilling
Tailors was well known. Under a property controller with a team of twenty-six
architects, entirely engaged in designing shop fronts, new shops were opened at the
rate of two or three a week on sites chosen in the best possible positions, on the best

sides of the main shopping streets. Cloth had to be bought from large firms such as John Crowthers and Mallinsons in the Colne valley and Bairstows at Silsden, and Henry Price bargained down to one eighth of a penny a yard. Sir Henry, as he became, never removed his account from the Keighley branch of the Midland Bank, although his takings of tens of pounds a week rose to thousands. When in the 1950s the business was taken over by John Collier, it had 285 shops.

The experiences of John Verity (1890–1975), born in Leeds in a street behind the Infirmary, illustrate aspects of the clothing industry formerly peculiar to it. His father was the wine steward at the Queen's Hotel, and his mother, the youngest of a family of thirteen, had worked as a child of eight or nine as a half-timer in the 'line garret' at Marshall's flax-spinning mills. When his father died following an accident, John Verity had to leave the grammar school to which he had won a scholarship, and after one or two other jobs he went in 1911 to David Littles, bespoke tailors of men's and boys' clothes, then employing some 350 to 400 people, and eventually becoming an order clerk in the Special Measure Department, he stayed there until retirement in 1952.

In his early days working hours lasted from 8 a.m. to 6.30 p.m. with an hour off for lunch eaten in the basement where there was a slow oven, a geyser for brewing tea and a trestle table. Trade fluctuated throughout the year, largely because men's suits were most in demand at Easter and boys' at Whitsuntide, so that from Christmas to Whitsuntide everyone worked late until 9.30 p.m. three nights a week. (This was allowed for up to thirty nights a year.) John himself in busy times often worked until midnight and sometimes until 4 a.m., but he had ten days' holiday with pay.

In the first decade of the century girls, almost always engaged on piecework, earned about 30s. a week, and during the summer after the spring rush had little to do. In the same period youngsters straight from school at thirteen began by soaping seams at 3s. a week of forty-five to forty-seven hours, and with overtime at 1d. a night could earn 3s. 5d. Because cloths were heavier than nowadays seams were then soaped and soaked, before opening out and ironing so that they lay flat. (In 1975 learners earned about £15 a week.)

Patterns of cloth changed very little, for example schoolboys' suits were made of grey herringbone, and men's suits of good quality blue serge, some of the best manufactured by W. E. Yates of Bramley. Serge, dyed khaki, was made up into army uniform during the First World War. Sometimes work was sent out to small firms, often Jewish, in North Street, Leeds, where perhaps a few relatives and neighbours worked in a bedroom, or an attic or a hayloft, using treadle machines, and with the women hand-buttonholing, finishing off and buttoning. Buttonholing machines, constantly being improved, were in fact introduced at Littles between the wars.

It was usual in those days for an order which reached them on Wednesday at noon to be completed and sent away on Friday. Once, about 1913, a tailor at Bentham, some fifty miles from Leeds, missed the post with a funeral order, so he sent it in a cardboard box by the milk train the following morning. The lid with the label blew off, and it was by chance that the order reached Littles at 9.20 a.m. With different sections sewn by different girls, the suit was finished and put on the Morecambe train to reach Bentham in time for the tailor to deliver it that afternoon.

Caps, those important items of men's and schoolboys' wear, make a postscript to the clothing industry. When suits cost 50s., caps sold at 1s. or 1s. 6d., and Henry Price refused to sell them saying that it took as long to sell a cap as a much more expensive suit. The demand for caps has been lessened by miners wearing safety helmets and by the general trend of wearing no headgear at all.

None the less four firms of cap-makers in Leeds and about twenty all over the country flourish. The firm of J. W. Myers was founded by the present owner's grandfather in Leeds in 1889. At that early date they made for example 'Polos', a roundcap resembling a bus conductor's out of corduroy or Donegal tweed, and a Tam o' Shanter with gold braid, worn by children with their sailor suits and sold to merchants who supplied shops such as Harrods and Swan and Edgar. When Mr J. W. Myers joined the firm in the period before the First World War, the heyday of the trade, if they sold less than 1,000 dozen caps a week, retailed at 1s. 6d each, it was considered disappointing. Caps, small in Edwardian times, increased in size and were made of eight pieces, then changed in style to a one-piece flat top or were varied with stitched fronts. In 1974 mock fur caps and 'Poms' in brightly coloured cloths, worn by golfers and others, were high fashion. Many caps go to Scotland, and instead of 2s. 6d. sell for £2 to £3, even £4, still small sums for the work and the material involved.

Lastly, a firm founded on a chance meeting of two men in a foreign country, the British Belting and Asbestos Company, whose headquarters is at Cleckheaton in the Spen valley. In 1878 William Fenton, a Scotsman, born in Perthshire, was working as a foreman in a cotton mill in Sweden, and W. W. Cobbett, a Londoner, was travelling there on business. The two men met and made friends. Fenton invented a solid-weave cotton belt, showed it to his friend, and encouraged by him returned to Scotland to manufacture it there. Cobbett undertook the marketing under the trade name of Scandinavia Belting. In 1901 the works, then at Lanark, were transferred to Cleckheaton, where 3,000 are now employed. With other modern factories in other parts of Yorkshire and England BBA make brake linings, clutch facings, general asbestos and glass fibre products, conveyor belting, and much else. At Cleckheaton, besides playing fields for various sports, a sea of cars belonging to the staff surrounds the factory.

So, too, at the Hunslet Engine Works the car park has had to be enlarged many times. No longer is there 'a tide of cloth caps' in Jack Lane as the many works loosed, nor, close up to them, built at all angles on every available plot of land, the rows of back-to-back houses to which the men were returning. Houses and many large works, such as Fowlers, have been razed to the ground, replaced by new roads, new factories and new housing estates.

9 Houses

IN contrast with a rural district the long application to industry has defined the shape of settlement in West Yorkshire. The very few mansions of the gentry, such as Temple Newsam, the sixteenth- and seventeenth-century halls of the yeomen-clothiers round Halifax, the houses of merchants, and clusters of old cottages, have been inundated by waves of building in the last century—the factories, the Victorian houses of all sizes, mostly in terraces forming ranks of streets and squeezed into a small compass for the unrestrained tide of people surging into towns and villages in search of work. To picture the country for instance between Leeds and Wakefield as 'very beautiful' as Arthur Young described it in about 1770 requires a feat of the imagination.

In the 1870s it was said of Leeds that on elevated ground north-west of the town 'wealthy merchants and tradesmen have thrown out a thick fringe of luxurious mansions and country seats'. As noise and smoke had increased, the exodus from centres had begun. In course of time houses in residential squares were abandoned for use as offices, and those in the old yards and courts became derelict. As new suburbs engulfed more and more countryside round the towns, a process continuing into the twentieth century, immigrants occupied the older districts and themselves moved on to be replaced by new groups.

A comfortable home is remembered by Mrs M. A. Hare (b. 1891) in Lambert's Yard, Lower Briggate, Leeds, where her father had a bill posting business. Near by were watch repairers, Bagshaw's the silver-platers, a woman feather curler re-curling ostrich feathers, Skelton's the saddlers in Queen's Court, Reynolds and Branson, pharmaceutical works and Goodall and Backhouse, makers of Yorkshire Relish, in Wormald's Yard, and premises elsewhere. In the early nineteenth century Mrs Robert Goodall, whose home-made sauce inspired the production of Yorkshire Relish shipped all over the world, lived in one of the Georgian houses in Park Place, now no longer residential, and her husband and Henry Backhouse then had a chemist's shop next to Trinity Church.

On the outskirts of most towns and villages the houses of the well-to-do, grouped in exclusive suburbs or secluded in their own grounds, range from the large semi-detached to the vast piles such as Cliffe Castle, Keighley (now a museum). Well built of stone, the larger ones have stables, conservatories, sometimes orchid houses; and were formerly guarded by a yard dog, often an Airedale. Inside are large lofty rooms, one for billiards or music, handsome staircases and elaborate mahogany woodwork enclosing fireplaces or framing oil paintings of Highland cattle. They have backstairs from the kitchens to servants' bedrooms in the attics, splendid cellars sometimes white-tiled throughout, and formerly wooden-slatted Venetian blinds (a penance to clean) for the windows, and furniture made by local cabinet-makers.

Life in these well-ordered homes followed a routine prescribed by the arrival of husbands returning home from work and by the employment of servants, varying in number, and for large houses, gardeners and coachmen.

Dr Phyllis Bentley, Halifax, believes that this orderly framework made life much easier and less uncertain than present-day easy-going habits, and that 'It is inaccurate to think of the bourgeoisie as lazy. Everybody worked very hard indeed. All the laundry and baking were done at home. My mother and a tailoress made all our clothes even the boys' sailor suits. For a middle-class girl it was not quite the thing to work for a living. I strongly disagreed.' Mrs H. Mitchell, too, whose father was the first Lord Mayor of Bradford and who herself was a sitting magistrate for thirty years, says, 'It was argued that you would be taking a job from somebody else who needed it more than you. We enjoyed a pleasant social life of balls and concerts [attended at St George's Hall in full evening dress]—very snobby. I had plenty of charitable work to do.'

In 1916 Miss C. E. Hepworth of Morley, one of three daughters, took the unusual step, barely tolerated by her mother, of entering her father's mill eventually to become cashier. 'My father had three interests—mill, chapel, and town hall.' When he retired she continued with the firm that bought the business, but no concessions were made at home to a new time-table, and her health broke down. It was not until 1948 after her father had died, aged ninety, that she was able to take up public work in earnest, and to become a magistrate, chairman of committees, and the first woman mayor of Morley. This convention of no work for the girls of better-off families often resulted in much the same frustrations and lack of fulfilment suffered by girls from poor families short of money for further education.

In these circles At Home days, set days once a fortnight or month, when mothers and daughters, at home to friends, provided afternoon tea, were customary. Ladies on arrival placed one of their own printed cards and two of their husband's on a silver salver on the hall table. 'My mother hated At Homes,' said Mrs Mitchell. 'Lady Tree who was acting in Bradford once came bringing a huge dog, which ate all the food off one of those three-tiered cake stands. I knew nothing about cooking. I couldn't even boil an egg. You weren't very welcome in the kitchen. If we entertained we had dinner at night, but usually we had high tea.'

High teas for special occasions, with salmon, chicken or Dover sole as the main courses, are remembered as delicious even sumptuous repasts. Holiday venues ranged from the Yorkshire dales, Scarborough, the Lake District, Blackpool, the Isle of Man, to Anglesey and the South of France, and were spent in rooms or for the rich at what we should now call second homes.

None the less thrift guided household management, and the rhyme beginning 'Waste not. Want not' was an oft-repeated warning to children. Nor did apparent means ensure immunity from disaster either personal or financial (*see Chapter* 2). From these Victorian houses some remember riding to work on horseback and throwing halfpennies to children turning cartwheels along the pavements in Hunslet Road. When many of these same people, the leaders and the better educated, moved still farther out into the country or sometimes migrated to southern England, the cities and towns were the poorer.

Besides these, and by far the largest group, were the vast array of houses of more modest size, often in terraces, occupied by people of a wide range of income, at the top end of the scale merging with the previous group. Possibly nowhere in England were there more of the middle-middle classes, because of the proliferation of independent units of work, than in the West Riding. At the bottom end of the scale came the slums in cities, towns and villages crammed with houses, at their best made the most of, and at their worst an affront to human dignity. Incredible as it seems now, they were disregarded by almost all except those who for one reason or another had occasion to visit them.

Before and during the period under review a series of housing, health and improvement Acts had brought some order into the chaos caused by too rapid an influx of people, and had ameliorated the indescribably insanitary conditions that had bred cholera outbreaks and prolonged epidemics of typhus and diarrhoea. No longer could parts of Leeds, Bradford and Halifax be described as 'a slimy bog' filled with 'sickening smells', nor everywhere even in villages were there so many back-to-back houses, tenements in yards, crowded lodging-houses, and the terrible cellar dwellings, the latter often occupied by old people for 1s. 3d. a week. Before the slum clearance campaigns of the 1930s there were 74,805 back-to-backs in Leeds and in 1955 30,000 in Bradford.[1]

[1] P. E. Razzell and R. W. Wainwright, *The Victorian Working Class. Selections from the 'Morning Chronicle', 1849*, 1973; J. Mayhall, *Annals of Yorkshire*, vol. 111, see 10 February 1866; J. N. Radcliffe, *The Sanitary State of Leeds, c.* 1870; A. Ravetz, *Model Estate, Planned at Quarry Hill, Leeds*, 1974.

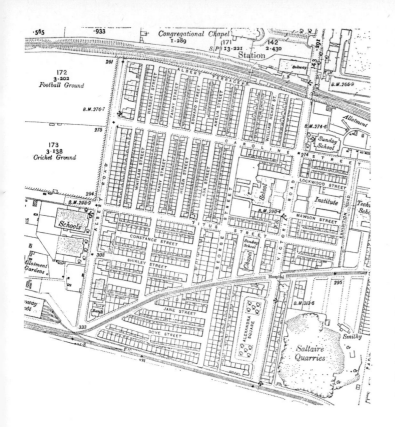

Model village: Saltaire, built by Sir Titus Salt between 1854 and 1872. There were then 45 almshouses and 850 houses, of which those facing Albert Road were larger than the others. The streets were named after his wife and children and Lockwood and Mawson, the architects. The mill is at the top on the right. Each house had a parlour, kitchen and three bedrooms.

Former slums at Camp Field, Leeds, close to the city centre, demolished about 1900. They originally consisted of four unbroken rows of back-to-back houses. Between the rows the spaces had been filled in with other back-to-backs, trough closets and ashpits.

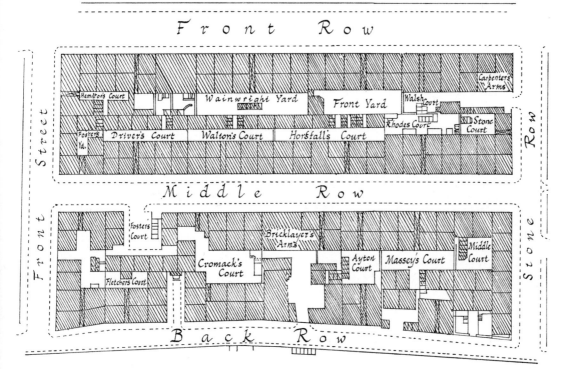

At Midgley, a village in Calderdale, 'When first we were married we lived in a one up and a one down in a cellar. I put up his jock in a red handkerchief on the sideboard overnight, and next morning rats had eaten t'jock and t' handkerchief.' [1] Remembered as particularly vile were Middle Row, Back Row and Front Row in Camp Field, Leeds, within a few minutes' walk of City Square, a ghetto of fifty-nine houses demolished after the 1890 Housing Act. 'People wouldn't go near them.' In 1904 complaints were made of the awful smell down Heaton Road, Bradford, where the fever van was often seen, and at Churwell, near Leeds, in the 1930s local councillors visiting houses in order to condemn them were sprayed with disinfectant.

Old houses everywhere, not only in city slums, were infested with bugs, and in consequence smelt like rotten apples. People stuck tarred paper on to walls to prevent them from penetrating from house to house. They stood bed legs in round glass cups filled with paraffin, speared them with pins at Gildersome, sizzled them on walls with a lighted candle at Holbeck. It was a heart-breaking experience for a newly married couple moving into a clean house to find bugs crawling in from adjoining ones. On the other hand in 1962 one old man who had moved from a slum area of Bradford into a new house, dogged by ill luck, returned to the old house before it was demolished, and collected some bugs in a matchbox which he kept in his pocket as a charm. They were the luck of the house.[2] Undertakers and upholsterers of necessity took precautions against fleas. The introduction of DDT was a godsend.

From 1907 a few Octavia Hill-trained lady social workers and housing managers were employed in Leeds. Mrs A. Maitland, formerly Brenda Hall of Leeds, remembers, 'In the 1930s old Quarry Hill was as verminous as anything I saw in London. The best way to look for bugs was to peel off the wallpaper by the fireplace. Layers and layers of paper on one wall I remember went back to a newspaper dated 1832. They were terrible houses, one room up, one down, back-to-back, long streets of them, and every so often two knocked down and a row of filthy lavatories in their place.'

'I would be given a block of forty to 100 houses and told that they were due for demolition in say six months. I collected the rents myself each week (3s. 6d. to 7s. or 7s. 6d. with debts of £4, £5, £6) as a means of getting to know the people, their families, places of work, and where they wished to be re-housed, and then gradually moved them into new houses which were handed over in batches every week

[1] Tape recording, 15th January 1956, Institute of Dialect and Folk Studies, University of Leeds.
[2] Anecdote from D. McKelvie, 'Some Aspects of Oral, Social and Material Tradition in an Industrial Urban Area', University of Leeds, PhD. thesis, 1963.

by the builders. The council did the move, collecting all furniture, clothes, belongings in the morning and delivering everything fumigated to the new home later in the same day. Coals in the bath were common. But almost all without exception wanted to get out of the slums.'

'Many were old. One woman shouting and swearing used to terrify me. Another, an old evil-looking woman with a deeply lined face, had living with her a slightly mental granddaughter, who was always having illegitimate children. They mostly disappeared, but the police were never able to trace where they had gone. An old couple, both nearly stone-deaf, possessed two old and mangy dogs and a parrot, not allowed in the new houses, and did not want to leave. I persuaded them to have the dogs put down and the housing manager to let them take the parrot. That parrot was the saving of them. Neighbours and children came to see it, so that they were never lonely.'

Thousands of terrace houses had been built before the 1840s and many in the 1890s. They are remembered costing £30, £40, £60 and £100 each, put up by speculative builders or mill-owners or by private individuals who built a row and lived in one. In a few cases five or six people joined together, and built a short row calling them Club Houses, to be seen for instance at Illingworth, near Halifax, and at Old Town above Hebden Bridge.

The demand for houses was such that it was commonplace to buy a key for £1 from the landlord (and for that matter to pay £50 for one for a council house). Most had a cellar, a living-room about 12 feet by 14 feet, with in one corner a stair-case leading to a small and a larger bedroom, and outside a shared privy. 'If you had a scullery house you were posh.' A cupboard recess on the window side of the fireplace held a tap and a sink and shelves for crockery. Many houses have attics. In Blackman Lane, Leeds, the back-to-backs have individual toilets in small back yards. But this was once a district for the better-off, who sometimes built a stable and coach-house in the garden.

From 1865 scavenging was carried out in parts of Leeds by the corporation, and tons of filth were taken to a depot by the river to be transported by boat or by railway trucks from luggage stations to farming districts. Night soil and midden men with horses and carts mostly worked during the night. An Act of Parliament in 1907 led to outside privies being converted to water-closets, but still families shared. 'You had a door with a key; there were eight of us and six next door, so— fourteen to a toilet. In winter the water froze.' At Hebden Bridge some tipplers still operate, a method whereby sink water is collected in a pan which when full tips over and flushes.

'They were all poor people living together in poor conditions, but they were happy. Old Hunslet had a spirit like the war; the conditions drew people together.' [1] 'As a child I lived in Domestic Street, Holbeck. Someone who came to live there brought a gramophone, and on a summer's night (and we used to have summers then) they opened their windows and people sat on the steps listening. Mother got a gramophone for us when we started work.' [2] 'I lived as a boy about 1922 in Hargreaves Square, Shipley. There were 171 back-to-back houses built by Hargreaves, a worsted spinner, and folk who lived there were known as Square-ites. Children ran about without boots and with their breeches' backsides hanging out. It was rugged—with women often fighting and shouting and a lot of drink. Yet I look back on it with happiness.' [3] 'At Hunslet the tingalary came on a Friday night after everyone had cleaned up. We flocked out and danced to the jazzy tunes. Local fellows borrowed them from Italians, Tomasso's, off the York Road. They paid so much and kept what they made over' (see plate 95).[4]

'When I was a boy we lived on Health Street down Commercial Road, Halifax, and the houses were back-to-back—one room up one down. My mother had to do everything in the one room, cooking, baking, washing, drying the clothes. We had our meals in that room, washed in it, lived in it and on Friday nights we had the old zinc bath up from the cellar to bath in it. [Some houses had set pots in which the water was heated.] In the house we had a good coal fire which was banked up at night with coal slack so that when we came down in the morning one jab with the poker and fire would be burning up. On one side was a small boiler and on the other a small oven, and the rule was that if you took any water out of the boiler you put some more in. My mother used to make all the bread we ate. On baking day the room had the smell of the bread—small flat cakes, large flat cakes, small loaves all laid out were a welcome sight when you arrived home from school on a winter's day.' [5] 'Everyone in Drighlington had huge roaring fires and kept the door open. My grandfather used to say "Oppen t' door. Oppen t' door". Coal was cheap. There were no indoors then. The neighbours all knew each other.' [6] 'We thought people were very poor if they didn't have a fire.' [7]

As the main bread-winners, fathers demanded full respect. A story, prevalent in more than one quarter, tells how when a son reached the age of twenty-one he came home and said, 'Now then we've got another prop in t'house'. But the father stood up and felled him saying, 'There's only one prop i' this house', or 'Thou sees t' house is still standing'. Whenever possible heads of households were

[1] Mr T. Sinclair, Hunslet.
[2] Mrs E. Hardisty, Leeds.
[3] Mr D. Larvin, Shipley.
[4] Mr T. Sinclair, Hunslet.
[5] Mr W. Gaunt, Sowerby Bridge.
[6] Mrs M. A. Collins, Drighlington.
[7] Mrs I. Humphreys, Gomersal.

indulged their favourite foods. 'My father used to go into the market every Friday after work, and bring home a bass full of fish and conger eel. He liked conger eel, and steaked it and picked out a few pieces for his tea next day.' [1]

The death of a man or his having an accident or absconding for one reason or another or his addiction to drink caused ripples of suffering which were of course not the prerogative of the poor. School careers and further training were time and time again the main casualties, and the youthful disappointments of the elderly have often been sublimated today in children's and grandchildren's success in their careers. Sometimes the overwhelming disaster of both parents dying left children homeless. Sixty years ago when this happened in a street in Morley, the neighbours each took one of the five orphans and brought them up as their own, so that they all stayed in the same street. 'It wouldn't happen now.' [2]

Mothers besides cleaning, washing and baking managed the money and mostly kept discipline. They were the recipients of wages, the dispensers of pocket money ($1d.$ or $\frac{1}{2}d.$ a week), and 'smacked and leathered us'. 'Mrs Wilkinson, of Armley, had three sons, a daughter and her husband all working. They came in and put their wages on the table. She had a jar and they had to put $2s.$ $6d.$ in for saving. She was very strict and wouldn't let her sons marry until they were about thirty.' On the other hand some managed less well. One woman with three or four grown-up sons all working went every Monday morning with a bundle of clothes to pawn and redeemed them every Friday.

'All women, your mothers and grandmothers, looked old. I can't remember many without shawls fifty years ago. We respected age and feared the law. If a lady come on a tram we were made to get up, and if a bobby come, we run. We did the same as these lads do, pulled trees down, pinched apples, and *chumped* for bonfires but we were frightened of the law. I won a scholarship when I was ten, but was not allowed to go to High School, because mi mother couldn't afford it. You'd to provide a uniform, which was only a blazer and a cap and $7s.$ $6d.$ for your books. She wanted me to work when I was fourteen. So when you left school, you'd no chance to get in anywhere. I was always a good figure man and school came easy. Father was a checker in the railway goods yard and liked a drink.'

'Usually the married women didn't work except by taking in washing. When I was about ten my mother started earning a little bit of money, and we moved to a bigger house. Mi mother was terrible for moving—always Armley way. She used to sing in clubs and pubs, and earned $10s.$ to $15s.$ a night. She took the *News of the World* because it printed popular songs, and she went to Woolworths for a $6d.$

[1] Mrs E. Nolan, Leeds.
[2] Miss C. E. Hepworth Morley.

record, pasted the words on brown paper and learnt them. There was a residential pianist and the customers joined in the choruses. [At the bottom of Call Lane, Leeds, was a pub called the George, kept by Mrs Simpson, where all the good vocalists of Leeds used to practise.]

'My mother always lit the oven on a Sunday night. I used to go for a pennyworth of gunpowder. Dad put this in its little paper bag, with the *News of the World* packed round it, and stuffed it right well under the oven. We all got behind the couch while he lit it. A terrific bang went off. Then mother lit the fire, and the heat was drawn under the oven.

'Even if you were poor nobody liked "Boots for the Bairns" because there were two big holes in the top and people knew where they were from. Free school meals were the same. Nobody wanted to go. Up to the age of eleven or twelve you never had a toothbrush, only a bit of rag used sometimes with soap or Sutton's Salt. Everybody was wearing cast-offs. The only time you were decent were once a year when everybody, choose how, however poor they were always had something new for Whit Sunday. If you'd nowt new, you stopped in. My father had a free pass on the railway, and we used to go for a day to Cleethorpes.

'As you got older, you had walks like up to the park looking for girls, and when you got one you walked them round. Before proposing you always asked your father, and you bought a cheap ring for 13*s*. or so. You'd to do your courting outside. Your mother couldn't afford to feed anyone extra for tea, and it was always could she manage the tea for a wedding. There were no houses and if there were, you couldn't afford the rent. Times were hard, but you were happy. There was always some fun.

'In Grannie's days they couldn't afford insurance, but I've two policies now mi mother took out when I was born for funeral expenses. I still pay it. Mi mother lived to be eighty and still sang to the last. She left sixty quid and a note which said, "This is to put me away nice."' [1]

Deaths cast gloom over the whole street. All blinds and curtains were drawn and children had to whisper until the funeral was over. Paying for this was not easy. Even in the early 1960s when a mentally defective daughter, one of a family of thirteen, had died in hospital, the father, who had worked as long as he could, drew £15 from the Rechabites. But it didn't cover the ham tea, two cars and the undertaker's fees, which the mother had arranged, costing £35, and expecting help from social security she waited indoors for four months until her plight was discovered.

The housing of the corpse, too, posed a severe problem. 'I [Mrs C. Greaves,

[1] Mr H. Bradford, Armley.

Halifax] was ten years old in 1912 when my mother died. We had only two bed-rooms and the body was laid out on the bed in the best bedroom in snow-white sheets and a handkerchief put corner ways over the face. We had to pass through every night to go to bed—five of us in one room for a week. Next day the visitors began to arrive and I was sent up with them to "view the body", lifting the hand-kerchief for them to gaze on the face quite a while. This went on for five days. On the funeral day relatives and friends wore deep mourning, but I being a child was allowed a white dress with a broad black crêpe armband, black hat, shoes, and gloves and coat. One hymn was sung: "Peace, perfect peace". We had a terrible week.'

At the present day whole districts of cities and towns have been demolished, and high-rise flats built. Two comments show the dichotomy of opinions. 'In 1974 I went back to look at the old streets. I got lost. They have all been pulled down and not before time.' 'When t'old square went summot else went wi' it that all t' posh tahn centres in t'world can't fetch back.'

10 Communities

IN the period under review local life was circumscribed. Cities were and are up to a point a series of villages, and towns a string of hamlets with their own identities. Towns with populations of 10,000 and even more are still referred to as villages. You were either a Top Ender or a Bottom Ender at Pudsey, and in the Pennine valleys, where in any case nicknames were essential to distinguish the ramifications of the indigenous families, you might be a Cragger in Cragg Vale or a Slowiter or a Marsdener in the Colne valley. Everyone knew everybody in their own little orbit, and others were outsiders. At the beginning of this century in remote places such as Heptonstall they threw sods at strangers shouting '*Scutch* up rotten pockets', a demand for pennies; and signalled their arrival by knocking from house to house on the backs of fireplaces.

Apart from work life revolved round chapel, church and home. Each community supported its own schools, clubs, newspapers, shops, hawkers and village idiots, and spoke slightly differing local dialect readily distinguished by a keen ear. In spite of the worldwide connections of its industries, life for most people was provincial.

Nor is the country usually far off. Many mourn the loss of the green woods and fields of their childhood, destroyed and covered by housing estates. 'We used to pick bluebells in Middleton Woods [near Leeds].' But blackberries may still be gathered for instance in Shibden Dale, nor are the freedom and enjoyment of the moors diminished. 'I've never heard larks sing like those on Haworth moors.' On fine summer days generations of people have walked up to the Ladstone, a millstone grit outcrop on Norland Moor above Sowerby Bridge. 'My grandfather used to take me to play on the moor. He always brought a tiny miniature mug, and put it on the springs which bubbled up like boiling water. They lifted it up. It was a delight to me.' [1]

Developing from the seventeenth-century Independents, Nonconformity had taken root in the Pennine valleys, and in the nineteenth century in the great

[1] Mrs S. E. Grayshan, Norland.

building era of the 1860s and 1870s a few churches and many chapels of all de-
nominations rose on every hand.[1] Huge edifices with lofty classical porticos in
cities and towns and small plain structures perched on Pennine heights were built
by the better-off who gave their thousands and the many who contributed their
mites in single-minded endeavour. Some individuals even built and ran their own
chapels and gospel halls. Remote situations such as that of Pole Moor chapel above
the Colne valley were sometimes dictated by the refusal of landowners to give or
sell land elsewhere. The names Brunswick, Eastbrook, Ebenezer, Square,
Providence, Zion, Mount Tabor, Upper Independent are as familiar to the elderly
in the West Riding as are the names of pop-stars to the young. Many, too, were
simply known by the name of the family connected with them, such as Henry
Brooke's chapel, Gomersal, or Pawson's at Morley, or the Primitive Methodist
Rigg's chapel at Rawdon. The latter was built in 1866 by Thomas Rigg, a butcher,
who collected money from the townspeople, and who when it was opened had his
ten children baptized there.

Except in cities where a majority did not attend places of worship, almost all
social life and popular culture centred round them. Nor was it uncommon for
attendance to be obligatory for employment. Men and women gave lifelong
service, and held simple beliefs. 'My father was organist at Norland for thirty-four
years morning and afternoon and only missed three times.' At Heptonstall Slack
Baptist church one old man prayed: 'We thank Thee, O Lord, that in heaven we
shall have crowns that need no fettling.' It is fashionable now to regard this great
religious climax as a panacea for then current social evils, yet it bred generations of
people of sterling worth and transparent honesty.

Famous preachers and ministers drew packed congregations, for example
Bertram Smith and Francis Wrigley, who in 1891, coming straight from college,
stayed until 1928 in a dual pastorate at Salem chapel (Congregational), Hunslet
Lane, Leeds, a chapel then deprived of its supporters by the exodus to the suburbs.
Amongst many innovations they started Men's Brotherhood meetings attended by
well over 1,000 men on Sunday afternoons, and At Homes for women whose
children were looked after whilst they enjoyed talk, music and a cup of tea. Here,
hymns sung in the streets on Sunday afternoons were accompanied by exhorta-
tions to 'Come to the chapel, dear brother and sister'.

Regular meetings filled every night and often afternoons: choir practice,
Christian Endeavour, Band of Hope, Bible Study, At Homes, sewing meetings for

---

[1] See for example, *Memorabilia in the History of Lydgate Chapel*, 1945; Upper Independent Church,
Heckmondwike, Historical Sketch, 1674–1924; *The Heptonstall Octagon*, 1764–1964; H. W.
Harwood, *History of Methodism in Midgley*, 1933.

bazaars, Girls' Friendly Societies, Young Men's Improvement classes. Less frequent events—anniversaries, socials and bazaars—involved special efforts. Bazaars were sometimes gargantuan affairs lasting three days, perhaps called the Egyptian, Sunrise or the Blue Bird, culminating in lavish teas and raising thousands of pounds. In many cases cricket, tennis, billiards and football clubs were church and chapel organizations, and provided venues at which young people often met their future husbands or wives.

Eagerly anticipated, especially by music-lovers, were the concerts and performances of oratorios in chapels and churches. 'After long hours at work we used to get washed and dressed and go to rehearsals, always arranged on moonlight nights.' Singers, instrumentalists, choir masters, organists, all were recruited locally. Famous soloists, also native—Mrs Sunderland, Walter Widdop, Norman Allin, Edna Thornton, for example—and an augmented choir performed *Judas Maccabeus*, *Elijah*, Haydn's *Creation*, and above all *Messiah*, often with readings interspersed between the choruses. 'I was a violinist in the King Cross Methodist Church orchestra for twenty years. At Christmas people came for miles and were sitting on the pulpit steps and up the staircases.'[1] Who can now conceive of the communal enjoyment, the pitch of excitement, the euphoria of these occasions, perhaps still experienced but more sedately at the Christmas performances of *Messiah* given in town halls by the great choirs.

Sunday schools, important on any count for their early role in education, filled a large part of Sundays. 'I went before I was ten. We started about 9.30 a.m. and had to say our collects, then we went to church. We had three marks for that, two for going in the afternoon and one for good conduct. Then I started teaching, taking a class alternate Sundays.'[2] 'At St Chad's, Hunslet, we used to go to Penny Romps in the autumn to raise funds for the Sunday school. We played singing games, "Bobby Bingo", "How Green the Grasses Grow", and "Mocking Bird" in which we sang loud and soft as a child searched for an object.'[3] 'We practised Whitsuntide hymns five or six weeks beforehand.'

Hymn practices heralded Whit Monday walks. 'Yes, Whit Monday, we looked for Whit Monday.' The first description of this annual event must surely be in the chapter entitled 'The School-Feast' in *Shirley*. These began early in the last century as treats to follow examinations then held in Sunday schools, and when they ceased after the foundation of Board schools, the walks continued as a reward for good

[1] Miss Pattie Smith, Halifax.

[2] Mrs I. Humphreys, Gomersal.

[3] Mrs A. Morrell, recalling Hunslet.

attendance and behaviour until superseded by coach trips.[1] In and near the Holme valley one or two walks still continue.

For the event printers prepared hymn sheets free of charge, dressmakers and tailors worked overtime making dresses and blue serge suits, farmers and coal merchants and others cleaned and decorated waggons and horses for the transport of children or pianos or harmoniums, and on the day Sunday school teachers assembled early to fill clothes baskets with long buns packed in paper bags. With local variations the programme followed the same pattern. A procession wound up and down and round streets and lanes, and stopped at pre-arranged points such as the town hall, big houses or those where someone was ill. At Gomersal 'My father was a Sunday school superintendent, so I always had to walk, trailing along feeling hot and uncomfortable.' Here, a small place but with several chapels, 'we never collided' as they did in *Shirley* with comical results.

The highlight was undoubtedly the tea, followed by sports and games. After the home-brewed ale era, tea or occasionally coffee 'laced with an egg dashed in at the last minute' or milk were provided together with buns, sometimes sandwiches, oranges and perhaps bags of nuts. In the Holme valley a bell was rung when it was time for the children to collect their buns, here called schoolcakes. At Hebden Bridge sweets were scutched, that is, thrown in the grass for children to scramble for. (In the 1860s scrambles for nuts were a customary treat at the ends of school terms.)

These rich tea-cake buns are well remembered all over and may still be bought here and there. A recipe used by the Dobsons, confectioners, of Elland for 'Whitsuntide Buns' made in 1884 gives: 24 lb. flour, 5 lb. butter, 5 lb. lard, 8 lb. sugar, 8 oz. salt, 20 eggs, 13 qts milk, 2 lb. yeast, 20 lb. currants, 5 lb. peel which made 180 10 oz. buns or 450 4 oz.

One Whit Monday at Drighlington Mrs M. A. Collins (b. 1878) remembers winning 3*d.* in a race at the sports, and on her way home she saw a pork pie in a shop window and bought it to give to her mother. But as she walked along, she thought, 'I'll try a bit, and then a bit and then a bit. My mother greeted me, "I reckon you've won t' race. What have you got?" I said, "3*d.* and I bought you a pie." "Where is it then?" I had to confess, but she only laughed.'

These Sunday school events burgeoned into the Jubilee Sings first held in the quadrangle of the Halifax Piece Hall on 14 September 1831, at the time of the

[1] Information from Mrs E. V. Chapman. Minute in 1818 from records of Birchcliffe Baptist Chapel, Hebden Bridge: 'On Whitmonday the children shall be examined in Reading the Scriptures, writing, and the Catechism, for a period not exceeding two hours, after which they shall be turned loose in Murgatroyd's field and given buns and milk with ale for the teachers.'

jubilee celebrations for Robert Raikes, the founder of Sunday schools. Tens of thousands of people flocked there to hear local choirs and bands led by well-known conductors rendering popular hymns, the 'Hallelujah Chorus' and other items. In all fourteen were held in the last century, that in May 1890 was attended by 29,897 people. A few other Sings followed up to the Second World War.

People speak with zest of childhood games and amusements. So little depended on money: pins, buttons, stones, bits of pot formed a ready currency if any were needed. Infrequent horse traffic menaced no one. 'The street was our play-ground', and the flagged pavements provided plenty of scope. Children *tilluped* (a hop then a stride) lightheartedly along them, or went 'hop a dock' with one foot on and one in the gutter. Chalk marks for hopscotch covered them, and children cried 'In a nick, out of the nick', as they sped along avoiding the cracks. On hot summer days globules of tar exuded between the stone setts of the roads, and when covered with fine dust and rolled into small balls they made temporary playthings.

In winter boys warmed their fingers on home-made hand-warmers, old cocoa tins with holes pierced with a nail at either end, filled at Hunslet with oily waste begged from railway engine drivers, or at Gomersal with cotton-band, round woven band used on spinning machines, which like the waste smouldered when lit. The cotton-band, called slow- or wheely-band, was wrapped in paper by youths to make foul tasting cigarettes, and a red-hot end of it was an essential accessory to November the Fifth celebrations for lighting fireworks.

At Shrovetide whips and tops, shuttlecocks and battledores, and marbles appeared everywhere. Peg and whip tops, called giant and monkey in Hunslet, could be whipped and bounced all over up and down the pavements. At Gomersal 'We drew circles with coloured chalks on them, so that when they spun round it was a lovely blur of colour'. For shuttlecock and battledore the girls at Hepton-stall, for this was a girls' game, started with wooden *braids* (bats), advanced to drum braids made of vellum, and later 'if we got a racquet wi' string on, it were wonderful'.

Taws (marbles) take precedence over all street games, and although mostly for boys, they were played by girls. Different versions abound: 'Knicks', 'Chivvy up', 'Three Oily', 'Bobby Longy' and others, and the actual marbles included plain glass ones from pop bottles, *stogs* made at local potteries, the large *dobbies* and beautiful coloured glass *alleys*. Pockets which mothers emptied at night bulged with them, or toffee tins or special home-made bags held them. A hole cut in an earth floor or a suitably broken flag made pitches. Allied to taws checkstones, called checks or checkers, was a girls' game, played with four or five checks (pot cubes) and a large marble or small ball. This consisted of picking up the checks

COAL AND CLAY

75. The Mortons (the potters) and others getting outcrop coal at Jagger Green, near Elland, during the 1921 coal strike. The seam was 2 feet thick below 2 feet of clay. Robert Morton on the left and Walker Morton, second from right, were throwers in the pottery. Albert Morton on the right was in charge (1921).

76. Mr L. Boothman making a Bradford Windguard chimney-pot at the works of W. T. Knowles, Elland.

77. The pit head at Walterclough Colliery, near Brighouse, worked by Joseph Brooke and Sons. The colliery was 100 yards deep, and fireclay and some coal were mined. The clay was ground and sieved to make bricks (1906).

COAL

78. During the coal strike of 1912 women look for combustible material on a dump left by an old chemical works or an industrial process at Cowrakes Lane, Lindley, near Huddersfield.

79. A collier getting coal with a pick at Eastwood Colliery, Nottinghamshire (1912).

CITY AND TOWN

80. Raising the bell 'Big Matthew William' (named after the then mayor of Bradford, Matthew William Thompson) for the town hall clock at Bradford. The bell, weighing 4½ tons, is the hour bell of a peal of thirteen bells forming the carillon (1873).

81. North Bridge, Halifax, soon after midday. The bookseller and printers on the left was also a Post Office. Across the road on the right was the Grand Theatre (1903).

STREETS AND INTERIORS

82. Main Street, Haworth. Groups of men and children probably waiting for the procession on the occasion of the Co-operative Society Gala held in June (c. 1903).

85. (Right) The interior of a typical working-class home of the early 1900s. The house in Hanover Street, Boothroyd Lane, Dewsbury, was back-to-back, one up and one down, and with an attic. Mrs Annie Eleanor Pickles sits crocheting and was photographed by her husband, a miner.

83. Women at the well, Heptonstall. In common with other places all water had to be fetched from wells (1890s).

86. (Right) The interior of a middle-class home. The drawing-room of High-cliffe, Eccleshill, a house built by Christopher Pratt, the founder of the firm of cabinet-makers and house furnishers of Bradford in the 1860s. The house had sliding doors opening up two rooms, a form of central heating and a bath with water laid on, features unusual in those days (1890s).

84. Bell Street, Leeds (c. 1901).

CHAPELS

87. West Lane (now Trinity) Methodist Church, Gomersal, decorated for the harvest festival, built by Edward Brooke in 1827. The hothouse plants are mostly from the conservatory at West House, the Brookes' family home (1890).

88. The Upper Independent Church, Heckmondwike (Congregational), built in 1890, architect Arthur A. Scott, Heckmondwike. It cost £10,976 8s. 11d., and followed other chapels built since the first in 1674.

89. All Souls Church, Haley Hill, Akroydon, Halifax, designed by Sir G. Gilbert Scott, built 1856–1859. The statue is of Sir Edward Akroyd.

SCHOOL FEASTS

90. Whit Monday walk at Heptonstall. The children carry flags, a custom later abandoned and replaced by men carrying a banner (1890s).

91. Sunday School Feast of Hinchliffe Mill Wesleyan chapel in the Holme valley, or a united sing with Hinchliffe Mill chapel, Holmbridge Church of England and Hall's School, Holmbridge, held about 1900.

STREET PERSONALITIES

92. (*Above left*) *John Mort, known as Johnny Lonkey, scissor grinder and umbrella repairer, who lived at Northgate, Heckmondwike. He performed many feats of endurance, for instance walking 1,000 miles treadling his grinding machine in 1,000 consecutive hours (c. 1880).*

93. (*Above right*) *Seller of hot peas in Westgate, Keighley. One such Keighley vendor who had a wooden leg was said to stir his peas with it (1890s).*

94. (*Below left*) *John Christopher Kennedy of Bramley delivered 5,000 copies of the (Bramley) 'Weekly Advertiser' every week in two days. He never missed from 1916 to 1940.*

95. (*Below right*) *Luigi Tomasso at Bowman Lane, Leeds, with one of the barrel organs which he made from start to finish. In the 1920s these were hired out at 2s. a day (1930s).*

whilst the ball was thrown up or bounced and caught with the other hand. Jacks or Five Stones played with small stones caught in some versions on the back of the hand was comparable.

The ringing sound of *bowls* (hoops) being propelled along the pavements echoes yet in the ears of the elderly. In the evening boys raced with iron hoops, guided by a *shirl* (an iron stick with a hook on the end), for miles across towns and cities. But girls, unless they borrowed from brothers, had wooden ones laboriously bowled along with a wooden stick, and felt this piece of sex discrimination keenly. Variations of skipping games, mostly but not necessarily for girls, became the craze in high summer. Duck Racing involved two girls who, perhaps living on either side of a street, each stood in their gateways winding the rope. A dozen or more girls and boys, even young women, dived in turn into the rope and skipped first once, then twice, and upwards to thirty or more. If you missed you were out. Often children skipped in bare feet to save their shoes.

'We played Diabolo, pillar box jumping, gas lamp swinging, stilt walking, train spotting, cricket with a home-made bat, and hide and seek on dark winter nights.' The latter played with a tin can in a chalked circle was variously called 'Tin Can Hiddy' (Shipley), 'Squat Can' (Batley), 'Kick Can' (Oakworth), and 'Kick Can and Hook it' (Halifax). Or children hid in all the best hiding-places like the yards where the dustbins stood near the outside toilets crying 'Relievo! Relievo!'. Or at Heptonstall the girls played a kind of 'Follow my Leader' round and round the village singing as they went, 'Through the long lobby we go, we go'. 'Buck Buck' or 'Ships', a wall game, 'Statues', pize-ball, similar to rounders, kite flying, and games with cigarette or football cards all filled leisure hours.[1]

Indoor round games included the well known 'Here we come Looby Loo', 'The trees are all covered', 'King William was King George's son', 'Poor Mary sits a-weeping', and many others. Less common are 'The big ship sails on the alley alley O', and a rhyme from Gomersal for a 'Drop the Handkerchief' game,

> I have a pigeon in my pocket
> If I haven't lost it
> Peeps in peeps out
> Peeps through the dish-clout.

At Rawdon they played a kissing game 'Here come three jolly jolly sailor boys/ Who've just returned to shore', for which the boys stood in a circle surrounding girls sitting on chairs. Three boys with handkerchiefs tossed over their shoulders,

[1] See for comparative descriptions of 'Tin Can Hiddy', 'Statues', 'Buck Buck', 'Drop the Handkerchief', etc. Iona and Peter Opie, *Children's Games in Street and Playground*, 1969.

walked round singing until they knelt on the handkerchiefs in front of the girls of their choice and kissed. They then linked arms. The girls proceeded to do the same and so on until all having chosen partners they paraded round the room.

A favourite forfeits game at Morley and in the Spen valley went:

> Here I come as stiff as a stump,
> Selling mi blacking a penny a lump.
> You must neither laugh nor cry
> But say 'I will'.

Miming an old woman leaning on a stick, the person in the centre of a ring addressed a catch question to a boy or girl sitting round, and if not answered adequately he or she had to take their place. Girls made a simple peepshow and recited 'Pin-a-sight, a sat a-sight, a pin to look in', or stuck cut-out pictures in a book and charged a pin a prick. If you pricked a picture it was yours.

For little children, sitting on a parent's knee, fathers used to recite:

> Hob shoe fellow fine
> Will you shoe this lad/lass of mine?
> Yes, sir, that I can
> As well as any other man
> This shoe's well shod, shod, shod.

On the last line the parent patted the shoe sole.

In the congested streets of cities and towns, hawkers sold their wares—'Long strong pins a penny' called a blind woman in Ivegate, Bradford. Most followed their particular rounds often on specific days. Moses Harrison sold 'wet yist' and skim milk on baking days round Thornton, near Bradford, and at Heptonstall William Hey brought round hardware—donkey stone, yellow stones, soap, block salt, pots and pans. The oatcake baker called once a week. They mostly came on foot, sometimes with a donkey or horse and cart. 'Grey peas all hot' were carried in a heated oval bucket or Pay Lionel at Gomersal brought them in a hand-cart. Dispensed with a mug, these were brown or pigeon peas eaten with vinegar. There were Pot Joe at Slaithwaite, Pie Sammy and Pie Tom at Hebden Bridge and Bradford. Pie and peas, this time dried green peas, was and still is a cheap satisfying dish (*see plate* 93). Up to 1914 good quality coal, sold at 9*d*. a cwt, was hawked and weighed on scales hanging at the back of the cart. Best coal rose from 11*s*. 4*d*. a ton in 1870 to 47*s*. in 1939.

At Heptonstall, Blacking Ab sold two pennyworth of blacking in a bit of paper. 'You put it in water and brushed it on boots and clogs.' In the Spen valley and elsewhere the old nettle woman came in the early spring with baskets of young nettles, bought for making beer, and porridge, called nettle cole, made with oatmeal. The hop ale man carted round brown stone bottles holding half a gallon of ale, made by one of the several botanical brewers. 'When the bottles were empty we used them as hot water bottles.' At Keighley railway station Freddie Gramophone played a tinny gramophone and held out a cap, and there were Joe Pumpwater and Sally Matchbox. Dancing bears with their attendants, organ grinders with monkeys, and German bands every now and again paraded the streets. In the 1920s in the spring in Briggate, Leeds, boxes and boxes of mimosa were sold at 3d. or 4d. a bunch. Gypsies and potters selling pegs and artificial chrysanthemums were occasional visitants to houses, as were elderly women or old soldiers after the First World War hawking bootlaces, elastic and reels of cotton from trays covered with black oilcloth.

More pathetic were the characters who were daily pottering round the streets. Many at Halifax remember Bull Pratt, a very strong man who went about barefoot, never worked, and who although harmless alarmed people, and also Grunter who grunted and Tabby Oggie who picked up cigarette tabs. At Morley they had Silly Edith and Silly Clifford, of whom the latter always dangled a piece of string, and at Gomersal Edwin Twe Twa and Little Jinny, who carried a doll dressed as a baby round the village.

The rag-and-bone man, the tatters, found fruitful pickings in the whole area, and still a fairly familiar sight, was important as a collector of rags for the shoddy trade. The experiences of one man, Mr Fred Bloomfield, now of Churwell, who was born at Diss in Norfolk, illustrate the life. Hearing that there was better pay in the north, he had come as a boy to live with an uncle in Morley, and eventually started with a horse and a flat cart collecting rags, bones, jam and pickle jars and scrap metal. He bought clippings from dressmakers, remnants from tailors, rags from housewives, and selling them to rag merchants at Batley at 1 cwt. for £1, could live on that for a week. At Christmas time when the women were making rugs from clips the supply dropped off. Since those days man-made fibres have confused the trade, and he sells four or five tons of rags for flocking, cloth, and cleaning rags (wipers) now important. Bones, often mixed up in the household rag bag, were sold at 3s. a cwt. Sometimes people concealed heavy weights such as cog wheels amongst the rags.

Scrap metal—pewter teapots, brass and copper kettles, brass candlesticks and fire-irons—were bought from midden and dustbin men, and he smashed up grandfather clocks for firewood and sold the faces as brass. Jam jars, wine bottles, pickle jars and broken glass, all could be sold at a profit to the respective factories or merchants. Sometimes he unwittingly bought coats with money or betting slips in the pockets, and people came running demanding them back. Fred Bloomfield has only had three ponies in a lifetime, and regrets the old days. 'I wish I could have one Friday, just one Friday before the war. . . . All rag men are not rogues.'

Lastly, what of the speech of these people? An easy answer would be broad, but it also has that 'comforting and coaxing inflection peculiar to Yorkshire folk'. When dialect faded, word-conscious families, who failed to find equally expressive words in current English, used: *tew* (to struggle), *thoil* (cannot bear), *moithered* (confused), *brussen* (bursting with self-importance), *nesh* (delicate), *peff* (a little cough), *chuff* (pleased with oneself) *minnin '-on* (a snack between meals), *frummety-sweat* (a state of trepidation or excitement), *soot wisel* (hanging spider's thread with soot on the end). They savoured phrases like 'Tha talks and says nowt' or 'I'm hearing through a foxglove' (muffled sound), or, said of a mean person, 'If she had a mouth full of gumboils she wouldn't give me one'.

One word, *'oile* (hole), perhaps epitomizes it all. There were and are face 'oiles (nostrils), snap 'oile (eating place), carring 'oile (place where men squatted gossiping on their haunches), best 'oile (sitting-room), Morley 'Oile (place-name), chip 'oile (fish-and-chip shop), a nice bit o' honeycomb (tripe) wi' vinegar i' every 'oile. 'Oiles describe all parts of a mill from scouring 'oile to tentering 'oile. A constituent visiting London in the last century managed to find his M.P. and, having been shown round the House of Commons, asked if he could see t' other 'oile.

11 Individuals

THE chronic lack of ready money for so many people was exacerbated by coal strikes and the desperate slump of the early 1920s which was worse in effect than that of the 1930s. During a coal strike 'We would meet during the day and arrange to go scratting. We went with barrows or sacks up to Middleton pit or tip-hills and dug into the slag and got out bits of coal. Scores of people would go in gangs. "Let's go scratting", they'd say' (*see plate* 78).[1]

'I started as a teacher in 1926, right in the middle of the General Strike, at Rye Hill, a colliery area, with huge classes of sixty pupils. The children, whose parents raised money for them by band playing and other means, had meals at school. Kippers and bacon and egg for breakfast was reduced as money became short to long buns and margarine.'[2]

'I was born in 1902 one of a family of thirteen. We lived in a house with a stone floor, one room downstairs, and one bedroom and a boxroom. We slept six in a bed. I always wore clogs; the only time I had boots was when I joined the army. In the slump of the 1920s I'd been out of work for a long time and was at my wits' end, for we were so very poor. On my daily travels looking for a job, I came across a lot of men standing by a wall outside an engineering works, and a man walking along was picking men out for jobs. I was only small, 5 feet 1 inch, so I found two bricks and stood on them at the back with the other men in front of me. Up came the works man and he says, "That big man behind. You can start in the morning." And from that day I was never out of a job until I was sixty-five. I still have one of my wonderful bricks, but I have had it gold-plated. In those days you were a millionaire if only you had a job.'[3]

'In 1922 my husband was out of work, and was told that the 19*s*. 4*d*. I was earning was enough to live on. After paying 6*s*. each week for rent it didn't leave anything for luxuries. We often dined on mashed turnips and dry bread with an

[1] Mr T. Sinclair.
[2] Mr C. Armitage, Batley.
[3] Mr Luke Crawshaw, Lightcliffe, Halifax.

occasional 1*d*. herring as a treat.'[1] 'In the 1920s I was wrapping 600 toffees by hand on piecework for 1½*d*. Your fingers bled, so you put alum on to harden them. When I was a girl my mother, a widow with no pension, got 7*s*. 6*d*. parish pay and earned about the same. She used to make a dinner for 2*d*. for five of us: a halfpenny worth of damaged potatoes, the same of savoury duck from the pork butcher's, with gravy if you took a basin, together with potatoes and water made a hash, which was followed by a halfpennyworth of bruised apples stewed.'[2] 'We had an old fitter [in Holbeck, Leeds] who had five or six sons who were sent down the street to get their suppers from other people's dustbins.'[3] At morning roll-calls schoolmasters looked out for children who might faint from lack of food, and 'many children had such poor foot-gear that they could not attend school in snowy weather'.[4]

'As a lad mi father used to go window tapping and all that sort of thing. They went up to Windy Top (near Thornton, Bradford) and in the middle house was a little old chap that lived by hissen. He were praying to the Lord to send him some bread. These lads listened for a bit and mi father ran home, got a loaf, wrapped it i' paper and tied it up wi' band, and they got on top of this little low cot and dropped it darn t'chimney. It made a din when it dropped on t'floor. He jumped up, oppened it out and "Praise the Lord! Praise the Lord!", he says, "I've gotten a loaf." He didn't know where it had come from.'

'My father was a quarryman and I'm seventh of a family of twelve. One week mi father told me he had to laike for fifteen week o' frost and got to t'bottom. "We went to bed," he said, "did me and yer mother. We hadn't a crust in t'house. We knelt at bedside and prayed, and at eight o'clock next morning when we got up, there were a horse and cart outside our door, and a chap brought a stone o' flour, a pund o' lard, sugar, tea, yeast, and ivverything we needed. After a fair while I picked it out mi brother had sent it." '[5]

In country districts poverty also struck the unfortunate. In the Holme valley 'We'd only a poor home, the walls were whitewashed, sand was on the floor, and we'd a long scrubbed table and a high-backed langsettle under the window. My father was once six weeks and never a stroke of work. I remember two or three of us sharing an egg plastered on a teacake, and we ate lumpy flour porridge with skim milk. My father came home drunk many a time. They'd nawt else to do. At

[1] Mrs S. Farnell, Halifax.
[2] Mrs D. Begley, Ovenden, Halifax.
[3] Mr H. S. Sykes, Leeds.
[4] Log-book, 23rd February 1923, St Paul's Church of England School, Manningham.
[5] Tape recording, May 1957, Institute of Dialect and Folk Studies, University of Leeds.

one time we owed a shop £20, and were taken to court and had to pay 1s. a week. As a lad [in the 1890s] I walked every Monday to Holmfirth court with a shilling.'[1]

Another story illustrates the problem of drink. In the Colne valley there were and are Wellhouse, Scarhouse, Ridings and Hoylehouse Cots, indistinguishable from ordinary houses. They are run by a secretary, a committee and a landlord, who formerly bought in barrels of beer. They had a coal fire and a bed upstairs for 'them as couldn't go home'. 'My father used to go on a Friday night and come back home on Monday mornings for his overalls.'[2]

Mr G. W. Atkinson of Morley recollects: 'Mi father was out of work, and he and my mother and three boys we'd lived on lard and bread for four days. I was nine. I heard mi mother weeping and saying to mi father, "We'll go and see our Walter tomorrow." Uncle Walter operated the first electric coal cutter, and in those days of twenty and twenty-six bob a week he earned £14 (probably paying about £4 to a mate). He was a millionaire. We set off for Castleford, some fourteen miles away, where he lived. My father borrowed 7d. which got us to Leeds on a tram, and from there pushing the younger ones in a little Tan Sad [make of push-chair] we walked to Oulton. A fellow came along with an old solid-tyred lorry and gave us a lift. He said to me, "Half a mile farther on, I shall slow down, don't make any mistake, shake hard because I shan't stop." Soon after I saw all these apples. Henry and me both jumped. We got thirty-four apples. My mother quite rightly said, "Two each and no more." Then we reached this old shop at Methley, and an old lady made us a pot of tea and gave us sandwiches with home-made potted meat in. My mother promised to come back to Methley to pay her, but the old lady said, "To see t' barns happy is my reward". And we walked from there to Castleford and got a wonderful meal with a tin of salmon at Uncle Walter's. I've eaten some expensive meals since, but none have tasted as good as that tin of salmon. He gave my mother £2 and sent us home by train which was terribly exciting.'

'In 1922 I worked in a bakery at Peel Street, Morley, making food for 100 impoverished children. Shepherd's pie was made of left-overs, corned beef, bits of tongue, ham, ham fat with plenty of potatoes, glossed over with fifty-six yolks of egg out of a tin at one go on top. We also took a huge container full of cocoa. When we went back to get the empties, one of the little tenpence halfpenny to t' shilling lads waited at the corner, and winter and summer ate all that was left of the shepherd's pie. Then we turned over the cocoa thing which was on wheels, and he lay on the floor and drank all that was left as I tipped it into his mouth.'

Children earned small sums in various ways: running errands, carrying and

[1] Tape recording lent by Mr Frank Burley, Mr W. Coldwell, Holme valley.
[2] Mr M. Taylor, Golcar.

minding babies, scrubbing shared lavatory seats, taking food to work, delivering newspapers on a paper round, always avoiding fights with other boys. Boys might buy bicycles out of their earnings. One girl at Sowerby Bridge, who was temporarily away from school, earned 5s. a week as a penny runner taking out telegrams for the Post Office. Favoured children took a mixture of oatmeal and sugar to school, so coveted by the hungry that it could be bartered say for a dozen taws.

On the other hand life on the farms, proceeding alongside and interrelated with industry, was less subject to fluctuating fortunes. In the Pennine valleys workers in the mills lived on smallholdings; manufacturers kept horses for transport and poultry for home consumption, and often owned farms as a hobby.

Many West Riding people living in towns look back on the idyllic days of childhood visiting farming relatives. Mrs Doris Rhodes used to go up to Crawstone Hall, near Elland, almost every weekend and every holiday. 'My grandfather went every day delivering milk and had a big cream round. How we loved haymaking time! When it was done we still had the fields to play in. We filled a milk can with blackberries, and took them to my auntie who made lovely pies. I used to sleep in a big bedroom. We used to take a candle up in a candlestick, and I can still remember the roses on the jug and bowl on the washstand. My other grandma lived alone on Norland Moor. When she was forty-two she was left a widow with eight sons to bring up. One was my father. They nearly all used to visit her on Sundays. I can see them now sat round her big fire. She was the most contented person you ever met.'

Farming on the Pennine hillsides resembled that in the rural Yorkshire dales; pasture and meadow rather than arable land predominated. It differed in that a larger population and a ready market was at hand to absorb dairy produce.

Mrs M. Murgatroyd lived as a child at Upper Hanroyd, near Midgley in the Calder valley. This was a farm of about thirty acres adjoining the moor and supporting some thirty cows and 100 hens, run by her father, Henry Fisher, with the help of an Irishman in hay-time and her tireless mother who helped to milk the cows, made 30 lb. of butter a week, cleaned, washed, cooked, sewed and knitted for a family of seven girls and a boy. The butter, made up into round pounds with a pattern of a sheaf of corn printed on it, together with eggs, was delivered to regular customers and sold at 2s. 6d. a lb. and 12d. a dozen respectively. 'We had a big vegetable garden with apple trees and gooseberries, raspberries, and blackcurrant bushes. We always killed two pigs for winter and made blood puddings and cured the hams.' In the spring dock pudding, fried in bacon fat, was a favourite dish eaten mostly at teatime, and pounds of bilberries gathered in the summer holidays were made into bilberry and apple jam. 'We were well fed.'

Clogs were polished every night ready for school next day. At one time five of the children, taking teacake sandwiches, went to Midgley school together, well over half an hour's walk. Chapel provided the chief entertainment. 'Eight from our house and twelve from a neighbour's attended Sunday school, more from what we call Midgley Heights than go there altogether now.'

The story of a farm dog comes from the Colne valley, told by Mrs G. E. Buckley of Delph. Her father, William Sharpe of Orchard Hey Farm, Marsden, used to buy stock from Carmarthen, and wherever he went so did his dog, Bowser. One day in 1921 returning home by rail, he found at Marsden station that the dog had been left on the train. He asked that a message be sent to the porter at Diggle, the next station, to put Bowser on the road facing Marsden, and as he had often driven cattle along it, he would find his way home. But the porter only put the dog on the platform, and he set off through Standedge tunnel. An express train coming through cut off his tail and damaged his rear legs, and workmen, finding and recognizing him, wrapped him up and took him home. He was nursed and nursed, and lived to be fifteen.

A ninety-five-year-old friend has a different story to tell. In the 1880s her father, earning 30s. a week, was the manager of a busy co-operative stores in Cragg Vale. The shop sold groceries, meat, crockery, drapery, corn, and employed a shoe-maker, a clogger with an assistant, and a dressmaker, for in those days eight cotton mills (formerly ten) flourished in the valley. The mills paid wages fortnightly, one group one week and the other the next, some on Wednesdays and some on Thursdays. On these nights her father and two or three assistants were occupied serving customers, who sat awaiting their turn on benches, until 11 p.m. The family lived at the back and above the store, and the child wearing a pinafore, shawl and clogs, went to Cragg Vale School.

'When I was ten, my father told me that I was appointed a monitor with a salary of 8s. 4d. a month. I was very excited.' Out of this her mother allowed her 3d. or 4d. a week, and she no longer wore clogs. Besides ability the reason for her appointment was that the other children were leaving to go as half-timers, and there was little for her to do. She was given homework and the teachers helped her, especially a newly appointed young headmaster who came at 8 a.m. and coached her with 'a respectable woman' present for an hour. 'Children really learnt then.' At fourteen she graduated as a pupil teacher earning 10s.

When she was eighteen her father had died. But her mother, determined that she should not go to the mill, encouraged her to take a Queen's Scholarship examination for the Stockwell Training College in south-west London. She passed number 816 out of 1,600, and set out on a first long journey for an interview. Lest she be overcharged she was warned to enquire the fare from King's Cross by hansom cab, and she returned to the station by horse bus, changing once and thus saving money. She was at college two years from 1898 to 1900, took London Matriculation, and could have taken a degree. But she had already cost her mother £100, 'all of which I paid back'. After training she taught at Hebden Bridge School, walking the three miles there and back daily, earning £70 a year. Fifteen years later when she left to be married, her testimonial stated, 'Never absent. Never late'.

Mrs L. Wardman (b. 1889), of Birkenshaw near Bradford, came of a family of four boys and three girls. 'We'd only three bedrooms, two girls slept in one, I slept in another, the boys in the third and my parents in a shut-up bed downstairs. Mother put up their meals in a red handkerchief tied on top, and I used to take two of 'em their dinners to Bottoms Mill twice a week and another of 'em their tea at Broadbent's Mill, Gomersal. When my mother fell ill I followed mi own folk and washed and baked for nine of us—4½ stone of bread and sixty teacakes, thirty currant and thirty plain. I answered an advertisement to sing at Tong Parish Church, twice on Sunday, morning and afternoon, and was paid 10s. a month. I enjoyed it. I always had a day off. I used to walk across the fields to mi uncle's at Cleckheaton and sing all t' way home. Men called out, "Good night lass"; and there was no fear. We were a lot happier then, and a lot freer. Life were different when neighbours helped each other. You don't get it now.'

'I had learnt to weave, and when I was twenty I returned to the mill. I went on after I were married and had 15s. a week on two narrow looms, and mi husband had 19s. 11d. Eggs were 1s. a dozen, mi milk were 1s., with a pint over on Sunday, rent was 2s. 3d. and rates 1s., and I paid 1s. to t'co-op for mi coal club. You could get a joint of meat for hef a crown. I could save 5s. to 6s. a week. My home cost me £44 for furniture, upstairs, downstairs, overmantel, and bed and fire-irons. It's all here barring that china cabinet. My husband had a rolling pin, a baking spittle, a baking board and summat else given him from Farnells [a saw-mill where he was employed]. Eventually he went to t' pit, but was off work wi' blood poisoning for thirty-two week. I never owed nobody nowt. You can't pay old debts wi' new money.'

Her husband became a lamplighter attending to gas lamps which from October to March were left on until 7 a.m. and the rest of the year put out at midnight. 'He had to put his head through a ladder and go round and wash 'em, and when he lit 'em and died 'em out his wage was 37s. 6d. a week.' She herself left weaving for charring and continued at this for forty-five years. 'I went to wash for some new people and was told to go to get mi dinner in the kitchen. I carved myself some meat, then saw a nice custard and ate that too.' But the family had company and had to say to their guests, 'We're sorry to tell you the washerwoman has eaten the custard'. She also took in three washings a week, and providing her own soap and using a charcoal iron she charged 2s. 6d. for washing 'and taking 'em back ready for t' drawer'. Her husband helped with putting the clothes through *nets* (clean waters). Some of her employers never forget her birthday and one or two take her for drives.

Now living comfortably but alone, she remarks that she has all her life given 10 per cent of her income to the chapel, and she looks philosophically back on the loss of one of her sons who was given a good education and had just passed his accountancy examinations when he was killed in the Second World War. 'I've had a long life, a hard life, but a happy life.'

Lastly, a romantic success story told us by Mrs V. Gaukrodger of Sowerby Bridge. 'My husband never played or signed on a day. I met him at work. As I was coming in at the entrance of the mill yard, he was filling the bunkers up with coal [for the boiler furnaces at Lock Hill Mills, Sowerby Bridge], and he used to wink at me. He wore a neb cap, and I used to think, "Oh heck, I wonder who he is". One Friday afternoon he brought me a bunch of green grapes on to my machine you know. I lived right up Norland and I thought no boy would want to walk me home all that way. Anyhow he came, and we were courting and saving up four and a half years. The first thing I had for my bottom drawer was some ebony for the dressing table. First I got the tray, then the brushes, then the candlesticks, and then the ringstand. I paid £48 for a bedroom suite. People used to say, "If you don't get a bedroom suite when you marry you'll never get one." Nobody was going to do me out of a bedroom suite.

'We got married in 1928, and lived on Pickwood Scar. I always used to look across as I came down at a hen pen on Sunny Bank, and after our little girl was three years old we heard that they were going to build thirty houses there. We put £5 down for one and watched it going up brick by brick. It was a middle house much warmer than an end one. Then we paid £50 and the house was ours. But the full price was £388, and we paid it off at £2 0s. 4d. a month. It took us fifteen years. We retired in 1966. John had forty-five years' work and I had forty-eight but out of that I had had eleven years off when the children were small.' They still live on Sunny Bank and since retirement they have been four times to visit relations in America.

12 Food

ALTHOUGH the regional dishes of the West Riding vary from district to district, from town to country and from class to class, a staple food was formerly oatmeal, eaten either as oatcake or porridge. By and large the same type of thin oatcake baked in the same way was made from the Saddleworth district adjoining Lancashire, northwards across the Pennines to the far boundaries of upper Wharfedale. 'The manufacturing parts of West Yorkshire', wrote Marshall in *Rural Economy* (1788), 'use principally oaten bread', and he adds that new oats making a good price were imported from the Vale of Pickering. Stiff porridge eaten twice a day was the diet in bad times, and up to about 1900 the chief breakfast food. The decline in the growing of oats locally began as early as 1800 when difficulty in ripening the crop seems to have been experienced.[1] Later, as the population increased oats were imported from Scotland, Ireland and elsewhere.

Oatcake was baked on three forms of bakestone—stone, iron and clay—of which the latter, a mudstone, quarried throughout the centuries in the Castleshaw valley near Delph in Saddleworth, is interesting for its antiquity.[2] To make the clay bakestones a huge block, euphemistically called a fly wing, was dislodged, immersed in the Hull Mill stream near the quarry, and the same day or within a day or two it was split with wedges into leaves half an inch to three-quarters of an inch thick. The under surface was chiselled and the upper surface scraped smooth (*see plate* 96). The bakestones, about 22 inches square, or made in sizes to fit specific ovens, were left in the stream, and after a few weeks stacked with the chiselled side inwards, and baked round a wood fire in an oblong pit in a small hut (*see plate* 97).

Crying 'Havercake bakst'ns' the maker hawked his wares in Yorkshire over the moors to the Colne valley and Calderdale. Two dozen formed a load, balanced on

[1] P. E. Razzell and R. W. Wainwright, *The Victorian Working Class, Selections from the Morning Chronicle*, 1849, 1973.

[2] Johannes Bakestoman appears under Quick (Saddleworth) in the West Riding Poll Tax, 1379, for which the returns were published by the Yorkshire Archaeological and Topographical Association in 1882.

either side of a horse or donkey or later carried by a horse and trap. They were sold by bargaining or barter, latterly at about 3s. 6d. each. For more than 100 years the Schofields of Grange, a hamlet above the quarry, were connected with the trade. It has been handed down that Tom Schofield, travelling with his wares during a cattle plague (rinderpest) in the 1860s, threw a sack over a *boskin* (partition) in the byre at the inn where he lodged and thus brought the disease back to Grange where some forty cattle were infected and died. Abraham Schofield, Ab o' Chit's, made the last about 1928.[1]

In the home the portable bakestones were placed over the fire for baking oat-cake. When ovens were introduced, in the Saddleworth district they were put in the bottom for baking oven bottom cakes, made of bread dough, here called 'mowfins', and were said to make them sweeter. Also, wrapped up in blankets, they served as bed-warmers. On the other hand Sally o' Ben's using a built-in bakestone is remembered baking oatcake in an outhouse at Crow Trees, Marsden, in the 1890s.[2]

In 1883 Easther wrote that 'Oatcake is seldom made by any but public bakers'[3] and already by about the middle of the last century Joseph Wright, ironfounder of Shipley, had invented a complete cast-iron bakestone, some of which had inscribed on the fronts in raised letters 'Evil be to him that evil thinks'. One, formerly at the Feathers' bakery at Haworth now at Cliffe Castle Museum, Keighley, was heated with coal, has two plates, one when in use hotter than the other, and measures 7 feet in length. Beginning by charging customers so much for baking a stone of meal, commercial oatcake bakers, usually small family concerns, started up in every town and village, and the occupation only completely ceased in the West Riding in 1968.

Basically the same method of making was employed as that in the home, except that in the bakery the batter was placed on and propelled by a tram, a mechanical roller on rails, fixed at one end of the bakestone (*see plate* 99). It was usual, too, to make muffins, *pikelets* (crumpets) and milk cakes for sale to shops or to hawk them with the oatcakes to regular customers. The flavour was all important, hence the demand for new oats which made the best.

[1] Information from Mrs A. Lawton and Mrs M. H. Gartside, Delph, Mr E. Schofield, Diggle. See also Ammon Wrigley, *Songs of a Moorland Parish*, 1912; E. Baines, *Directory and Gazetteer of the County of York*, 1822, Vol. 1. p. 270, gives 'Schofields and Co. Bakestone delf, near Delph.' A good example of a bakestone may be seen at the Saddleworth Museum, Uppermill.

[2] Mr Joe France, Marsden.

[3] A. Easther, *A Glossary of the Dialect of Almondbury and Huddersfield*, 1883, describes the process of making oatcake. See also Marie Hartley and Joan Ingilby, *Life and Tradition in the Yorkshire Dales*, 1969, and Miriam Lord, *The Yorkshire Havercake*, 1961.

As oatcake bakers are not listed as such in directories it is difficult to be precise as to numbers. There were said to be forty in Bradford. Like cloggers they are remembered by name in every locality, where they travelled on their rounds with the oatcakes in baskets, covered with white cloths, slung over each arm or balanced on their heads. Mr and Mrs L. Feather, the last bakers in Yorkshire, to whom we are indebted for information, retired in 1968 (*see plates* 98–102). Hird Lord (1860–1950), an early Christian Socialist, worked almost up to his death in his bakery at Worthington Street, off City Road, Bradford. He bought meal from Scotland, used milk for mixing to improve the flavour, and gave misshapen cakes away to poor children. At Highburton, near Huddersfield, five Oldroyd brothers ran an oatcake and bakery business combined with a smallholding from about 1920 to 1941. They kept three horses and carts for delivery to surrounding villages. When they retired, the recipe, in all cases always a secret, went too. When his niece asked for it, Alfred Oldroyd replied, 'Aye, it cost me a lot o' brass to learn that. I'm not telling thee for nowt.'

Asa Nicholson of Thornton, near Bradford, then a quarryman, took up baking after the rigours of the winter of 1898. He bought a second-hand iron bakestone with a tram for £2.10*s*., and learnt how to make oatcake from a baker in Mount Street, Halifax, who charged him £5 for the tuition plus ¼*d*. for every cake he spoilt. The ¼*d*. fine was not unreasonable, as throwing the batter from the tram by cranking a lever requires considerable practice. He soon bought a Galloway, a spring cart, two hawking baskets, and medium oatmeal from Ireland. In 1918 when his son, Mr J. C. Nicholson, joined him, they delivered far afield. Oatcake ceased to be made by them in 1939, but a bakery flourishes at Denholme Gate.

The cost of meal regulated the size of oatcakes so that comparisons of prices do not hold good. However, in 1814 they were sold at 1*d*. each, in the early part of the century at 4½*d*. a dozen or four for ½*d*., and in 1966 at 3½*d*. each. Innkeepers served them with stew as 'Stew and Hard'. They were linked with a traditional riddle: 'What is edged all round and not a stitch in it?' At Outlane Billy Breead Hawker's old horse, which had 'three pot legs and a wood un', was said to have a gait like 'hard breead running on a bakestone'.

Two practices shared in common by most classes were high tea, eaten about five o'clock and deriving its importance and timing from the return home at the end of the day of the workers of a family, and home-baking undertaken by the mother during the day, by the working wife at night after a day's work, or by servants in middle-class households. 'My mother thought they were sluts if they bought bread.' 'We never had anything out of a tin.' Thursday or Friday was baking day, followed the next day by cleaning-up operations.

In consequence flour was a much needed commodity. Every Friday morning Miss A. Jones, shopkeeper, at Delph End, Pudsey, used to weigh out forty stones of flour into stones, half stones, quarters and pounds for Yorkshire pudding-making. At the Akroydon Cash Stores, Halifax, Miss Pattie Smith, then a child, helped her mother weigh up three types of flour, Best Snowflake at 1s. 1d. a stone and two cheaper kinds, all milled at Raventhorpe Mill, near Felixkirk. People fetched flour in white cotton bags which they carried away in big blue or check handkerchiefs or sometimes balanced them on their heads.

In households where workers needed packed-up meals teacakes which were readily cut for sandwiches took pride of place. Some housewives to earn a little extra money made them for sale, and others were baking them all day with one or two loaves for week-end consumption. A delicacy for those who liked caraway were seed teacakes, which split and well buttered were warmed through in the oven and eaten for tea (Morley). 'My mother baked on Thursdays ten loaves and about twelve teacakes, a sweet cake of some kind, either madeira or currant, and always a thin cake which we ate with bacon for tea. The bread was stored in a big crock, glazed outside but not at the top' (Mirfield). At Thorpe, near Wakefield, Mrs G. M. Brears baked gingerbread almost every week throughout the year in a tin 12 by 9 by 2 inches. Here and there we have heard gingerbread called *moggy*. Parkin, a different form of ginger cake, was always in some homes cut with a fork, and baked for November the Fifth.

The thin cake—variously called thin, flat, new, oven or oven bottom cake— already referred to, was made in all households. At the end of the kneading of dough for bread, a piece was set aside, rolled out round and flat, a hole made in the centre, and baked in the bottom of the oven, turned after ten minutes with a baking spittle. They were then leant to cool against the doors of houses on well-scoured doorsteps to be ready for tea. 'You could look down the street and see them at nearly every door.' 'When new cakes were there kids congregated on the doorsteps. A place called Simpsons sold fish and chips, $\frac{1}{2}d$. for each, and children sat on the pavement edge or on the doorsteps eating this with new cake.' [1] The cakes, never cut, were riven into triangular pieces and split into two for buttering. Many took oven cakes to work for snap with the favourite 'mucky' fat spread inside. Or in the early years of the century delicious 'skull-draggers', a hot steak placed inside a small oven cake which soaked up the juices, could be bought in Leeds.[2]

[1] Mr G. W. Atkinson and Mr R. Dennis, Morley; Mrs E. Nolan, formerly of Holbeck, near Leeds; Mr T. Sinclair, Hunslet.
[2] John H. Wilkinson, *Leeds Dialect Glossary and Lore*, 1924.

Yorkshire pudding scarcely needs elaboration. Suffice to say that traditionally it was made not in small individual tins but in large ones and then cut up, and it was served with a thickened gravy as a separate course before the meat. Seasoned pudding, similarly baked in a large tin, and made of oatmeal, white bread-crumbs, onion, egg and herbs, was served before pork, duck or goose. In upper Calderdale suet cakes, a dough with currants or sultanas and sugar, were eaten warm for breakfast or after dinner 'to finish off with'. Fritters, resembling small oval thick pancakes with currants added, were eaten on Ash Wednesday.

Some foods had their origin in the country, where as seen in Chapter 11 farming families benefited from having their own produce. But formerly pigs were kept by many even in the slums. In upper Calderdale the tradition of making dock pudding, so called from the main ingredient, *Polygonum bistorta*, picked in the fields, continues. The similar Westmorland Easter pudding differs only in that barley meal is used instead of oatmeal, and in Littondale, off Wharfedale, the local name for the Bistort, 'pashdocken' with its reference to Easter, the time when it is picked, suggests that once the pudding was made there.

At Mytholmroyd, Midgley, Hebden Bridge, Heptonstall and thereabouts the young leaves are gathered in early spring. A recipe, which may vary from family to family, consists of 2 lb. fresh dock leaves, 2 large onions or 2 bunches of spring onions, a knob of butter, $\frac{1}{2}$ lb. nettles, a handful of oatmeal or more if required, salt and pepper. The onions are chopped small, the leaves well washed, the stalks removed, and all boiled with seasoning until tender. With oatmeal added the mixture is then boiled for some twenty minutes, strained and stored in a jar. Usually it is eaten for breakfast, fried with bacon, but many enjoy it at any meal.

A very different food is rhubarb, grown on the lowland farms within an eight-mile radius of Leeds, chiefly between Leeds and Wakefield, where 95 per cent of the forced rhubarb grown in Europe is produced. It is a strange concentration in a once beautiful countryside despoiled by man. The land, too, is man-made, for in the past thousands of tons of night soil from privies and middens, as well as sewage and shoddy waste, have enriched it. This and the once cheap coal near at hand to heat the forcing sheds to 50 to 60 degrees, and a clay soil cold in late October and November when the dormant roots are brought in from the fields, make ideal conditions for cultivation. Started 100 to 150 years ago, this has grown from small men, often colliers, and their families planting and later splitting a few roots in back gardens and allotments, building a shed for forcing, acquiring land and building more sheds, to the 110 growers of the present day, half the number of fifty years ago, combining with rhubarb the growing of sprouts, peas and broccoli to give a rotation of crops.

A thousand roots produce thirty-seven cwt of rhubarb, and in the dark sheds—dark to preserve the cerise colour of the sticks—it grows audibly, to those attuned to hear it, at the rate of an inch a day. W. G. Smith & Sons of Thorpe Lane Farm, near Wakefield, grow ninety tons a year and send it to London, South Wales, the Midlands, Glasgow and Edinburgh; and the women of the family, competing with others, formerly made jam and rhubarb pies for local shows. The Asquiths, based on Brandycarr Farm, Kirkhamgate, near Wakefield, have seven farms, and eleven sheds 200 feet long and 10 feet high to the ridge, each holding 5,500 roots, which each are groomed to produce six *fangs* (sticks).[1] Several days old forced rhubarb compares unfavourably with that freshly picked obtainable in Yorkshire. Soaked in sugar overnight, gently stewed, and eaten with a runny egg custard, it is a delicious Yorkshire sweet.

Either cooked or uncooked onions were relished. Raw onion sliced up in vinegar, with if available a little cucumber on top, was an accompaniment to cold meat, and offered in the past at fairs with roast beef sandwiches. At Delph oven cake was 'best eaten with raw onion'. Onion and potato pasty, with the filling sliced up raw between the pastry, then baked, made a tasty winter's tea. At one time in Methodist circles at Sowerby Bridge it was tantamount to a declaration if a boy bought a girl a present of onion pasty.

Tripe, sheep's heads, frozen Australian rabbits without heads and Egyptian eggs at twenty-four for 1s. provided cheap meals. Both honeycomb and seam tripe were popular—the former in a thick white sauce for high tea. 'I used to go night after night for my father's supper, and was told to say, "A quarter of thick seam for someone who's poorly." He never had a day's illness in his life.' Because easily digested, tripe was in fact given to invalids, as were *pobbies*, a bed-time food for both children and adults, made from cubes of white bread covered with boiling milk, with a dab of butter and seasoning added. Brown peas, as already described, were sold by hawkers and made a satisfying dinner boiled with a ham shank. Cockles and mussels, more of a treat, were sold by greengrocers at so much a pint, and boiled in large iron pans ready for supper. 'In the 1890s my father used to have a dozen oysters, brown bread and butter, and a pint of stout for 1s.'

Fish and chip shops, fish 'oiles, abounded and still do, although diminished in numbers. At Hebden Bridge twelve are remembered (now three), and at Queensbury six (now four). In some streets there might be three in 100 yards. Many fish friers started in wooden huts, of which a few still function. Prices varied according to the quality of the fish. At Hebden Bridge fifty years ago they were 2d. for fish,

[1] Information from Mr N. Asquith. 5,000 tons of forced rhubarb was produced in 1970, see R. A. Giles, *Forced Rhubarb in the West Riding of Yorkshire*, University of Leeds, 1970.

1*d*. for chips with perhaps a few scraps on top for nothing, 1*d*. for a 'bit' (a child's portion), 1*d*. for a steak or collop (three or four slices of raw potato fried in batter), and 1*d*. for cakes or sandwiches (little pieces of fish cooked between a potato cut in half). Other recollections give 1*d*. for fish and ½*d*. for chips. Formerly too brown peas were on sale with them in canisters standing on gas rings, and were taken away in pint or quart pots. 'If you were really poor you could just order chips with pea gravy.' Fish friers cooked special batches of fish and chips for husbands returning home late to take as peace offerings to their wives.

Although fish and chips were cheap, they cost 2*s*. for a family of eight—'a lot of money'. 'When father got his money on a Friday we all got fish and chips for Saturday dinner.' 'For mill orders we used to pack them in cartons, with salt in a paper and vinegar in a pop bottle. Those were the days. They were fish and chips then.' Harry Ramsden led the move away from the solely take-away shops, when he abandoned his wooden hut for a large restaurant started in 1931 at White Cross, Guiseley. Now open six days a week, twelve hours a day, and run by a staff of between 150 and 160, it is nationally, even internationally, famous.

The grocers, greengrocers, butchers, pork butchers, confectioners and sweet shops, individual to each town and with individuals as proprietors, are remembered vividly. Grocers were noted for their tea, cheeses, hams and bacon, and now banished to the suburbs, were a feature of the centres of towns. At Ellins, grocers, down by the Kirkgate market, Leeds, people were allowed to sample the huge mounds of butter and huge cheeses on show all round the shop by nipping a bit out with a 6*d*. Maypole shops, now gone, are remembered for their sawdust on the floor, and a continuous sound of Scotch hands slapping pounds of butter into shape. Corner shops whose proprietors knew the characters and finances of their customers gave 'tick', as did Thrift Stores in Leeds up to Friday. Greengrocers sold slices of raw coconut, liquorice root to chew, locusts (the sweet pods of the carob tree) and pomegranates in the autumn.

Pie shops were well known such as Gosnay's in Wakefield and Roberts' with its outsize imitation steaming meat pie in the shop window in Godwin Street, Bradford. 'When we were children we used to go with my father to Bradford market. It was a red letter day. We ate pie and peas, or *trunnel* pie with peas on top, stood up at a stall. You helped yourself to mint sauce. My father used to have warm black pudding, and there was a big dish of mustard to put on it.' Trunnel pie, eaten hot, had boiled chopped-up tripe as a filling.[1]

On the other hand there were the pork butchers. 'We always had brawn and a big stand pie for Christmas from Etheringtons at Birstall.' 'As a boy I reckoned to

[1] Mrs A. Marlow, Gildersome.

get ½*d.* change out of a tanner—5 Woodbines for 2*d.*, a gill of beer for 2*d.*, and a pork pie for 1½*d.*' Craps, the rendered down pieces of fat from pig *leaf* (inner layer of fat), eaten with mustard sauce, made occasional teas, and slices of hot pork in gravy, fetched in basins, were bought for dinners. About the middle of the last century German pork butchers settled in many towns, for instance the Zieglers, Gebherds and Hoffmans at Wakefield. F. M. Keitel, who came to Colne in 1879 as a boy of sixteen, when he married bought a shop in Rothwell, with a slaughter-house and a building for cooking in the yard behind. In the First World War they encountered hostility; some left, and others anglicized their names.

Confectioners, too, ran special lines, such as Parrots of Batley, who advertised malt bread and made penny parkins. Gregson's ecclescakes and Miss Smith's cream cakes at Dewsbury were 'out of this world'. Collinsons at Halifax was founded in 1834 as a tea and coffee business by Thomas Collinson, a Westmorland Quaker. It is related that he used to ask an assistant to turn off the coffee grinder, so that he could hear the German bands in the street. His sons opened cafés in Leeds, Halifax and Huddersfield, and his grandson, Edward, started Beech's chocolates. The cafés have now closed and the business has been taken over.[1] Woods, confectioners, with a café above the shop, in Commercial Street, Leeds, and presided over by Mrs Wood, was known far and wide for sausages and first-class confectionery, whilst the foreign confectioners who came to Bradford at the end of the last century made 'wonderful cream cakes'. Bought cakes were in fact a treat.

Hundreds of sweet shops flourished in this sweet-loving county, and local sweet factories, often begun on a small scale in houses, were numerous. The Smiths in their shop at Akroydon always sold boiled sweets especially mint drops from Bottomleys of Keighley, and toffee from Turner and Wainwright of Brighouse before Mackintoshes had made their name. In the last decade of the last century there were four sweet manufacturers in Halifax—Binns, Moore, Bancroft and Mackintosh. As a means of advertising, one used to scutch sweets from his front door to passing school children on Fridays. Mr Arnold Townsend (b. 1882) remembers John Mackintosh, not to be outdone, asking him to scutch a box of sweets for him from his pastrycook's shop where he was then beginning to make toffee in 1890.

Joseph Dobson and Sons, founded in 1850, still a family firm, make boiled sweets at Elland (*see plates* 103-7). They hailed from York, where they were connected by marriage with Bayldon and Berry, a firm from which Terrys developed. They, too, started as bakers, and were famous for their sponge cakes. An undated recipe book shows that amongst other confectionery they made common

[1] Mrs E. Hyde-Welch, née Collinson.

peppercake, brandy snap, bride cakes, moggy and various lozenges such as opium for curing tickling coughs.

Nowadays horehound, cassia and oil of cloves are some of the ingredients in the cough candy, which together with voice tablets, were invented by Thomas Dobson, Joseph's youngest son. Joseph made conversation lozenges which had phrases like 'I love you', 'Be mine', and 'Will you be my sweetheart' on them. They have a shop in Elland and stalls in Halifax and Huddersfield markets. Formerly the boiled sweets were taken to the markets in 28-lb. cans by horse and flat cart and tipped on to the long sloping counters, from which they were served with a shovel and scoop at 1 lb. a time for about 2½d. Yorkshire Mixtures, for which they are famous, contain about twenty varieties.

Children only spent their Saturday pennies or halfpennies after considerable thought. 'For a halfpenny you could buy a kali sucker, which consisted of a paper with kali [sherbet] in it, with a piece of liquorice telephone wire stuck in it.' Lucky packets or bags, too, about 2 inches in diameter, sometimes triangular, contained sweets, a trinket such as a tin brooch or ring or a small toy, and cost 1d. or ½d. It was said that some had a 3d. piece in the bottom, but this was never found. There were coconut chips or aniseed balls at so many a halfpenny, and lamb, green peas and potatoes, little red, green and white sugar sweets. At Heptonstall Palm Sunday Fair Roseanna actually rolled rock in sugar on a little table in the street. Tiger nuts (*Cyperus esculentus*) were bought and chewed for their juice, and all types of liquorice confections—pomfret cakes, telephone wires, boot-laces and shoe leather (squares) were ever popular. Chopped up black liquorice sticks bought from chemists, shaken up with water in medicine bottles, made 'Spanish', a pleasant childish drink.

One of the biscuit firms of Yorkshire, Fox's Biscuits at Batley, now a public company, originated from the sale of brandysnap to stallholders at fairs. The firm began with Michael Spedding, who in 1853 having started a small confectionery business launched out into the making of brandysnap then curled by hand. In 1882 F. E. Fox joined him as a boy, and in 1897, having married the daughter, took over the business. Even up to the 1930s all the family worked overnight at fair times. Orders were sent on a postcard, and canisters of brandysnap delivered to fairgrounds by horse and cart. It was always heaped up on the stall, never laid out neatly, because people preferred to buy it from a pile. Modernization and expansion, begun after the First World War, continued, with the introduction of new machinery including a brandysnap curler. Sixty types of biscuits, many of them sold at 6d. a lb. up to the Second World War, are supplied all over the world, for people are prepared to pay high prices for British biscuits which are the best.

However disparate the food of the better and the less well-off may have been, all shared an appreciation of flavour—of the taste of new home-baked bread, ham, oatcake, chicken, rabbit pies—flavours that to some of us seem to have gone for ever. Home-baking largely ceased during and after the Second World War owing to a combination of the need to supplement rations by the purchase of confectionery, increasing affluence that enabled people to buy the more expensive cooked and baked products, and of women of all classes going out to work.

13 Shops

AFTER the Industrial Revolution, when quantities of goods became available, shopkeepers entered a golden age. They were then, like Swiss hoteliers, individuals providing individual service and before the Shop Hours Acts were passed open early and late. Shops were of their era, and often only lasted the lifetime of their owners. Small- and medium-sized shops with narrow frontages of different designs and with goods massed against the glass of the windows were the rule. The last century saw the building of those early pedestrian precincts—arcades, covered markets and department stores, as this has seen the spread of the chain store, the multiple tailor, the supermarket and the hypermarket. Shops were and are both a necessity and an entertainment.

Consider the Grand Pygmalion, the first department store in Leeds, established by Alexander Monteith, a Scotsman, in Boar Lane, a main shopping street. In March 1888 he bought a building with a 90-feet frontage, framed large windows in ornamental brasswork, built a new staircase with flights off to right and left, made two entrances, and in three weeks' time was partially open. The departments included women's and children's clothing, dress goods, lace, millinery, upholstery, haberdashery, dressmaking, carpets, furniture and later toys. Two features were that the ground floor sloped upwards from Boar Lane, and that cash was sent in wooden balls and change returned on an overhead railway, working by gravity, to and from a cash desk high up like a 'floating gondola'. Monteith was joined by his brother-in-law, Andrew Hamilton, and by his son, and became Monteith, Hamilton and Monteith.

The store was both in advance of and of its time. The merchandise could be handled and purchases could be exchanged or the money refunded. But in the old style the fourth floor was entirely devoted to staff quarters, with dining- and living-rooms and mostly separate bedrooms for fifty of the 100, later the 200 employed, and superintended by a housekeeper and a housemaster who doubled as floor walker. Employees stayed for years. The sales ladies wore black dresses even in summer, and high collars stiffened with little whalebones. The head of the toy department, T. B. Duncan, the first Labour Lord Mayor of Leeds, not only acted as buyer but mended anything including the eyes of dolls which refused to shut. To people who remember them there never have been such toys nor such Christmas toy shows.

For Christmas 1892 before an electricity supply existed, the Pygmalion and a few other shops were lit by electric light from a John Fowler engine stationed in a side street working a generator. The Pygmalion lasted only thirty-nine years, yet it impressed itself permanently on the memories of the adults and children of those years. Following the slump of the 1920s and the deaths of the two elder partners, the shop was sold to C. and A. Modes in 1927.

In Leeds Schofields, at the present day the only family controlled store in the city, attracts shoppers living in times of more widespread affluence. It was founded by Snowden Schofield (1870–1949) who was born in Bradford, where he was apprenticed at the department store of Brown, Muff's. After working in London and Liverpool, he had saved £300, and with a view to starting on his own, he visited Blackburn where it snowed and Leeds where the sun shone, so that he plumped for Leeds, and for £50 a year rented a two-windowed corner shop in the newly built Victoria Arcade, in what was Upperhead Row not then the main shopping area (*see plate* 111).

He opened as a fancy draper and milliner, with two full-time assistants earning 10s. a week and others part-time, on a beautiful spring morning in May 1901. On that day he took £62 3s. 4½d., £43 10s. of it in gold. By 1910 he had built up the nucleus of a store by renting shops as they became vacant in the arcade, and he gradually acquired buildings near by including the Red Hall, one of the old halls of Leeds, the Leeds Hippodrome which had closed, and in 1946 the entire arcade of twenty-four shops on either side for £250,000. Meanwhile the Headrow, the first major rebuilding project in Leeds, had advantageously brought a new main shopping street past his door. When Snowden Schofield died in 1949 the staff numbered 700. Never forgetting a face, he cared for them all, and had introduced a welfare service, a house journal, annual garden parties and outings. He had also pioneered in Leeds advertising on the front pages of newspapers—the first was for nappa (capeskin leather) gloves sold at 1s. ¾d. a pair, on which he made ¾d.

Schofields was carried on by his son Ronald who supervised the complete rebuilding of the store between 1956 and 1962. Part of this included the old Theatre Royal which was alongside the Hippodrome in Lands Lane. Ronald died in 1971 and was succeeded by Mr Peter Schofield. In recent years the store has added a multi-storey car park, an out of town warehouse, and in 1972 another family business, Cockaynes of Sheffield.

One of the most remarkable of success stories which, as it originated in Leeds, must be mentioned in passing is Marks and Spencers, for it was here that Michael Marks came from Poland in 1882. In the Leeds covered market he first sold goods for a penny, from which developed a chain of Penny Bazaars, and out of these eventually came the chain of superstores. The trademark, St Michael, was registered in 1928.

Whilst in Leeds, let us look at a shop specializing in china, pottery and glass: Doyles, the story of which has been told to us by Mrs Maggie Doyle. In 1842 James Alfred Doyle had opened a little shop on Leeds Bridge, where he sold domestic ware made by the Castleford Pottery. When in the 1870s Leeds Bridge was rebuilt, he moved to a shop in Boar Lane, and stocked it with a more varied class of goods. James Alfred, a handsome autocrat, thought that women engaged in trade were not only out of place but immoral, and when he died he left the business to his son, Sydney, and the premises to his three daughters. Maggie Doyle, who had married Sydney, was shortly left a widow, with two children, no pension, a small insurance and total ignorance of the shop business.

However, she was invited to Staffordshire by Major Frank Wedgwood, the head of that famous firm and an old friend of her husband's, and encouraged by him she decided to take over the running of the business. But first at Wedgwood's invitation she returned to Staffordshire and toured all the important potteries including Minton, Coalport, Doulton and Stewart's Glass Works. At the shop, the chief assistant left, and eventually her husband's sisters gave notice that they wished to sell the premises. This was not altogether disastrous, as they were on five floors, so that when anything was sold a whistle was blown, the order whispered, and it came down on a lift on a pulley. In 1937 she moved to Albion Street, and as an attraction had early morning tea-sets wrapped up ready to give away to the first customers. But the opening coincided with the Abdication and no one claimed a set.

This inauspicious beginning only served to emphasize later success. Amongst her many customers she particularly remembers the gypsies, always women, who, carrying baskets of pegs and bringing children with them, ordered goods worth £50, £60, even £100. They had catalogues and knew exactly what they wanted, and the prices. Often these, Crown Derby or Worcester ornaments, plates and so on had to be ordered and sent on, and were not paid for. Instead they deposited jewellery in her safe, until they came round again and had saved sufficient money to pay. When Maggie Doyle retired in 1963, she was presented with specially made gifts from all the potteries.

Two shops in Bradford, Brown, Muff's and Lingards, illustrate how different shops developed under the personal imprint of their owners. Brown, Muff's has a long and distinguished history, for it was founded in 1814 by Mrs Elizabeth Brown who opened a small draper's and outfitter's shop in what was later to become Market Street, Bradford, selling underclothes and fustian goods. Her son, Henry, joining her, ran a circulating library and bookshop, and he married a cabinet-maker's daughter, Betsy Muff, whose brother Thomas eventually came into the firm. In 1845 the two men, described as woollen drapers and tailors, entered into partnership as Brown and Muff. As Henry Brown had only one child, who died, the connection with that family ceased, and Thomas's sons became partners—as their descendants are today.

In 1871 they opened a fine new store near Mrs Brown's first little shop when they were described as drapers, silk mercers, tailors and outfitters. A boy's suit then cost £1 3s. and two pairs of blankets £2 16s. About six apprentices used to live in. Milliners, tailoresses and men tailors were employed as well as carpet fitters and mattress-makers. Bridal dresses were a speciality. In those days when lino was required a roll was taken to the house by horse and cart, laid out in the street, cut, fitted, and the rest of the roll carried back.

Brown, Muff's opened a restaurant in 1923, an innovation comparable with developments in London and other stores, and like them they also had a small orchestra. Formerly, the high quality goods for which they are renowned catered only for 'carriage folk'—a distinction that has not applied since the Second World War. A separate furnishing store near by, warehouse and service departments have been added, and large new stores opened in Skipton in 1963 and in Doncaster in 1975.

Another Bradford draper's shop, Lingards, was founded by Henry Lingard (1839–1903) after he had prospered as a stall-holder, at first in the open market, then in Kirkgate market when it was built, and as a warehouseman selling *fents* (short lengths of cloth or remnants sold cheap). A pioneer in the fent trade, still prominent in local markets, he was one of the first to realize the potential of the business, and it is said that he once climbed over a gate into a field to cut up his long lengths and so did better trade.

Built in 1875, the shop was intended to resemble a market, and was without display windows on to the street. Two large wide entrances led to the ground floor open to a glass-domed roof, with two tiers of balconies, so that sitting in the café on the first floor shoppers could look down into the shop. Averse to ostentation, Henry Lingard neither advertised nor held clearance sales. His employees eventually numbered some 200. About 1920 his eldest son, Asa (1872–1956), built a modern store with windows which for some ten years more were painted over, and he flourished like his father. The shop was sold to the United Drapery Stores in 1938, bombed in 1940, rebuilt on a different site in Westgate, and still continues.

By and large the big family drapery stores were the exception. There were the first-class outfitters and dress shops such as John Holmes in Manningham Lane, Bradford, where children going to boarding school were fitted out, also Madame Neil who, like Madame Arthur of Bond Street, Leeds, supplied the well-off with model dresses. We should not forget the branches of Marshall and Snelgrove at Leeds and Bradford whose very name spelt high-class clothes. Nor must men's shops be omitted—the tailors, shirtmakers and hat shops flourishing before the arrival of the multiple tailors and chain stores—Hardy, Bissington, John Wales Smith in Leeds, all individualistic.

Every town had its modest but well-stocked drapers, such as Manchester House, Elland, founded in 1900 by Thomas Forrest and so-called because goods were regularly bought from Manchester wholesale warehouses, and in 1975 still run by Miss D. Forrest. Or Waterloo House, which has gone, at Holmfirth, owned by John Beardsell, who employed eight girls as tailoresses and milliners living in a dormitory with a housekeeper to look after them.

Or consider Mrs E. Barrett (1869–1965) who because her husband was delicate (he died in 1918) rented a shop in Thwaitegate, Hunslet, in 1916, and started with a stock of drapery bought on a month's credit from a wholesale trader's warehouse, where a brother-in-law who could vouch for her worked. Later she went regularly to Leeds to buy material, carrying it home on the tram. She made ladies' and children's underclothes, dresses and men's shirts on a sewing machine in the back room, and at Whitsuntide worked all night long. Her daughter, too, with a second-hand machine provided for her, helped for many years sewing up to eight, nine or ten o'clock.

Emma Barrett lived in a poor district and was 'right soft' so that many people owed her money, paying part off, then owing more again. To help she ran a club to which people paid 3d. a week and after so many weeks had saved enough to have a garment made. Eventually she joined the well-known Provident Clothing Club for which she paid a collector a commission. He called weekly on householders who paid 1s. a week for twenty weeks and a further 1s. for the cheque, which presented to shopkeepers such as Mrs Barrett purchased goods. The cheque was sent to headquarters where a percentage was deducted and paid out at the month's end. In 1933 moving to a better shop, eventually run by a daughter and son-in-law, she still served behind the counter when she was ninety.

Various systems, of which one is club cheques, have evolved especially in the poorer districts of cities and towns to obviate the shortage of ready money. One group is the travelling draper or credit trader, originating from the old packman, Scotsman or tallyman who kept accounts on his stick. Usually dealing in drapery, clothing, furniture, sometimes hardware, they range from one person running a club to a nationwide firm such as the Provident Clothing and Supply Company started in Bradford in 1880 by Sir Joshua K. Waddilove, who was a deacon at the Wesleyan Methodist church in Carlisle Road, Bradford, and wished to help the poor to obtain much needed goods on credit.

The small individual credit trader may have a shop and employ collector salesmen. Both he, members of his family and the paid collectors spend their time 'doing the round', calling at houses delivering goods, collecting the weekly shillings, maybe more, showing samples and taking further orders. He charges fifty per cent profit on the goods for the credit. He and the customer both keep a book. Many are proud of this, 'a picture with not a payment missing', but some irresistibly fall into debt, and a few 'pay nowt nor nobody'. A trader makes discreet enquiries before taking anyone on, for unlike hire purchase he cannot reclaim goods for non-payment. He may buy a book of 'deadeyes' (debts) at 15s. or more in the £1, which gives him an inroad into a district, and by fair trading, recommendation, a personal approach and a 'gift of the gab', builds up a connection. On his rounds, undertaken in all weathers, he meets other collectors: rent, club, bad debts, even of doctors' accounts, all of whom share a mutual fellowship.

Besides these, the other main group are the many catalogue agents acting for the big mail order firms such as Grattan Warehouse or Empire Stores, both based on Bradford, which differ from the above by issuing huge catalogues and themselves carry a very large stock of branded goods. Club agents for one scheme and another, perhaps more than one in a street, in the mills and in other works still abound.

A chain of shops, already referred to from time to time, are the Co-operative Stores, started in the hard times of the first half of the last century, and returning profits to the customers in the form of dividends. The bald statement disguises the determined effort and selfless devotion behind the movement. For instance at Honley the first shop was begun by twelve men who walked to Huddersfield, brought back cheese and sold it at a profit of 1d. a pound. That at Slaithwaite in the Colne valley was opened in 1858 in a remodelled cottage rented for 2s. a week. As at other places they transferred to new enlarged premises, opened department after department, ran libraries, provided services such as coal deliveries, undertaking and life assurance, and organized outings, and concerts in the winter months. By 1908 Slaithwaite had five branches and by 1922 ten.

Another type of shop, the pawnshop with its distinctive sign, has greatly diminished in numbers. Between Hunslet and the centre of Leeds sixteen might once be counted, now two, and at Huddersfield fourteen, now one. Before the days of social security they played a vital role in society. Traditionally they have two entrances, one at the front leading to the counter selling new goods, and the other at the side or the back for pawnbroking.

New goods form a large part of the trade. In 1900 Horatius Lloyd, who had run a pawnshop in the Quarry Hill slum area of Leeds for fifty years, had advertised throughout that period, and made the most profit from sales of jewellery. Jewellery, especially wedding rings and watches, were traditional stock, as may still be seen in the window of Claude Hill's pawnshop in Huddersfield. In the past mostly shawls and cord trousers for men were the new goods stocked, and heald rugs, already mentioned. List rugs, hanging up outside, may still be bought at Beethams in Mabgate and Hunslet, Leeds.

In the past almost anything was pawned: men's suits, overcoats, boots, freshly washed and ironed bedding bundles, silver Albert watches and chains, all kinds of musical instruments, even a piano to pay for a family holiday. About 1911 at Beethams a concertina in a box was brought in each week and each week redeemed, so that from familiarity they did not trouble to check it. One week it was not redeemed, and they found that the box was empty. At one time people even brought in a tin or earthenware bowl full of dough. In the 1930s slump a queue fifty yards long and six people deep waited outside, and so many parcels were strewn all over that they had to walk on them. Eventually they were sent unseen to auction with their tickets still attached.

Nowadays Tuesday rather than Monday is a busy day, and some of the commonest articles 'shoved up the spout' are typewriters, radios, electrical goods and men's wear. In 1973, rather than lack of money, the usual troubles were mismanagement, compulsive gambling, stealing, drug-taking, or the buying of jewellery beyond the purchaser's means. A pawnbroker must be ready for anything. A man came into a shop not long ago, wanting to buy a bag and a suitcase for very little money and leaning over the counter said, 'We've got guns now'.

Again catering for the enormous influx of people various patent medicines were manufactured at considerable profit to their promoters in the West Riding. Zambuk was made by Frank H. Fulford, a Canadian who came to Leeds in the early part of the century, and Teasdale's Chlorodyne mixture for coughs and colds by George Teasdale at Bramley and sold all over the world. They operated against a background of self-medication, stemming from poverty, and the habits of country people flocking to the towns who were used to folk medicine. Herbalists, too, supplied this need, and the early exponents 'Dr' D. I. Coffin, an American, and

John Skelton, herbalists, made Leeds a centre for their itinerant practices and the publication of literature.

The original J. W. Clapham of the herbalist's shop of that name in Vicar Lane, Leeds, founded in 1859, was an American. Mr W. Rutter who came to live with his aunt over the shop in the 1920s describes those days. Then, pickers with hand carts explored the surrounding countryside, reported on their finds, and if the herbs were required, brought them in. Paid by the pound, they collected for example elder flowers, which had to be picked in dry weather, ragwort, used for bathing, burdock, a blood purifier, eyebright, for eyes. If a mandrake with its huge roots were found, it was displayed on the counter before being sliced up and sold as good for black eyes, bruises and rheumatism. After Christmas Claphams bought cheap any mistletoe left over, whose leaves and stalks were good for the nerves.

The herbs were dried on dated hand-made trays, then, with the thick stalks removed, they were chopped into small pieces in a chopping machine, weighed out and sold. The buyer scalded the soft herbs and boiled the hard ones. They also made pills, powders and herb extracts. The ingredients of, for instance, stomach and liver pills were mixed, kneaded, put through a worming machine, then a pill machine, cut and coated with simple liquorice powder. They also made Slippery Elm food mixed in a long narrow trough, and a bath and poultice powder, made from mustard, bran, ginger and cayenne, which when scalded was used for bathing the feet and to keep the temperature down. Today, regulations control what may be made and sold. Herbs are imported from abroad, and pills, especially for indigestion, literally bought by the ton for sale.

14 Craftsmen

WHETHER craftsmen lived in town or country, they found their jobs usurped by machines and their ranks depleted by economic pressures. A few were engaged in rare occupations. In the 1930s Tom Riley, as his father and grandfather had done before him, carved rocking horses at a toy-makers, Whiley Bros in Camp Road, Leeds. Matthew Henry Sunderland's life's work until retirement in the 1940s was the making of thimbles at Charles Horner's, gold- and silversmiths at Halifax. Horners in 1884 had obtained a patent for what were to become their Dorcas thimbles, constructed with a sandwich of steel between two layers of silver so that they did not easily puncture.

In 1822 Leeds supported sixty-five cabinet-makers by which time Thomas Chippendale, born at Otley, had been dead forty-three years. One of the Leeds makers, John Kendell and Company of Mill Hill, established in 1760, was bought by a partnership, Marsh and Jones, later Marsh Jones and Cribb, whilst another, Josiah Teale and Son, established in 1789, first in Lowerhead Row and later in Upperhead Row, Leeds, worked continuously until the 1920s.[1]

Chippendale represents the London cabinet-maker furnishing the great country houses; Marsh Jones the provincial firm catering for magnates such as the Salts; and Teales the local craftsmen supplying well-designed furniture to the less wealthy. In other towns, too, many cabinet-makers of good standing flourished such as Simpsons of Halifax, Eldwicks of Wakefield, and Pratts of Bradford who still function.

The Pratt family hailed from Gunnerside in Swaledale, and moved in 1830 to the then growing town of Bradford where Christopher Pratt (1819–1903) was apprenticed to Joseph Nutter, a cabinet-maker. After his marriage he started in business on his own, and in 1850 after Nutter's retirement he leased, with another craftsman, his house, workshop and showroom, now part of the present premises in North Parade, Bradford. These were extended in 1874 to house piece masters,

[1] *Furniture made in Yorkshire, 1750–1900*, Temple Newsam, Leeds, 1974; L. O. Boynton, 'High Victorian Furniture: The Example of Marsh and Jones', *Furniture History*, vol. III, 1967.

specialist craftsmen who, employing journeymen, were provided with timber and other materials—an individualistic system which worked well, but ceased about 1914 owing to trade union opposition.

At the turn of the century, the firm's heyday as cabinet-makers, they were employing 200 men, and providing a complete furnishing and decorating service for houses, town halls, banks and churches. Like others they signed their furniture by affixing paper labels on each piece, after 1913 replacing them with brass plates. In this era when trifling sums were allotted to the equipment of kitchens and servants' bedrooms, a seven-bedroomed house could be well furnished for between £175 and £200. Pratts is still a family business offering a comprehensive service and making fitment furniture, with workshops and a design studio attached to their extensive modern showrooms.[1]

Clock-makers add up to a far smaller body of craftsmen. One firm flourishing as cities, towns and transport expanded was Potts of Leeds, famous all over the north of England for their public clocks. The family originated from Berwick-on-Tweed, and via Darlington were drawn to the West Riding to settle at Pudsey in 1832. By 1840 they were making turret clocks, and about 1862 William Potts (1809–86) moved to Leeds, where three of his sons joined the business of clock-makers and jewellers.

In the last half of the century they made roundhead wall clocks for the stations of the Great Northern, Midland and other railway companies. Apart from the dials, cases and springs, these were all hand work and finished to perfection. They made and supplied floral clocks, ones for schools and offices and above all turret clocks for town halls, works, cathedrals and churches. Potts are thought to have been the first in the field to illuminate dials. They also installed the two mechanical clocks, with moving life-size figures, in Thornton's and the Grand Arcades, Leeds. In 1907 a staff of forty-seven were employed, ten of them engaged on small clocks, fifteen including a foreman, a tuner and labourers on turret, and two as a blacksmith and a striker.

They also repaired old church clocks, often after difficult journeys having to mount rickety ladders leading to belfries deep in bird droppings and with mechanisms covered with flies. They contracted for the winding of clocks, no mean task when for instance all the clocks in Leeds Infirmary were wound by hand. For this job the winder took a boy to hold the ladder steady on polished floors. Latterly

[1] L. W. Pratt, *Yesterday Our Ancestry*, 1929, reprinted 1969; Christopher Pratt & Sons, *Small Hints on Furnishing*, 1893; Day books and Catalogues; *Victorian and Edwardian Furniture by Pratts of Bradford*, exhibition catalogue 1970, Bradford City Art Gallery and Museums. All lent to us by Mr C. B. Pratt.

Potts installed automatic electric winding for and fitted cut-out apparatus to the striking mechanisms of many public clocks, for example that on Leeds Town Hall. In the 1930s the old name and the firm were sold to John Smith, clock-makers of Derby. Charles, grandson of William, started on his own account, and in 1964 Cecil, the last of the Potts family of clock-makers, retired and this business was sold to a London firm.[1]

A still more rare occupation and one totally unmechanized, dependent on touch and eyesight, is that of organ builder, engaged especially in the Victorian era in putting organs in the many newly built churches and chapels. Formerly firms were to be found in several West Riding towns, added to by apprentices who having served their time set up in a small way as pipe-makers or voicers, the two trades that together with the fabrication of the consoles and chests go to the completion of an organ. Every part was made except the keys, a specialist's job. Apprentices earned $6\frac{3}{4}d$. a week. Workmen and journeymen were constantly on the move, travelling from workshop to workshop, or to distant places to assess the acoustics of a building, to enquire what type of music was required, and eventually to put the organ in, perhaps a three-weeks' task for two men. 'When you built an organ you put up a memorial to yourself.' Now the decline in religious observance has lessened demand.

The works of Peter Conacher and Company, a firm founded in 1854 at Springwood, Huddersfield, were purpose-built after a fire in 1910, and resembling a vast chapel, was one of the largest organ factories in England. When Mr Brian Hirst, who showed us round, came here in the early 1930s a constant flow of whole new organs was leaving the works. Many were sent to Ireland and many more to the chapels in the Welsh valleys. Then followed the demand for cinema organs, rush jobs which sixty or eighty men, including twelve engineers, laboured night and day to complete. Formerly a steam engine running all day drove the wood-working machinery. Now the firm is part of a group under Henry Willis, organ builders of Petersfield, and the four or five men employed were in 1974 engaged in rebuilding the organ for the city hall in Johannesburg. Mr Farrar was voicing and Mr Gillhouley making components for the consoles. Mr Hirst engaged in soldering pipes, was attuned, as we were not, to hearing the cry of tin, made by solder with a high tin content (*see plate* 116).

At Bramley an enclave of pipe-makers has sprung up in the wake of the now defunct but formerly well-known firm of J. and J. Binns, organ builders, established here about 1881. In 1974 Fittons, Rogers and Booths were to be found there engaged in their skilful and delicate task of pipe-making and voicing. Mr

[1] Information supplied by Mr W. A. Potts, son of Charles H. Potts.

MAKING BAKESTONES

96. James (Nipper) Mills shaping bakestones with a length of scythe blade near the quarry at Delph. Many finished bakestones are hardening off in the water of the Hull Mill stream. The men had a hut and grindstone, but most of their work was undertaken out of doors (1910).

97. Arthur Schofield and James Mills firing bakestones in the hut or kiln at the bakestone quarry at Delph. Inside the hut was a pit in which wood or anything available was burnt, and the bakestones were reared up round it. Schofield and Mills are given as bakestone-makers in 1838 (1910).

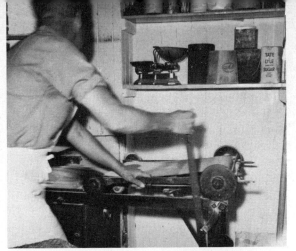

OATCAKE AND MUFFINS

98. Mr L. Feather in his bakery at Haworth pours a ladleful of batter on to the scored bakboard which is made of mahogany, and has been sprinkled with semolina (1965).

99. Having transferred the batter on to the cloth of the tram he pulls a lever which jerks the tram forward to throw the batter on to the bakestone.

100. He turns the oatcake with a bent knife, after which it is transferred to the cooler end of the bakestone shown on the left. Mr and Mrs Feather working together made eight dozen cakes in an hour.

101. Mrs Feather weighs out the dough for muffins and Mr Feather kneads it.

102. The dough is dropped into a ring on the hot bakestone.

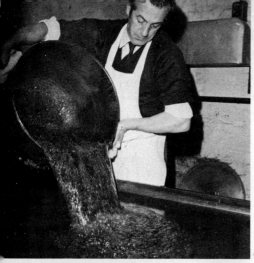

SWEETS

103. Mr R. Berry at Joseph Dobsons, Elland, making boiled sweets. He pours the boiling mixture on to an oiled steel plate which has a cold water jacket below.

104. A length has been cut off with scissors, and is being pulled first one way and then another until it appears white from the many air bubbles.

105. Mrs J. Whalley and Mr R. Berry striping humbugs by cutting lengths of candy and laying them across a main lump.

106. A length is put through a roller with dies which press on the right shape of the sweets. It comes out in narrow strips of thirty-two sweets, which when cold are easily broken up into individual sweets.

107. The various rollers which are used to shape the sweets—round, fish-shaped, oblong, pear-shaped, square, ridged and so on.

MARKETS

108. Halifax Market.

109. Mrs E. Stanley and helpers in her café, a booth in the old Kirkgate Market, Bradford.

110. A corner of Dewsbury Market.

111. *Schofield, Milliner and Fancy Draper. A postcard captioned 'One of the sights in Victoria Arcade, Leeds'. Schofields has developed from this one shop to a huge department store (c. 1905).*

112. *In 1822 Manoah Rhodes walked to Bradford from Morley and took work with John Allott, a watch- and clock-maker, and there in 1836 set up his own business which became one of the best known gold- and silversmith's establishments in Yorkshire (date unknown).*

113. *McKitrick Bros, Huddersfield, a present-day firm founded by Abel Hellewell, brazier and tinner, in 1819. It was taken over in 1855 by C. W. McKitrick, then aged eighteen, later joined by his brother (1890s).*

CRASTS

114. (Above left) Mr Bill Clarke and Mr Charles Lofthouse from Potts of Leeds repairing Leeds Town Hall clock (1956).

115. (Above right) Mr J. Gledhill and Mr W. Cook, apprentice, outside the printing works, in Town Street, Beeston, Leeds. They published the 'Beeston Gazette' (1910).

116. (Below left) Mr B. Hirst of Peter Conacher and Co., Huddersfield, soldering an organ pipe, a skilled and delicate operation.

117. (Below right) Mr Norman Fitton of Bramley voicing an organ pipe.

CRAFTS

118. Mr Albert Smith, a cooper's apprentice, at the Melbourne Brewery, Leeds, undergoes the custom of 'trussing out' at the end of his apprenticeship. He is covered with wood shavings, rubbish and a bucket of water, then rolled round the yard (1960).

119. Mr H. Beckett shaping a cricket bat with a draw knife at the works of International Sports Co., Horbury Bridge. Bats have been made in these works for many Yorkshire cricketers.

120. The rope-walk at Coates and Sons, St Ann's Ropery, Nottingham. A branch of the Coates family came to Carlton, Wakefield, in 1929, and took over a ropery established in 1812. The figures in the foreground are William Coates, George Coates and another William. From left to right operations being performed are twisting, spinning by hand, polishing, balling and twisting. The rope-walk at Carlton closed down in 1954 when machines were substituted (1860s).

POTTERIES

121. Mr Harold Morton and his sister, Mrs Ethel Lockwood, making plant pots at Lindley Moor Pottery, Salendine Nook (1946).

122. Isaac Button, the last potter at Soil Hill Pottery, Ogden, between Halifax and Keighley, standing by the kiln, ready for one of the last firings (1964).

123. Slipping a mixing bowl—coating the inside with light-coloured clay (1961).

CLAY PIPE MAKING

124. Mr Samson Strong, Leeds, making clay pipes. The first process—rolling with the hand board (1938).

125. The shanks were pierced with a wire.

126. The rolled clay has been put into a cast-iron mould and pressed in the gin-head (on the right). This operation also hollows out the bowl, and was called stopping down.

127. Trimming off the clay which had oozed over the seams in the moulding process.

CLOGS

128. Mr Leonard Sharp stacking clog soles in drying racks at Maudes, Clog Sole Works, Hebden Bridge. They are left for some two months, whilst warm air circulates above and below (1962).

130. Clog iron makers at Thomas Greens, Silsden. The man with the beard is Frank S. Green, son of Thomas and head of the firm. Three of them eventually completed over sixty years' service, others were musical. Note the white smocks and fustian trousers (1897).

129. Mr Willie Moss at Maudes, hand shaping a clog sole with a stock knife (1960).

131. Mr H. Schofield, Walton Bros, Halifax, is fixing a steel toe-cap to a safety-clog (1961).

CUSTOMS

132. *Heckmondwike Fair, held on the green the first week-end in May, was typical of the fairs and feasts of every town. B. Powell's Swiss Mountain High Flyers on the right are worked by a steam engine, and a marionette exhibition and other side-shows are on the left (1889).*

133. *A rushcart in Oliver Lane, off Garfield Place, Marsden in the Colne valley. They were built there by the firm of Pinder's. A man is sitting astride the top, but instead of the traditional boughs a decorated triangle has been substituted. Men hold up the stangs with which it was drawn (c. 1903).*

134. *The Pace Egg play being performed at Luddenden by the boys of Calder Valley High School on Good Friday, 1973.*

BANDS

135. Young members of the Black Dyke Mills Band in practice, with the professional conductor, Major Peter Parkes, in the band room at Black Dyke Mills, Queensbury.

136. The local reading-room and the garden of the family of Oliver Ainley, seen here, were meeting-places for sing-songs which developed into the Thump Sings held at Nab End Tower, Longwood. They were the first of the Sings (c. 1880).

BANDS

137. The Heckmondwike English Concertina Band playing on the occasion of a royal visit to Heckmondwike on 10 July 1912.

138. Hepworth Silver Prize Band playing at Holmfirth Band Contest in Victoria Park, Holmfirth. Although they had uniforms, it was not then the custom to wear them at band contests, only at School Feasts, galas and park engagements (May 1923).

139. Morley Parrock Nook Band. One of the several comic bands which performed at fêtes, sports and so on (1907).

OUTINGS TO THE DALES

140. Choir trip from Rehoboth Chapel, Morley. The members halt for refreshment part way up Ingleborough. It was a very hot day and they did not reach the top (c. 1910).

141. Shop trip from Pratts of Bradford to Bolton Abbey in 1876. The picture includes—middle row: far left, the yard foreman, fourth from left the cabinet foreman, fourth from right the polisher foreman. Front row: second from left the designer draughtsman. Others are a carpet planner, a wood turner, an upholsterer, eleven cabinet-makers and, top centre, the errand boy who had stowed away.

LEISURE

142. The children of West Lane chapel, Gomersal, in their decorated waggon at the celebrations for the Coronation of George V (1911).

143. Playing billets near Scout Road, Mytholmroyd (c. 1919).

144. Early picture house (cinema). The Royal Electric Theatre at Hebden Bridge (1913).

HOBBIES

*145. Mr J. Akers judging Old English Tulips at the spring show of the
North of England Tulip Society at Wakefield. Mr H. V. Calvert, secretary,
is in the centre.*

*146. Bowls. A veterans' match, Hebden Bridge v.
Mytholmroyd at Mytholmroyd.*

*147. Mr Maurice Westmoreland, retired miner,
in his greenhouse at Rothwell.*

Norman Fitton, whose father, William, was linked with Binns and apprenticed to Conachers, and who made complete organs, now has a workshop adjoining his home which was once a clothier's house with a blocked up 'takin'-in' door. By the time he was eighteen he had travelled all over the British Isles putting in organs.

Fittons used to buy their pipes from Rogers, a firm founded in 1897, now run by the Buckle family, who employ six or seven men, and who in 1974 were engaged in making 5,000 pipes for an organ in Ghana. Small organs may have from about 300 to 1,500 pipes which are made of alloys, usually of lead or tin, with zinc in large ones, and copper for display pipes, all cast in the works by melting the metal in a crucible, transferring it to a skillet and pouring it on to a special casting bench. The higher the tin content the better the ring, and the more lead the sweeter the note. Pipes are shaped round mandrels, planed up, sized inside, turned and knocked down even, and then soldered down the joint using tallow as a flux and solder with a slightly higher tin content than the metal of the pipe.

The voicer needs to have perfect pitch. (People who cannot sing in tune are said in the trade to have cloth ears.) Like a human being a pipe has a body, foot, ears, toe and mouth with a top and bottom lip, and is said to speak, and there are two kinds, reed and flue, in the proportion of one reed to ten flues. A stop of reed pipes, sixty-one, may be voiced in three days. By enlarging the mouth, paring, nicking the languid in the mouth of the flue pipe, blowing and trying it out on a small organ, the voicer slowly attains his note (*see plate* 117). We were told that reed voicers used to have a pint of ale on the bench.

Another craft, printing, with its long and distinguished history, was established in the last century in every town. Men set up on a small scale, sometimes beginning in an attic or a cellar with a hand-fed machine and a case of type. They printed the yearly almanac, the weekly advertiser, church, chapel and school magazines, posters, invoices, hymn sheets, show catalogues and so on.

One such firm was founded by William Witts (1838–1914), the son of a Gloucestershire weaver who came north and found employment in Leeds as an overlooker at Gott's mill at Bean Ing. After apprenticeship to a printer Witts came to Bramley where in time a descendant, Mr William Murgatroyd, first ran then bought the business, now continued by his son. He remembers learning his case, soaking and stretching paper, the Columbia Press in use, and that ten or twelve posters, occasionally huge ones made up of six or seven pasted together, were usually printed every week.

In 1896 Mr C. Roberts's father started the *Colne Valley Guardian* (now taken over by the *Huddersfield Examiner*) a four-page paper sold at ½d., and composed with loose type, used, washed, cleaned and replaced to use again. He had settled at Slaithwaite because no other printer was there.

On the other hand when in 1885 Mr A. Charlesworth began his printing works and shop at Holmfirth two others had started at much the same time. In addition to the usual work the Charlesworths ran a circulating library, and sold decorative greeting cards with photographs for which the printer's own young family acted as models. His son, Mr N. J. Charlesworth, remembers that as a boy he delivered handbills as far as six miles on a wheelbarrow. Barrows, hand carts and horses and carts for the quick delivery of orders were in fact usual transport for the rush jobs so frequently associated with the printers' trade, even for the despatch of paper by merchants.

Mr W. Cook, whose parents left Middlesbrough for Leeds in 1910, was apprenticed to a small printer, J. Gledhill, in Beeston, Leeds, for 3s. a week, and developing a flair for composition fell in love with the craft. He attended classes at the then Leeds Printing School, where he was later to teach and examine for the City and Guilds candidates in machine work, and moved about to gain experience. Although it was said that if you could set and print a parish magazine, you could do the same for the Bible, some men were kept for years at composing nothing but railway time-tables or hymn sheets. In 1927 he started on his own, and in time entered into partnership in the firm of Whitehead-Miller, formerly known for chess publications and music printing, but now for general work and colour.

In a long lifetime printing has been transformed and the demand for it increased a hundredfold. Gone are the days of hand-setting, treadling, the Eagle presses, even of the Wharfedale Presses, once made at Otley and worldwide in use, or of the one ink manufacturer in Leeds, who made the ink while you waited and asked for cash on the spot. From small one-man firms large ones have grown such as Alf Cookes, E. J. Arnold and Son, and Waddingtons, Leeds, specializing in particular spheres—packaging, educational publications, playing cards and games. At Bradford Lund Humphries are world famous for high grade work and Sharps for their greeting cards, and at Idle, near Bradford, Watmoughs, beginning by publishing sporting magazines, now work round the clock printing huge fully coloured mail-order catalogues.

One after another almost every craft has been transformed by new machinery, new developments, fashion and other factors—none more so than tanning. About 1840 Thomas Smith, tanner, of Ouzlewell Green, Rothwell, employed several tailors and supplied local people with tough leather suits and the army with leather breeches. Other tanneries existed and still do in other parts of West Yorkshire. In 1822 Leeds had one tanner, but by the latter half of the century it was the tanning centre of the country with twenty firms situated on the Meanwood Beck, a tributary of the river Aire running through Leeds. About the turn of the century the trade gradually began to drift away southwards to settle near the then expanding boot and shoe factories of the Midlands and elsewhere, until now only four firms remain.

Of the original twenty, Harold Nickols, the best known, supplied hides for upholstering motor cars, railway carriages and so on; William Paul made the well-known Beaver leather stuffed with grease for country boots; J. Bateson and Sons dressed sheepskins for lining women's shoes; E. B. Balmforth made golf club and tennis racquet grips, Thomas Wright leather for book-binding and jewel cases. W. H. Ingle and Sons, a large firm which moved to Churwell, has only recently closed down, and W. and H. Miers, still very active, were amongst the first of the chrome tanners of calf.

One of the remaining firms, Charles F. Stead and Company, was established in 1823 by Wilson Walker, who built the present tannery at Sheepscar in 1863. Charles Stead, who began as a traveller with Thomas Wright, a firm on the Meanwood Beck, invented the use of East Indian Persians (the fine skin of hair sheep from Southern India) in the construction of gas meters, and flourishing on his own account, he bought the Sheepscar tannery in 1904 and formed a company. When his son, Mr Philip K. Stead, joined the firm, machines were still simple, tan pits filled the yard, and sumac but not oak bark was being used. Also at that time tanners employed *puer* (dogs' droppings) in the bating process to make the leather flexible. Selling this was a huntsman's perk, and people collected it for sale in buckets in the streets. Calf and ox hides were British, and large quantities of goat and other skins were imported mostly from India. Glazed kid, made from goat skin and used for women's shoes, is now too costly to produce.

Instead of men laboriously scraping the skins with knives over a beam, machines quickly remove the flesh; synthetic materials, not puer, aid the curing; mineral tanning with chromium salts has replaced oak bark in pits, and dyeing has become so sophisticated that the once basic five or six colours have increased to as many fashionable shades as in textiles. The large companies still operating produce as much leather as did all the original small firms, and one such as Steads makes 10,000,000 square feet a year, an amount unheard of in the past. They run a laboratory for research and development and make chrome tanned leather for shoes, for clothing, especially suede, and for industrial gloves.

Although in the early days they were to be found in cities and towns, rope-makers, because of the flat farmland available and the proximity to growing centres of population, came to be concentrated in and near Wakefield, where twenty-seven flourished in 1838. The first Ordnance Survey map of this area shows rope-walks running alongside hedgerows which gave shelter for work then undertaken in the open and dependent on the vagaries of the weather. Wells, too, were sunk for washing the yarn and for sizing. In 1822 there were four rope and twine spinners at Carlton, near Wakefield, one of them, John Dobson. It was this business that the Coates family, which originated in Nottingham and had moved first to Shipley, bought in 1929.

Mr Eric Coates recollects that when they came there had been a heckling shop where hemp was dressed with oil, beaten and straightened on steel pins, and that his father, so as not to waste it, spun half a ton of hemp in the old way by tying it round his waist, walking backwards paying it out by finger and thumb, whilst a boy wound a wheel at the other end to twist it (*see plate* 120). Men were employed for rope-making and drum polishing, and women for twisting and balling. They had a covered rope-walk until the 1950s, and made packing twine for baling, loom cords, waggon ropes, plough lines, halters, whipcords and gaskins for soil pipes. Clothes cords, too, were sold to Woolworths in competition with Calverts, another rope-making firm at Potovens, near Wakefield. Now, different types of twisting and balling machinery, some made by Fairbairn Lawson, have replaced hand work, and the firm, sold to H. Barnett and Company of London in 1951, make twine for butchers and the furniture trade.

Lastly the ancient craft of coopering, once a closely guarded secret and for apprentices after they had served their time culminating in a trussing-out ceremony (*see plate* 118). At Joshua Tetley and Son, Leeds, they employed thirty-six coopers in 1919, fifteen or sixteen in 1948. In the early 1960s they ceased to make new casks, and in 1974 had three coopers engaged in repair work.

Here, too, in the vicinity of Tetleys, were the premises of William Waide and Son, a firm noted for its dairy equipment. William Waide, a farmer, lived in a Leeds surrounded by farmland where bees swarmed and crops grew, and in February 1840 he wrote down in his 'Working Book' the length of staves and the dimensions and prices of spirit and wine casks, peggy tubs, piggins, tub and barrel churns. In the 1860s he began to specialize in dairy equipment and from the 1880s onwards in churns, in particular the Victoria Churn, which had an end-over-end action and of which Waide's were the inventors and sole makers. Gold medals and prizes were awarded them at the great dairy shows held both in England and on the Continent. In the late nineteenth century they were selling 6,000 to 7,000 a year. Many went to Ireland where William's son, Richard Waide, went round for orders in a jaunting car. They had agents in Germany and Japan, and before the First World War sent fifty to sixty churns at a time to Russia, some huge ones to the Siberian salt mines, with instructions in Russian. Later trade moved to East, West and South Africa, Egypt, and India where churns were used for making ghee. Waides exhibited at agricultural shows from 1860 up to the end, and with their churns dairymaids competed in making the most butter in the shortest time. The winner often bought the churn. If kept washed, this could last for sixty years.

When English oak, at one time grown and sold from the Bolton Abbey estate, became scarce, Memel oak from Russia was shipped to Goole and brought up the Aire and Calder canal. Later oak was imported from America, Poland and Persia. When Mr D. G. Waide was apprenticed to his father in 1927, some eighty men were employed. If he was satisfied with the finished barrel, and only then, did a cooper put his initials on the bottom. The firm closed down in 1966.

15 Pottery Chimney-Pots and Clay Pipes

WHEN considering so richly endowed a Riding, clay must be added to stone, coal and water. Clay, fireclay in particular, found in conjunction with the coal seams of the exposed coal-field, especially in the Leeds and Halifax districts, led to the establishment of important potteries, the making of chimney-pots, bricks and sanitary ware and of clay tobacco pipes.

Although they had existed long before, potteries come into focus in the mid-eighteenth century. From then onwards and throughout the nineteenth century a widely stratified society created a demand for pots, fine and coarse, ornamental and useful. At one end of the scale were the potteries using white clay suitable for fine quality pots, and at the other end clay, which because of its iron content turned terracotta when fired, for coarser wares.

Amongst the makers of fine earthenware several were grouped in or near Hunslet, Leeds. Of these the Leeds Pottery, formerly in Jack Lane, was not only the earliest and the best but its creamware, noted for quality and beauty of design, now ranks with the products of other notable eighteenth-century potters. Its best pieces were made when it was Hartley Greens during the last twenty years of the eighteenth century, and it virtually ceased in 1878.[1]

Two potteries in a different class, one at Wibsey and another at Eccleshill, near Bradford, of which the first was founded in 1770, and the second lasted until 1867, when it became a brick works, made well-moulded figures and good examples of salt-glazed brown stoneware. The so-called Eccleshill jug at Bolling Hall is so large that it may well have been made to celebrate the marriage of Queen Victoria and Prince Albert in 1840 (*see drawing on page* 137). Burmantofts at Leeds, flourishing as a pottery from 1862 to 1904, entered an altogether more modern era

[1] For further reading see J. and F. Kidson, *Leeds Old Pottery*, 1892; 'Pottery' by Maud Sellers, *The Victorian History of the County of York*, vol. 2, 1912; Donald Towner, *The Leeds Pottery*, 1963. The Leeds museums contain excellent examples.

making art pottery and architectural tiles, and in its day employed a host of people, some mining clay and iron on the spot, others engaged in design and manufacture.

The redware-makers rooted in tradition and aesthetically on a different level, provided households of all walks of life with pots for domestic and horticultural use, such as baking bowls and plant pots. They also made ornamental wares, usually decorated with slip, which appealed to the unaffected taste of humble folk. Amongst the salt kits, tea caddies, frog mugs, tobacco, money and knife boxes, were cradles and two-handled loving cups given as significant presents for christenings and betrothals, and puzzle jugs, which had been made in Tudor times and which puzzled because it was apparently impossible to drink without spilling from the numerous spouts (*see drawing on page* 137).

These potteries, some again near Leeds, were early grouped on the hillsides north and south of Halifax at for instance Blackley, Woodman House and Ainley Top near Elland, and at Ovenden, Ogden and Denholme between Halifax and Keighley. Almost twenty might be counted flourishing at one time or another. The oldest, Howcans, near Ovenden, although not always precisely on the same site, was run by the Halliday family from the mid-seventeenth century until 1889.

Often family concerns, the potteries frequently occupied a small farm which had mineral rights for the coal and clay on its land and space for kilns, clay mills and drying sheds. Brothers, sisters, cousins, aunts and uncles, as well as hired help contributed—the skilful as throwers, others as labourers, and often the women as decorators.[1]

At Salendine Nook, south of Elland, Lindley Moor Potteries were also long established, founded in the seventeenth century by the Mortons, a Scottish family of potters who fled here from religious persecution. In 1739 Joseph Morton gave land for the first Baptist chapel there, described a few years later as at Pot Oven. About 1834 the family split into two firms, Joseph Morton and Son and Enos Morton and Sons, housed in adjacent buildings. It is related that Joseph in busy times waylaid labourers at Enos's and offered them 6*d.* more to work for him. In 1887 he was making bowls of all sizes, cream pots, stew pots, pie dishes, plain and fancy tree-pots, and rhubarb and seakale forcing jars.

Although on a greatly diminished scale, Mr Harold Morton, a descendant of Enos, was making some pottery at Salendine Nook in 1973. Fifty years ago this was a busy place. Thirty-three workers, including six or seven members of the

[1] For further reading see Oxley Grabham, *Yorkshire Pots and Potters*, 1915, reprinted 1971; P. C. D. Brears, *The English Country Pottery: its History and Techniques*, 1971. Examples of the work of the country potteries may be seen at the Yorkshire Museum, York, Shibden Hall Museum, Halifax, Cliffe Castle Museum, Keighley, and Bolling Hall Museum, Bradford.

family, were employed. They had an 8-h.p. steam engine, known as 'Whoa Emma' because to start it Aunt Emma used to have to put her foot on the flywheel and quickly release it. This ran clay mills, four potters' wheels, and a hay chopper for horses' fodder. Horses and carts, with chain horses for the steep hills, fetched clay from Holywell Green three miles away. Coal and clay was dug from day-holes with a 22 feet drop to reach the Halifax Hard and Soft beds (*see plate* 75).

To prepare the clay they stacked it, poured water on it, and trod it wearing clogs until they knew by the feel of the suction that it was the right consistency. After this it went through the pug mill to mix the clay to a plastic form. The clay was then moulded into balls the correct weight for the goods to be made. The largest, bowls 20 inches in diameter, were thrown in two parts. The kiln, which had seven fires and took thirty-five to forty-eight hours to heat, held 7,000 large and small plant pots, and as each fire took three or four hodsfull, by the time a man had gone round and recovered his breath it was time to start again. Harold Morton began stoking when he was thirteen and a half, and if a factory inspector came round, he hid under the flue. After a good firing they used to say 'What a gloss they have on!' but if 600 to 700 pots fired badly 'We could be weeping'.

They kept horses and carts to carry pots, packed in straw, to Lancashire and Yorkshire towns, sometimes returning at two o'clock in the morning, and Harold Morton's father travelled as far as Scotland, always taking orders written down in dozens. Many people came to the pottery to buy, including gypsies who wanted seconds. It is remembered of these that they once put a tiny child in straw in a bread pot to keep it warm on the journey back to Bradford.

In those days 3½-inch plant pots sold at 2*s.* 9*d.* for sixty (*see plate* 121). They despatched them to Bermuda, South Africa and the Bahamas, insuring them for breakages. An unusual line was gilders' pipkins, made in three sizes, and sent to middlemen in London who sold them to firms in Ireland, France and Belgium. Sometimes they made cheap marbles, stogs, sold at schools at sixteen for 1*d.*

Another potter, Jonathan Catherall (1740–1807), had migrated from North Wales, and eventually established near Ogden Soil Hill Pottery taking its name

1 Puzzle jug, Howcans Pottery. 2 Rustic log basket, Lindley Moor Pottery. 3 Flask, Eccleshill Pottery. 4 Vase, Wibsey Pottery. 5 The Eccleshill Jug. 6 Money box (1846), snail horn ware, Howcans. 7 Teapot, Denholme Pottery. 8 Cradle, Howcans. 9 Tea caddy, Howcans. 10 Cup (1907), Woodman House Pottery. 11. Knife box (1853), Denholme. 12 Rocking chair, Denholme. 13 Flower pot (1868), Soil Hill Pottery.
1, 2, 3, 8, 13, Yorkshire Museum, York; 4, 5, 10, 11, Bolling Hall Museum, Bradford; 6, 7, 9, 12, Shibden Hall Museum, Halifax.

1

2   6¼"

3   8"

4   8"

5   21"

6   6¼"

7   6½"

8   8¾"   2⅞"   1802

9   M G

10   4"

11   13¾"

12   7⅝"   1871

13   7½"

from the hill behind it, 1,320 feet above sea level. It continued in the family's hands until the 1880s when the Button family who came from Roberttown near Heckmondwike took it on. The Catheralls sometimes fired the kiln with bracken, and Jonathan of the third generation used a hand wheel turned by his grandson. As late as 1939 thirteen men worked at Soil Hill, but latterly Isaac Button, the last member of two generations of large families, ran the pottery alone until 1964, when it closed. The largest vessels in regular production were brine pans that took 70 lb. of clay. Isaac could throw a huge vase on a wheel in about six minutes, and make a ton of clay into pots in a day (see plates 122–3). Both the Catheralls' and Buttons' houses and the pottery building that the Buttons built may be seen on a scarred hillside.

The last pottery to be started was at Pepper Hill, near Shelf three miles over the tops from Soil Hill, begun by John Pickles Sunderland and from 1926 run by Sam Bradley (1890–1964), who had been apprenticed to Arthur Button, Isaac's brother, at Soil Hill, and had worked for Eliot and Rhoda Morton, Joseph's descendants, at Salendine Nook. In their heyday in the late 1930s the Bradleys, then making mostly domestic earthenware, had three throwers and employed three labourers. A donkey engine ran the potters' wheels, a blunger (a machine with revolving knives), and a pug mill; but coal had to be bought at 18s. to 19s. a ton. The kiln held 8,000 3- to 4-inch plant pots, and they once fired thirteen times in thirteen weeks. Sixty 3-inch pots sold for 3s.

People visiting Pepper Hill bought mugs with their names put on in white slip. Sometimes a rhyme was scratched on a square of the slip on puzzle jugs, for example:

> From mother earth I claim my birth
> I'm made a joke by man
> So now I'm filled with good cheer
> Come taste me if you can.

They also made clay pigeons, and pot knurs for the game of knur and spell. Delivering to a few places in Yorkshire, they sent small lots of goods up and down the country. The pottery closed in 1958.

These men and women formed a community of craftsmen whose passing may be deplored. Some of them were buried in the graveyards of the Nonconformist chapels on the moorland heights. Local potteries had been dealt mortal blows by cheap wares imported from Staffordshire, by the cessation of home-baking, and finally by the change from clay to plastic plant pots.

Potteries and brick works were interlinked. Men turned to making what was needed. When Gillroyd Mills, Morley, was being extended in 1845, notices were put up at the Waggon and Horses, Holbeck and the Green Man, Hunslet, 'for a person to make two hundred thousand bricks'. The Buttons made their own for their new pottery buildings, and Joseph Morton ran a brick and tile works at Cinder Hills, Siddal, near Halifax. On the other hand large firms developed round Leeds, Wakefield and Halifax.

The Elland hillsides on both banks of the river Calder have been torn by brick and sanitary and drainage pipe works. On the one side Wilkinson's clay works cover up the sites of some of the old potteries such as Kitsons and Woodman House, and on the other W. T. Knowles and Sons mine a six-foot seam of clay half a mile into a hillside honeycombed with workings, meeting up with the Marshalls' quarries at Southowram.

Knowles employ skilled hand-moulders who with the aid of moulds used to make the intricate chimney-pots of the West Riding, fashioned to break the wind and to forestall downdraughts. Every corporation or borough favoured a different pattern. There are the Bradford and Halifax Windguards, the Carlisle Blow Down, the Hooded Leeds, and others named after the chessmen they resemble: Little Bishop and Long Knight, as well as Tulip Top Tall Boy. Especially after a severe gale many would be ordered, in the old days sent by horse and cart and a *teamer*. Now the two or three hand-moulders left chiefly make gullies of clay ground up as at the potteries but on a huge scale, and fired in kilns so large that the pipes and gullies can be barrowed in.

Whereas clay mines and makers of chimney-pots and the like operated on a large scale and were not numerous, in the last century every city, town and even the occasional village supported one or more clay tobacco-pipe-makers. In the seventeenth century a few existed at Hull, York, Wakefield and Halifax. The Gill family flourished in the two last places from 1709 to the mid-nineteenth century. Thoresby says that the craft was introduced to Leeds about 1700. By 1837 there were for instance six in Bradford and sixteen in Leeds, but when in 1950 the last maker in Yorkshire, Samson Strong (1873–1953) of Leeds retired, his nearest rivals were in Manchester and Edinburgh. By then cigarettes had become fashionable and briar pipes had superseded the clay.[1]

As we have seen in other crafts families passed on their skills from one generation to the next. Both sides of Samson's family were clay tobacco-pipe-makers: his

[1] Thomas Sheppard, 'Early Hull Tobacco Pipes and their Makers', *Hull Museum Publications*, No. 6, 1912; Simon Lawrence, 'Clay Tobacco Pipe-Makers in West Yorkshire', *Yorkshire Archaeological Journal*, vol. 45, 1973; W. White, *History Gazetteer and Directory of the West Riding of Yorkshire*, vol. 1, 1837; *Slater's Directory of Yorkshire and Lincolnshire*, 1849.

grandfather, another Samson, in Derby, and his mother's people, the Pickles, in York. His father, Frederick Strong (1832–95) had moved to Leeds to work for his wife's sister, Jane Wilson, née Pickles. Later Frederick and Angelina his wife buying moulds and equipment started up in Cottage Street, Leeds, where the one-storied workshop continued in use to the end. They had eight children, of whom Samson was apprenticed to his father in 1884. From 1895 when he took over, aunts, sisters and cousins all worked under him, and the youngest brother, John Frederick (b. 1892), remembers that times were hard. About 1900 when they had three kilns in use, fifteen people were employed, and in 1920 about ten.

Clay was not obtained locally as in Thoresby's day. China clay from Cornwall came by sea to Hull, and at Leeds was stacked in balls up to the ceiling in the clay store, one of six places into which the building was divided. The others contained the kiln, the packing, drying and moulding rooms, and a bottom place where the clay was prepared. For this the balls were broken up with a hammer on a block with a $\frac{1}{2}$-inch thick steel top, then left in water in a big steel tub for two days. The clay was thrown back on to the block and belaboured from side to side with a heavy wooden beating hammer, chopped into pieces by hand, rolled, patted and put on the bench with wet sacks round it. If a little dry, Samson took a mouthful of water and sprayed it.

'Grip your clay! Grip your clay' he used to exhort his helpers as they took a nip the correct size and weight to make two pipes. This was rolled on a rolling board, broken in two, doubled again, so that a nip of clay was in either hand. Each was then rolled by hand, making it as long as required and tapering at one end, and put side by side the two were rolled with the hand board (see plate 124).

The rolls, placed on dozening boards which held sixteen to allow for breakages, were put on drying racks to await moulding for which a gin-head and cast-iron moulds, which were greased with a mixture of paraffin and sweet oil, were employed. First the roll was ducked in water two or three times, then pierced with a wire which had a small twisted end, called a button, and the end of the roll was bent, fitted into the mould and slipped into a slot in the gin-head. The handle was brought down, called stopping down. After this the wire was removed, and if it came out with a little plop they knew that the hole was clear. Finally the pipes were trimmed with an iron smoother, and dried on racks all over the workshop, even on the roof of the building, or on orange boxes in the street.

The kiln held 150 gross, with the shanks arranged uppermost round three inverted bowls one above the other. Fourteen to sixteen pipes were handed to Samson at a time until he had potted up. Stoked with best coal in three fire-holes, the kiln took sixteen hours to fire, and a day and a half later they emptied it, taking out six pipes at a time. If a lot of churchwardens came out soft, called 'pink', it was a catastrophe.[1]

For years a little old man, Jack Hayes, came in at 7 p.m. to make Dandies, and was gone by morning. Another, a big Irishman, called Tom Doyle, who lived in lodgings and moved on with his belongings tied up in a muffler, was asked to make say a dozen gross of Acorns and stayed until he had finished them. Another, Benjamin Wilson, one of the cousins, taught by Samson, was always the first to use new moulds which, bought from Turpins of Macclesfield, had to be handled carefully. A good worker could make about forty-eight pipes an hour, some 3,000 in a week, and in 1900 the total weekly output was about 36,000.

They made Cutties: Thorn, Basket, Ship and Anchor, Soldiers, Auld Lang Syne, Acorns, the ribbed Cutty, with no heel, and the plain, the cheapest and smallest. The Miner with sloping head was sold in Durham. Footballers had a heel in the shape of a foot kicking a football, and Kitcheners had the Field Marshal's head on them. The last to be made were bubble pipes for children, sold at $\frac{1}{2}d$.

Sometimes when the kiln was being burnt, Samson started off with the horse, Tommy, and a cart-load of pipes packed in boxes, and travelled from town to town in North Yorkshire. Or he took pipes round to local inns, where they were given free with a pint of beer, so that he used to say, 'You couldn't expect a big price when they were given away'. The price was 2s. 6d. a gross, even 1d. each. Trade boomed during and after the First World War, but after that came the slump and trade gradually faded away.

[1] The equipment is to be seen at Kirkstall Abbey Museum, Leeds and the Castle Museum, York. Mrs E. Hope, Samson Strong's daughter and Mr J. F. Strong, his brother, have described the processes for us.

16 Clogs

CLOGS, associated with industry, are none the less an ancient form of footwear for long in use on farms. First worn by mill-workers in Lancashire at least by the early nineteenth century, they rapidly commended themselves to operatives elsewhere in mills, breweries, quarries, pits, potteries and foundries, for they were cheap, warm and waterproof. But in this century they began to be looked down on as a sign of poverty and were frowned on by school teachers for the noise they made. These factors, and the introduction of Wellington boots, the wearing of silk stockings, and the diminishing number of agricultural labourers, all conspired to a decline in their use.

In the first half of the last century cloggers (clog-makers) often combined their craft with patten-making. The similes 'As elate as any midden cock on pattens' and 'As bad as a cat in pattens' perpetuate the memory of their use. Early in the century the numbers of cloggers, although never so great as that of boot- and shoemakers, increased until every village had one or more, towns between ten and twenty, and co-operative stores clog-making departments.

Formerly to obtain the wooden soles the maker himself felled suitable trees (alders), or gypsies and other family groups camping in woods partially prepared and dried them in stacks. However, in the latter half of the century, as a result of invention and improvements to machinery, the Maude family in upper Calderdale developed a clog sole-making business which together with a firm at Snaith in Yorkshire near Goole supplied the needs of a wide area.

About 1870 James (1844–1919), the son of John Maude, a wood-turner, at Jerusalem Farm, Luddenden, began to make clog soles at Hawksclough near Hebden Bridge, and ten years later he erected there a purpose-built mill, subsequently enlarged, between the Rochdale canal and the river Calder. Later James's son, John R. Maude (1875–1964), bought a small engineering works across the river where machinery was made.

Up to 1900 they bought logs cheaply from southern Ireland, and then ran a sawmill on the Duke of Devonshire's estate at Lismore in Co. Waterford, where wood was cut up and roughly band-sawed into shape. But when freight charges doubled after the First World War, they erected a mill with an 80-h.p. engine at Raybeck on the Raby Castle estate near Barnard Castle, where T. Place & Sons, timber merchants of Northallerton, felled and delivered trees. Here, under James R. Maude, grandson of the first James, forty people were employed, and machines—roughers, side cutters, shankers—partially shaped the soles, which were then dried in brick steam-heated chests which each held 300 dozen pairs. They were despatched to Hebden Bridge where a similar number of employees were engaged in finishing them.

Until the First World War a dozen to fifteen hand-makers using stock knives were kept busy, each known for their own particular shape of soles. For hand-making alder was used, but beech 'kind to machinery' and some sycamore replaced it. Up to 1954 a steam engine ran the machines which were simple but numerous, at least six, each performing a different stage in the shaping of the sole.

Soles were air dried for about two months, then stacked in racks containing the different sizes—the smallest, size two, 5 inches long, and the largest, size fourteen, 13½ inches. (Clog sizes are three sizes larger than shoes.) They were then matched up in pairs. These in the early 1920s sold at 10d. a pair, a sum corresponding roughly to the hourly wage of a man, and as many as 50,000 dozen pairs might be kept in stock. Eventually customers who had once asked for 100 dozen pairs of one size alone reduced their orders to a gross in all (*see plates* 128–9).

Usually clog soles were sold to grindery merchants, such as Greens of Silsden, near Keighley, or Horsfields of Bradford, who stocked leather for uppers, also tacks, clasps, toe-plates, clog welting and irons, of which the latter were sold in pairs in two parts, fronts and heels. At Silsden a nail-making industry, started there in the middle of the eighteenth century, led to the making of clog irons, and both crafts continued side by side from about 1850 to 1919. Ill-paid jobs, they suited the independent way of life of farmers and hand-loom weavers who needed supplementary employment.

About 1850 it was a nail-maker who gave impetus to the making of irons by developing a series of mechanical processes and at the turn of the century there were four clog iron smithies at Silsden. They are remembered as hot and dirty but companionable places where men brought their books and pets, and discussed theology and current affairs.

Thomas Greens, founded about 1874, had at one time sixteen to twenty hearths in use making ten to fifteen gross a week. They specialized in Colne irons, a pattern introduced from Colne with flat sections on the fronts. Formerly mild steel rods, 12 feet long, were bought in Birmingham, but after 1918 these were obtained more cheaply from Belgium. The iron was worked red-hot in all the processes. In the 1920s a man on piecework earned 18*s*. to 28*s*. a week, and boys often put in two or three years at primary tasks before going on to mills or engineering works (*see plate* 130). The Greens, by then the only makers in Silsden, made their last Colne iron on 2 August 1950, and Mr C. T. Green gave the tools to Cliffe Castle Museum, Keighley, where they may be seen.

Horsfields, who at one time employed 100 men and issued catalogues, not only supplied Yorkshire, Lancashire and Cheshire clog-makers, but sent goods as far north as Dumfries and to London and Wales. Founded by James Horsfield in 1867, this business too succeeded because of the invention of machines manufactured on the premises and perfected by James's son, Walter (1868–1950), who had trained as an engineer. After 1914, when trade had declined, they turned to the making of clog uppers, usually in two patterns, Derby and Balmoral, made from waxed splits, which were split hides of which the flesh side was used, tanned again, waxed and blacked. In 1919 Horsfield's output of clog irons was 300 gross sets a week, that is 300 times 288 heels and the same number of fronts, sold at 23*s*. a gross. When the firm closed in 1962 it had dropped to a tenth of that amount.

Acquiring the necessary parts from the grindery merchants, the cloggers in different districts supplied different styles, chiefly based on the shape of the sole. The many shapes included common, mostly worn in Yorkshire, wide common, round duck, peculiar to Lancashire, London which had a wide square toe and was favoured by brewers, a Leeds and a Halifax shape which were variations on the duck, and spear points used for Sunday clogs. Besides these there were three strengths in each—strong, medium and light.

Formerly the clogger used mostly black leather with some brown for clogs worn at night. George A. Wilde, who had come from Lancashire to be manager of the clogging department of the Slaithwaite Co-operative Stores, advertised himself as the only maker of the Lancashire one-piece clog. This, with one-piece uppers sewn down the back and spear-pointed soles, had designs of birds or flowers scored on the leather. These clogs, highly polished and with brass nails, clasps and toe-plates, were worn on Sundays, and cost 10*s*. a pair in the late 1920s. Women's and children's had brass tacks, clasps and toe-plates, whereas men's usually had steel tacks and sheet-iron plates.

All cloggers employed a square clog size-stick for measuring the foot, with a gauge for clogs on one side and for shoes on the other, and they also hollowed out the soles for deformities, hence the continuing popularity of clogs with some orthopaedic surgeons. Based on Lancashire, the Amalgamated Society of Master Cloggers published a series of tables setting out wages and prices, just as the makers of clog-irons had a society with offices at Birmingham. In the 1920s a pair of child's clogs cost 2*s*. and good men's, said to be double the price of the uppers, 6*s*. 6*d*. Cheapness was the prime object. 'It was a right poverty job.' 'If clog soles went up 1*d*. a pair it was the end of the world.'

Many children had, besides their clogs, only one pair of shoes to their name. At Heptonstall school each morning they toed a chalk line to have their well-blacked clogs examined. At Queensbury the children owed Fred Firth 'who had the co-op clogging, many a penny' for putting on irons. Boys revelled in striking sparks on setts and pavements with their clog-irons, or in winter sliding on the ice. In time children wearing them were shouted at by their school fellows. 'They called me Cloggy Dick and I went home and cried.' Clog fights disfigured feast and other events. Each contestant stood on opposite sides of a fixed horizontal bar, and held it whilst kicking each other until an opponent was brought down.

Two family firms, Waltons of Halifax, established in 1910, and Walkleys of Huddersfield, started in 1946, still make a variety of industrial and safety clogs in standardized shapes. When Mr W. Walton (b. 1888) came out of his apprenticeship to a bespoke boot-maker in 1909, mass production had taken over. However, after starting at Siddal, near Halifax, in a small way he bought with his savings a shop in North Parade, Halifax, for £30, and developed a wholesale trade in clogs. At this time, although uppers cost 1*s*. 10*d*., soles 10*d*., irons, nails and tins 4*d*., laces 1½*d*., and the employee's pay 7½*d*., they sold at 3*s*. 9*d*. a pair. He also made 'old top' clogs, always in great demand, by knocking the soles off old boots, adding a wooden sole and oiling them. Or he bought old boots from a repairer in the East End of London at 3*d*. a pair, and could sell clogs made of these for 3*s*. Increasing trade, buying shops and inventing the trademark, 'Walco', Waltons had in 1974 forty-four retail shops for all kinds of footwear and leather goods in Lancashire and Yorkshire.

Mr F. Walkley, who started with a small repair shop and remembers travelling round with sample clogs on a bicycle, has adopted the trademark 'Eliminax', and employing about twelve people at Huddersfield makes some 40,000 pairs a year. In 1972 he bought the Maude's mill at Hawksclough and there installed new lathes.

When shoes were rationed during and after the Second World War, clogs enjoyed a revival. But now the sources of supply for toe-plates and tacks are reduced to one firm. Clasps as fasteners and clog hoops for protecting the backs of clogs have gone. Clogs are laced, and moulders' clogs with quick release patent fasteners are worn in foundries and a Wellington wooden-soled boot in fish docks. They are sent to Wales for the steel industry, to Cornwall for the China Clay Works, even sometimes to Singapore. Enquiries come for clog-dancing and Morris dancing clogs. Now as expensive as boots, they may cost from over £4 to over £8.

17 Recreations

'ALL their dearest associations cling round their own hillsides', wrote Mary Jagger of the people of Honley, near Huddersfield, a sentiment applicable only to old communities. The thousands who came to settle in the West Riding brought their own habits and traditions, but they were also assimilated into a vigorous life already there. Perhaps the textile industry forged the strong continuous link. Formerly all the manifold activities of the leisure hours of the peoples revolved round the age-old seasonal events, as time went on added to by new departures such as brass band contests and carnivals in aid of local hospitals.

Those once indispensable gatherings—fairs—included the ancient events of Wibsey Fair, Bradford, Lee Gap Fair, near Morley, and Adwalton Horse Fair, near Drighlington, between Bradford and Wakefield, the first two still held in a very minor way. Some were primarily horse fairs, some marts for cattle brought down the drove roads from Scotland and for merchandise of all descriptions. Within memory Atherton or Adwalton Fair took place on the Friday of feast week, the week after Whitsuntide, when horses for farmers and dray horses showed their paces up and down the main road, and every gateway and open space held stalls selling brandysnap, nuts and sweets. Accompanied by a pleasure fair, it was and had been for centuries 'together with all other fairs' the occasion for reunions of families and friends who were regaled with vast quantities of food, usually cold beef and pickles.[1]

Sixty years ago at Haworth Tide the streets and lanes were filled with pens for sheep, some being driven down to Derbyshire for the winter, gypsies trotting horses, geese and crates of pullets from Ireland.[2] Feasts, wakes or tides, the holidays originally based on the feast days of the saints' days of churches, still signify the holiday weeks, as do rushes and thumps, derived respectively from rush

[1] Mrs M. A. Collins, Drighlington.
[2] Mr J. H. Gill, Haworth.

bearings, always occurring at feast times, and thumps literally from people thumping each other.[1]

Those chiefly remembered today are the pleasure fairs with, in the past, travelling theatres, such as that erected at Halifax Fair, the huge Parish's Temple of Thespis, which had a lofty proscenium arch with classical columns and a pediment, an apron stage and open auditorium. In 1897 William Scruton complained that the fair at Bradford had altered for the worse with the coming of pea saloons, shooting galleries and fat women.

In the Leeds district Woodhouse and Holbeck feasts were so large that 'they were as good as Christmas week for the shopkeepers'. At Churwell Feast or 'Churrill Thump' a string of lads swinging great sods tied to cotton bands snaked in and out of the crowd. Gomersal Fair, held in March, was 'the next event to look forward to after Christmas'. Here Harry Ashington's marionettes performed such barnstormers as *Maria Martin or The Murder in the Red Barn*. At all of them were helter skelters, Shamrock and Columbine swing boats, roundabouts, cake walks, coconut shies, hoop-la and brandysnap stalls, pie and pea stalls with monkeys running up and down poles, and the bursts of gay music and the dazzling lights of the steam organs.

Rush bearing, when fresh rushes were strewn on the earth floors of churches at the time of feasts, developed in the eighteenth and nineteenth centuries into an elaborate ceremonial of the building of rushcarts in Cheshire, Lancashire, and the south-westernmost corner of the West Riding. Originating in rivalry between villages, they consisted of pyramids of bolts of rushes skilfully built up in the manner of thatching on a cart, then hung with sheets on which were fixed flowers, paper rosettes, ribbons, tinsel, even silverware. They were topped by boughs astride of which sat one or two men. These extraordinarily decorated vehicles, at times up to seven or eight of them, were drawn to churches by men holding stangs attached to the cart, accompanied by musicians, and sometimes Morris dancers.[2]

How far the custom penetrated into Yorkshire is not easy to ascertain. They were certainly made for Almondbury and Brighouse Rushes and in the Holme valley.[3] At Uppermill, Saddleworth, the ceremony continued to about 1890, and

---

[1] *The English Dialect Dictionary*, vol. VI, 1905, ed. Joseph Wright.

[2] A. Burton, *Rush-Bearing*, 1891; Ammon Wrigley, *Annals of Saddleworth*, 1905; 'Rush Carts of the north-west of England', Alex Helm, *Folk Life*. vol. VIII, p. 20, 1970.

[3] A. Easther, *A Glossary of the Dialect of Almondbury and Huddersfield*, 1883; Horsfall Turner, 'Brighouse Feast', *Leeds Mercury Supplement Local Notes and Queries*, May 1889–Sept. 1890; H. J. Moorhouse, *History and Topography of the Parish of Kirkburton*, 1861.

at Marsden over the hills in the Colne valley the last was built in 1903 (*see plate* 133). Having lost all meaning the whole procedure deteriorated and faded away. In recent years a rushcart has been made for the Saddleworth Festival.

The Pace Egg play, performed every Good Friday in the neighbourhood since 1949 by the senior boys of the Calder Valley High School, enacts a revival of a version of a play deriving from age-old celebrations of the renewal of life with its roots in antiquity. Although the words and characters are now an accretion and a jumble of folk memory, they none the less illustrate renewal, and listening to it stirs deep memories. The play was once performed all over England, and in Yorkshire a text of the words then extant was printed in Otley in 1840. It owes its revival in Calderdale to H. W. Harwood and F. H. Marsden, who collected the words and details of costume from old people, resulting in the boys of Midgley school playing it in the 1930s.

The characters are the Fool, St George, Bold Slasher, the Doctor, the Black Prince of Paradine, the King of Egypt, Hector, and Toss Pot, of whom five carry swords and are attired in brightly coloured clothes and exuberantly conceived headgear (*see plate* 134). The play begins with the Fool ringing a bell, walking round and exhorting the crowd to remember that ''tis Pace-Egging time', and the plot turns on the exploits of St George who wounds Slasher, kills the Black Prince and wounds Hector, all of whom are revived. The verse, remembered elsewhere in Yorkshire,

> Here come I Little Devil Dout
> If you don't give me money
> I'll sweep you all out

is not part of the Midgley version, nor is the character of Beelzebub, found in other similar mummers' plays. Instead of him is Toss Pot who collects money (once eggs) from the audience.

As the play was forgotten, the custom turned into mumming or guising on Old Year's Night (now New Year's Eve) when boys and girls dressed up or disguised went round singing carols. Collop Monday, before the start of Lent, was an occasion for children to beg for collops, slices of raw bacon, saying 'Pray, dame, give me a collop'. A multitude of local rhymes attached themselves to November the Fifth but not the making of a guy, and on Boxing Day married children and their families came back 'to the homestead'.

It was a matter of pride for those who could afford it to go for holidays in feast weeks to Blackpool, Morecambe or Scarborough. Morecambe at one time was known as Bradford-by-the-Sea. For the less well-off bedrooms only were booked in advance, and every item of food—joints of meat, eggs, bacon, bread, butter and so on—was packed into a tin trunk and handed to the landlady on arrival.

On the other hand by means of the then fully operative and cheap railway system marathon days' outings, often for educational purposes, were possible. For example round the turn of the century the Sowerby Bridge Flour Society and the Hebden Bridge Manufacturing Society in co-operation with the Lancashire and Yorkshire Railway Company ran annual excursions from upper Calderdale in July to Chester and Llandudno, Scarborough, Liverpool, Southport, Bridlington, Windermere, Grimsby and Cleethorpes, Lincoln, Boston and Skegness, Lancaster and Morecambe, Redcar and Saltburn. The train left the first station at 4 a.m. and was timed to start back about 6.30 or 8.55 p.m. The fare varied from 5s. 6d. to 10s. 6d., and the comprehensive descriptions in the handbills listed the points of interest, the walks, brake drives or steamer excursions.[1]

Nearer at home members of choirs, groups from shops, works or mills set off for the day to the Yorkshire dales to see the Strid on the river Wharfe, Aysgarth Falls on the river Ure, or even to climb Ingleborough (*see plate* 140). Many aimed for the Tennant Arms or the Anglers Hotel at Kilnsey (*see plate* 141). In the 1890s the proprietress of the latter, Mrs Horner, catered for the annual foremen's excursion from Hattersleys at Keighley, led by the head of the firm, Alfred Smith, on Boxing Day, 1898. Taking the train to Skipton, they then proceeded by open wagonettes to Kilnsey, and on this occasion went on to Hawkswick in Littondale. Breakfast cost 2s., 'a very good substantial dinner' 2s. 6d., cigars and a good deal of beer were consumed, and they left Skipton at 10.25 p.m.

Simpler outings on foot sometimes started with a short train or tram ride. On Whit Tuesday, 1900, a beautiful day, up to 20,000 people, some having arrived by train, cycle or wagonette, walked to Hardcastle Crags at the head of Calderdale. Huddersfield people came similarly to Marsden, and set off for the moors, to the inns, Nont Sarah's and the Isle of Skye for ham and egg teas at 1s. 3d. For a special treat Leeds families went by train to Weeton and explored Almscliffe Crag, Cockers Dale and Howley ruins, near Morley, Gildersome, and Gomersal. Shipley Glen, and Shibden Dale, near Halifax, drew people into the country, in some cases to cottages or tea gardens for tea.

Walking, although a pastime in itself, was inevitable for those who attended some of the innumerable activities—the lanternist for instance who at lectures operated the magic lantern. This, together with the cylinders of oxygen and hydrogen necessary for the limelight, was often transported by milk float. Societies, many fostered by the mechanics' institutes, ranged from 'Lit. and Phils.' with

Posters lent by Mr L. Barker, Co-operative Wholesale Society, Hebden Bridge.

their own libraries and distinguished lecturers, to naturalists'. The Heckmondwike lecture, founded in 1761, still functions as an occasion in the calendar of the
Spen valley. There are the dramatic societies, the Bradford Civic, the Halifax, and
the Huddersfield Thespians and others, some with their own theatres, which as
well as entertaining foster talent for the professional stage. Or take the Ovenden
(near Halifax) Naturalists' Society whose annual subscription in 1944 was 2s. 6d.
and who organized twenty outdoor meetings and seven indoor with subjects such
as Mendelism and Microscopy. Occasionally a few of the members of these groups,
the less privileged so far as education was concerned, have made important contri-
butions to knowledge on rare subjects.

Arising from the early spade husbandry and land societies started in times of
stress, grew the many allotment associations, a movement accelerated in the 1890s.
We met an elderly allotment holder in Leeds, who by selling produce and bunches
of flowers had in ten years saved £250, enough to buy a house which he eventually
sold for £4,500. Other groups still flourishing specialize in chrysanthemums,
auriculas or tulips. The development of the Leeds Paxton Society points to social
change. It was founded in 1886 to exhibit chrysanthemums by professional
gardeners then employed by the wealthy Leeds families, and is now supported by
amateur gardeners, women as well as men, with small gardens and allotments.

Or consider the Wakefield and North of England Tulip Society whose members
since the first society, with a different title, was formed at Wakefield in 1836 have
always been working men supported by the better-off as patrons. At their spring
show, although classes for other tulips have been introduced, the real interest lies
in the different types of Old English Tulips, the Bizarres, the Roses and the
Bybloemens, the species seen in Dutch flower paintings. Traditionally they were
shown in salt-glazed stoneware containers made by local potteries, but as these
have been broken or lost they are now exhibited individually in small beer bottles
(*see plate* 145).

Indoor hobbies are different again, and here the attics of the terrace houses serve
a useful function containing many likely and unlikely collections. One of the
suppliers of collectors' items is Bamforths at Holmfirth, publishers of calendars,
views and comic seaside postcards. The firm originated when in 1870 James
Bamforth started making lantern slides to illustrate lectures, stories and songs
using local people as actors posing against backcloths painted by himelf. From
this cinematograph films developed, some of the first to be made in England,
employing local talent in the same way, taken on location in streets, shops, banks
and railway stations. When the craze for collecting picture postcards developed,
sentimental cards were printed from negatives copied from the lantern slides, and

following these Edwin Bamforth, James's son, conceived the idea of the comic card, vulgar, funny and topical, drawn by special artists. Again these are a commentary on the times, for more outré jokes than formerly are admissible nowadays.

Often comic, too, with Buster Keaton, Fatty Arbuckle and Charlie Chaplin featuring, were the early silent films, at first shown in makeshift buildings (*see plate* 144), then in newly built picture houses sometimes with frontages faintly resembling the white marble façades of Italian cathedrals. Mr H. Ambler remembers the first moving pictures coming to Queensbury, and that the apparatus was brought by tram and pushed on a wheelbarrow to the Hall of Freedom. Mr J. E. Hardy of Morley, an early cinema manager, recollects that he took the tickets, ran upstairs to tear them in two, dashed back to put through the film and played the piano in the interval. He was the first in the neighbourhood to show the early cliff-hangers featuring Pearl White.

Week by week children from the slums, paying 1*d.* each, flocked to the Saturday matinées, and although the advertisements on the safety curtain as well as the films (always breaking down) were an attraction, extra inducements were gifts of sticks of rock, an orange or a lucky packet. At Armley some used to wait for a huge woman to arrive to be swept in unseen under her voluminous skirts.

Different theatres catered for all tastes. Touring companies visited the Leeds Grand and the Bradford Alhambra where many people first saw *Peter Pan*, Sir Frank Benson and his company in Shakespeare's plays, Sir Martin Harvey and his company in *The Only Way*, seasons of Shaw plays, Gilbert and Sullivan, and the British National Opera Company conducted by Sir Thomas Beecham, as later generations see similar and different programmes performed by a new breed of artistes. One ninety-year-old lady of our acquaintance remembered that she was allowed to go and see Wilson Barrett at the Leeds Grand in *The Sign of the Cross* only because of the play's religious content. At or around Christmas most families went to the pantomime, at Leeds weighing up the reported merits of those at the Grand and the Royal. Few saw both. Mr H. Ambler at Queensbury, near Bradford, one of eight children, says that his family only afforded to send one child a year, and still remembers his two visits with delight.

Music was above all the great outlet for joyful expression developing from singing to bands, to orchestras, to musical festivals, such as that at Leeds founded in 1858. It cost nothing to sing; people clubbed together to buy scores; inns served as meeting-places as they did for many hobbies; church and chapel choirs trained by their organists acted as forcing houses, and enthusiastic audiences filled the assembly rooms, and mechanics' institutes, churches and chapels and later concert rooms of town halls. Even children knew the arias of oratorios from hearing their elders practising. On 29 September 1818, Thomas Cook of Dewsbury Mills wrote in his diary, 'At Wakefield this day at our Oratorio in the Church, the Messiah much gratifying.' Over the years *Messiah* has become associated with Christmas, and is performed annually by the many choral societies, the Halifax, the Huddersfield, the Bradford, the Holmfirth, the Leeds Philharmonic and others.

The Colne valley may be taken as a focal point of musical fervour. There were glee and madrigal societies, a string band attached to the Slaithwaite Mechanics' Institute, the Crosland Moor United Handbell Ringers, who in 1912 toured Australia and New Zealand. The Slaithwaite Philharmonic Society was founded in 1891 to form a band, as early orchestras were often called, and after struggles and poor attendances at concerts was transformed by its conductor, Arthur Armitage, into a fine orchestra continuing at the present day. There was the Longwood Philharmonic conducted by the village cobbler, Eli Brearley, which played all the Beethoven symphonies including the Choral. Although not precisely in the Colne valley but not to be omitted because it is the oldest is the Huddersfield Philharmonic orchestra which celebrated its centenary in 1971. Many professional players of one instrument and another, born in the area, have made their names elsewhere. Seven silver bands are still in being, and the Colne Valley Male Voice Choir, founded in 1922 and conducted for forty-four years by George E. Stead, has won innumerable prizes and trophies at festivals and eisteddfods including the 'Mrs Sunderland' competitions.

It was at Longwood on the north side of the Colne valley that the Sings (not to be confused with the sings connected with Sunday schools), for which the whole neighbourhood became famous, were started in 1873. They grew from small groups of friends and relations gathered together to make music in particular in the garden of Oliver Ainley, a violinist, at Longwood (*see plate* 136). When Nab End Tower was built near by and an open air theatre made, the Tower Sings began on Thump Sunday, and from these arose many others taking place annually on Sundays in different villages. To Longwood people flocked from far and wide walking or arriving in wagonettes; even famous professional singers returned home for it.[1] Choirs, bands and orchestras sang and played hymn tunes or excerpts from oratorios, and collections for charity, often hospitals, were substantial. Sings began to dwindle in the 1950s, but that at Longwood has celebrated its centenary and still continues.

As well as these, brass bands, most later to become silver bands, were everywhere being formed. In the early half of the century some such as Silsden, Saddle-

[1] Information from Mr George E. Crowther, formerly of Huddersfield.

worth and Cleckheaton started as reed or reed and pipe bands. There were town, village, mill, works and colliery bands which competed in local contests and at the public competitions at Belle Vue, Manchester, and the Crystal Palace. They played on every conceivable occasion from Whitsuntide walks to musical festivals, gave concerts in local parks, in town halls, and recently have taken part at the Proms. Some were disrupted and not re-formed after one or other of the two World Wars, and several were affected by the coming first of radio and then television.

In the Holme valley five bands still flourish: Hepworth, Holme, Hade Edge, Hinchliffe Mill and Honley, and an annual contest is held, as one is at Dobcross, Saddleworth, staged in different villages. Some bands are household names: Black Dyke Mills, Brighouse and Rastrick, Grimethorpe Colliery and Hammonds Sauce Works bands.

Black Dyke Mills Band, winner of world and national championships, was founded in 1835 by John Foster, himself a player of the French horn, who converted the Queenshead (later Queensbury) reed and brass band into all brass. In those days, although not obligatory now, all members had to be employees of the mill, and it used to be said that 'half came out of the machine shop and the other half out of the wool-sorters'. One man, a collier, migrated from Rotherham to Queensbury in order to work in the mill and join the band, and his son, Mr E. Keaton, followed on and played the E Flat bass in it for fifty years.

It was and is a way of life. After performances far afield bandsmen thought nothing of arriving home in the early hours of the morning, and although if very late they were allowed the day off, one is said to have reached Queensbury at 5 a.m. and to have been at work an hour later. They may at times be away for weeks, and when in 1972 they visited Canada for six months, they started by each putting down £50 and finally broke even. In the old bandroom, still used, framed photographs hang on the walls of bandmasters with the dates of their years of service and the money prizes won—Phineas Bower, a euphonium player, bandmaster for twenty years, and the famous Arthur O. Pearce, for thirty-seven—as well as the blue banners awarded to the champion band of Great Britain.

Coming on to the scene later were several concertina bands which also competed in local and national contests playing test pieces: 'La donna è mobile', Handel's Largo, waltzes and the 'Hallelujah Chorus'. Amongst them the Heckmondwike English Concertina Prize Band founded in 1902 won more prizes than any others at contests at Shrewsbury, Belle Vue, Manchester and the Crystal Palace. Fred Tyne, a miner, took a leading part, and his daughter, Mrs N. Power, who plays the concertina herself, tells us that neighbours used to sit on their doorsteps listening to practices. A tour of America had to be cancelled in 1914, and the band finished at the beginning of the Second World War.

Comic bands, too, flourishing in the early part of the century and into the 1920s, consisted of groups of men dressed up and with painted faces who made their own fantastic instruments out of cardboard and thin sheet tin incorporating tommy talkers down which they blew the tune. (The tommy talker acted on the principle of a comb and tissue paper.) They too entered contests and played at carnivals and charitable functions. The Morley Parrock Nook Band included one performer on a hobby horse with a donkey's head harking back to Morris dancers (*see plate* 139). We may picture the members of the Hunslet band, called either the Wiffum Wuffam Band or the Nanny Goat Lancers, as was usual standing up in a waggon, playing *The Death of Nelson* (composed by John Braham) and one by one falling down in turn and disappearing into the bottom of the waggon. In one of the last contests the Jungle Band at Holbeck won with this piece not because they were better musicians but 'because their conductor deed better'.

Hunting in the Pennines, especially on the hills round Halifax, the Colne valley and the Saddleworth district, has accumulated as much lore—poems, and stories of hunts and huntsmen—as in other places more generally associated with hunting. When he died, Ab o' Chit's, the Delph bakestone-maker, was buried in full hunting regalia with cartridges in his coat pockets and a gun in his coffin.

Another sport, racing pigeons, also had and has its devotees. In 1852 it was said to have become a nuisance in the Huddersfield district where 'swarms of children from six to twenty years of age gather to test the powers of their pigeons'. In the last century in the Colne valley rival fanciers arranged matches called 'Cote to Cote and Run'. They employed their own runners and threw up the pigeon at their antagonist's cote. It flew to its own cote where it was caught and put in a bag, and the runner ran with it to a halfway mark between the two cotes. The one to arrive first was the winner.[1] 'It used to be quite a gala day did that.'

Until budgerigars ousted them from favour many people kept or bred canaries, of which there is a particular Yorkshire variety. Again in *Shirley* is the description of twenty cages containing as many canaries hung above the tables at the school feast 'whose piercing song . . . amidst confusion of tongues . . . always caroled loudest'. Fred Tyne's wife, distracted by the constant trilling of her husband's canaries, once opened all the cage doors and the windows and set them free.

Sixty or so years ago arrow throwing matches were a pastime at Gomersal and in the colliery districts as were the games of piggy, billets and knur and spell, all venues for betting. The arrow, 30 inches long, was loosely attached with a length

[1] Mr Joe France, Colne valley.

of string to the finger of the contestant who ran to a mark and threw it with the string still attached.

Knur and Spell enjoyed its zenith in West and South Yorkshire in the last decades of the last century and was still played in the 1930s when it lost its appeal until revived in a minor way in the 1960s. Champion players used to be as revered as many a present-day sportsman, and crowds followed the two participants, taking bets and eagerly marking where the knur fell. It was not unknown for someone deliberately to tread a knur into the ground. At Greetland on the hills above Halifax, Mr Tom Ellis still makes *pummels*, the sticks and their heads, and speaks of the participants at knur and spell as *laikers*. Each player is followed by a *baumer*, a kind of caddy, and a knur sent farther than an opponent's is a *cut*. How old, we wonder, are these terms in the life and traditions of the West Riding?[1]

[1] F. Atkinson, 'Knur and Spell and Allied Games', *Folk Life*, 1963.

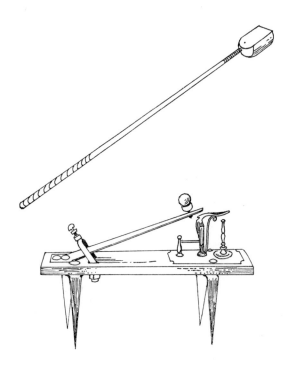

Index

Numerals in italics indicate page numbers of drawings. Photographs are indicated by plate numbers at the ends of entries.